T.P. BURNS
A Racing Life

Guy St John Williams

HILLGATE PUBLISHING LTD
The Village Pump
Batterstown
Co Meath

ISBN 0-9541819-1-3

Printed in Ireland by Colour Books Ltd, Dublin

Design & Layout by Eugene Donovan, Donovan Printing Ltd.
This book is typeset in Garamond 11/14 pt.

Cover Portraiture by Padraic Deasy, Deasy Photographic

If I were to begin my life again, I would go to the Turf for friends.

They seem to me to be the only people who really hold close

Together. It may be that each knows something that might hang

The other - but the effect is altogether delightful.

Harriet, Lady Ashburton

We yet retain

Some small pre-eminence, we justly boast

At least superior jockeyship, and claim

The honours of the Turf as all our own.

William Cowper – The Timepiece

ACKNOWLEDGEMENTS

Hillgate Publishing Limited is indebted to the generosity of the under-named. Without their help T.P. BURNS – *A Racing Life* might never have been afforded the opportunity to make its significant contribution to the slender written history of Irish racing. By their generous support the tradition of Irish racing history being essentially an oral history has – in this instance – been transcribed to the printed page.

Ballylinch Stud

Bolger, J. S.

Coolmore Stud

Cox, Dermot

Fleming, John

Irish Racehorse Trainers' Association

Leopardstown Club Limited

Moyglare Stud

Mulvany, Seamus

O'Brien, Dr and Mrs M. V.

O'Neill, Desmond

Richard Power Bookmakers

Rogers family, Airlie Stud

Weld, D. K.

The author's thanks are due to the following people who kindly contributed in various ways to the production of T. P. BURNS – *A Racing Life*: Sarah Lady Ainsworth, Jim Bolger, Dick Brabazon, Tommy Browne, James Burns, John Burns, Stella Burns, T. P. Burns, Ted Curtin, Padraic Deasy, Eugene Donovan, Patsy Egerton, Tom Gallagher, Harty family, Mary Healy, Healy Racing, Eva Kauntze, Vivian Kennedy, Bert Kerr, Virginia Kerr, Michael Kinane, John Murphy, Jean Neil, Caroline Norris, Dr M. V. O'Brien and Mrs O'Brien, Paddy Power, Mr and Mrs Cyril Ryan, Dr Tony Sweeney, Rosaleen Tonson-Rye, Liam Ward and Mary Weld.

FOREWORD

To most people he is known as T.P., to Vincent O' Brien as Tommy and to me when greeting him as Tom but otherwise as T.P. Burns. Nowadays he can be found at the entrance to the parade ring at The Curragh Racecourse resting his left arm on the woodwork and facing the activity before and after each race, pen in hand – result, distance and time recorded. His is a constant presence at said location since his retirement from the saddle in 1975. Any trainer, post race, who is told by T.P. that he has a 'real one there' had better treat it as such. After St. Jovite won the Anglesey Stakes as a two year old T.P.'s comment was "you'll have him back here next June". I am told that his predictions after he dismounted were a source of great hope to some and to others a severe dose of realism. On work mornings no trainer relished being told that he had a 'Thursday horse' but would be invariably happy to take the assessment in the full knowledge that his charge was better suited to a five-day week. Few could put one asleep like T.P., whether one and a half miles on the flat or three and a half over fences, and only occasionally forget to ring the alarm bell which 'omission' would be corrected with devastating effect on a future excursion.

T.P. is a man of strong faith in the Almighty, influenced by his Mother and his education by the Dominicans. His faith in his own ability was almost on a par with that which he has in the Almighty. In his riding days he showed great self discipline and adhered strictly to his spartan diet and strict lifestyle. He never embraced alcohol or nicotine and maintained a high level of fitness. His lifestyle contributed greatly to ensuring that he never lost his nerve, and was as daring in the twilight of his career as he had been at the outset.

Away from the racetrack T.P. was risk averse, careful and thrifty, though he always stood in good leather, invariably brown and well maintained. His tweeds were from the top drawer and he will always be synonymous with best quality cavalry twill. Though he would have 12 stone 7 lbs in my handicap of the most competent pound minders, closely followed by two, whose paths intertwined, there is nothing cheap about T.P. Burns. A dedicated family man, he is very proud of his children and freely acknowledges the help and support of his wife Chris. He is also very proud of his own achievements having hung up his boots with few unfulfilled ambitions.

Guy St John Williams beautifully captures the essence of this great man with no less insight and artistry than that displayed by T.P. during his brilliant riding career, whether over the banks, fences, hurdles or on the flat. It has been suggested to me that whoever, in future, can combine the riding qualities of T.P. and his contemporary Toss Taaffe will most certainly be destined for stardom.

T.P. is unassuming, retiring, even shy but once on horse back he metamorphosed into a completely different character. Though many modern day dieticians would hardly approve of the flask, the brown bread sandwich and the water biscuits, he showed that they were just what the doctor ordered. I wish him many more good days at the Curragh, Leopardstown or wherever the bus pass takes him.

J. S. Bolger.

PREFACE

The beauty of a race consists in detecting the how, and the where. The how it was lost; the where it was won. It is highly interesting to observe a race won out of the fire, solely by fine riding; - by the jockey slipping his opponents, or by taking the off chance by lying away, when the struggle was made too far from home; the forced pace, too unnatural to last the distance, by which, the superiority of his antagonists succumbs, and the man wins on an inferior animal, solely by his patience and by his knowledge of pace. The knowledge of pace to a jockey is as important to a jockey as the judgement of distance to a fencer, or to a boxer, it must emanate from a natural genius, and can only be self taught.

All the famous jockeys were eminently famous in this respect. It is the very criterion of race riding. The most trying task a jockey can be set, is to ride a jady horse against an antagonist known to possess superior speed with doubtful bottom; and his object, consequently, is to ride the distance steadily against time, alias, to come the best pace the horse can maintain, without forcing him beyond his natural powers of endurance, and at the same time to keep a reserve to land the horse in the final struggle. In this instance, if the jockey be not a perfect judge of pace, his chance of winning is a forlorn hope.

Riding a horse of acknowledged superior speed is a very easy task, and only requires a fine hand and patience. The jockey has the advantage of waiting; nineteen horses out of twenty follow on better terms than when they take the lead. If the jockey has any doubt on the subject of comparative speed, he must go up to his adversary at a certain distance from home and ascertain the fact; if he discovers it is all right, he draws his horse back and waits till he measures his length on the post; if, on the contrary, he finds the other horse can go as fast or faster than his own, there is no remedy but to fight the battle without loss of time, and to ride him home.

This is the A, B, C, of riding races.

Horse Racing – Honourable Captain Rous, R.N., London, 1852

Chapter One

IN FATHER'S FOOTSTEPS

"Tommy Burns, the ex-jockey, who is now a trainer, will have very pleasant recollections of the meeting, for his two sons, Tommy and James, who are apprenticed to himself, each rode a winner. Tommy just steered Prudent Rose to victory in the Apprentices' Plate, and James, on Kilglass, rode strongly to snatch a sensational victory in the Welter Plate.

In each instance these very promising boys revealed in marked degree good judgement, coupled with a strength and determination in getting the utmost out of their mounts. Their many friends will hope that in the near future they will be emulating the brilliant jockey-ship of their father."

That report referred to the 1938 Irish Derby meeting. 'Young Tommy' was fourteen. In another interview the boys' proud father observed that he had retired from the saddle, "to give the boys a chance." It was only partly true, for things were seldom quite as they appeared with Tommy 'Scotchman' Burns, one of the jockey trio that dominated Irish flat racing for almost half a century - Canty, Burns and Wing.

Twelve months previously the 'Scotchman' had been assaulted by the 'establishment' Newmarket trainer Jack (later Sir Jack) Jarvis in the jockeys' dressing room after the Ascot Gold Cup. Jarvis had called the jockey "an Irish bastard," accusing him of deliberately sabotaging the chances of Fearless Fox, Jarvis's runner in the Gold Cup.

The 'Scotchman' first reported his assailant to the Ascot stewards, who fined the trainer. However, the jockey then initiated legal proceedings for defamation and slander. The stakes were high. Failure would bankrupt the 'Scotchman'. To strengthen his case he had retired from the saddle, evidence that Jarvis's allegations had ruined his riding career.

Young Thomas Pascal Burns - or TP as he has ever been known professionally – thus learned to live with pressure from the outset of what was to become a racing career of remarkable endurance, in which so much so often depended on his judgement and ability. Unlike so many successful jockeys, TP was born to ride, thus the importance of setting his story in its rightful context.

Chapter Two

The Burns family originated, appropriately, on the west coast of Scotland, in Ayr – Land o' Burns – where Thomas Burns, horse dealer, supplied innumerable horses of all descriptions to the inexhaustible Glasgow market in an era when the horse was the principal mode of transport. Following the example of fellow horse dealer William Wyllie, the first recognised trainer in Ayr, Thomas began training a few of his own horses, competing on the Scottish circuit – Bogside, Hamilton Park, Lanark, Paisley, Penrith and especially his annual home event, the Western Meeting at Ayr each September.

The Ayr racecourse was then located at Belleisle, alongside the route supposedly taken by Tam O' Shanter on his way to Alloway Kirk. Robbie Burns, Scotland's national poet, associated with prominent racing men of his day, receiving £25 from the Royal Caledonian Hunt on publication of his 1781 collection of poems, for which the RCH subscribed for one hundred copies. Ayr racecourse moved to its present location in 1907.

THOMAS BURNS, TP's great-grandfather.

With that relocation Ayr became the principal racecourse and training centre in Scotland. Historically, Gullane, on the east coast had been the seat of Scottish racing power and influence, producing three training dynasties destined to leave an indelible mark on racehorse training, initially in Scotland and subsequently in Newmarket – the Dawsons, the Ryans and the Waughs.

Thomas Burns was succeeded in the 1890s by sons John and James. The former specialised in form and betting, while James concentrated on the horses' welfare, galloping them on the adjacent strand. Jack Fairfax-Blakeborough, racing official and tireless chronicler of northern racing, was always a welcome guest of the Burns family in Applehirst for the Western Meeting. He recorded Watch Tower as being James' first training success at Hamilton Park in 1895, the year in which James married Jane Tait. Their wedding certificate noted James's profession as 'Horsedealer'. In due course Jane produced five sons John, Thomas (born 11 February 1899), James, William and Reginald, together with five daughters Jane, Anne, Bessie, Cecilia and Muriel. A further five children failed to survive.

The mischievous element in Thomas's make-up later induced him to adopt February 14th as his date of birth. He preferred to think of himself as a child of St Valentine's Day – more romantic. And that was just the beginning of the amalgam of fact and fiction Thomas Burns was destined to become.

Jane, the eldest girl, married Billy Neil. Their daughter, Jean, lives in nearby Mauchline. Neither Anne nor Betty ever wed,

JAMES BURNS (1874-1954), TP's grandfather.

Anne instead becoming her father's indispensable assistant and financial comptroller.

R. B. Dobell and then Edward C. 'Ned' Clark became principal patrons of the Applehirst stable. The Burns brothers concentrated mainly on laying out horses for selling races, then the staple fare on all but a handful of the major courses. Even at that exalted level the 'seller' formed an important part of any racecourse's potential income. In 1910 James Burns was credited with two winners, rising to three the following year, during a period when *Ruff's Guide* listed just two Ayr trainers under the heading 'Principal Trainers and their Employers'. These were Gilbert Steele, Clyde House, and Robert 'Ruby' Thomson in Craigie House. Though numerically more successful, neither John McGuigan nor James Burns merited inclusion.

Meanwhile, the Burns boys, when not attending Ayr Academy, where young Thomas enrolled in 1903, were becoming increasingly involved in the workings of the Applehirst stable. As they did so the fortunes of the stable increased, yielding five winners of nine races in 1913. By that time Thomas was apprenticed to his father, while James, his brother, was indentured to Felix Leach in Graham Place, Newmarket. Thomas was entrusted with the mount on First League when the three-year-old daughter of Athleague made her racecourse debut at Ayr in July 1913. Unquoted in the betting, First League finished down the field behind her stable companion, the well-fancied Half Caste, ridden by Newmarket apprentice George Pullin.

Half Caste thereby completed a hat trick in selling plates and was retained by connections for 160gns; wisely, as time would prove. First League, on the other hand, proved very expensive to follow in subsequent outings. Starting favourite or nearly favourite each time and ridden by more experienced jockeys, First League failed to realise the promise she showed in home gallops under young Thomas Burns. The boy became increasingly convinced that he held the key.

In October First League was duly despatched by train to faraway Thirsk, North Yorkshire, to contest the Thirkleby High-weight Selling Handicap over six furlongs, worth £100 to the winner. As the school year was in full swing, young Thomas had to beg leave of absence from the principal. To his dismay, his polite request was firmly refused.

Fortunately for Thomas, his father had also become persuaded that his son might indeed be the key to transmitting First League's home ability to the racecourse. They travelled to Thirsk together. On Saturday, 18 October 1913, in the third event on a six-race card, T. Burns jumped First League smartly out of the gate, making all to win by one and a half lengths and one length, returned at 7/1. As soon as Thomas Burns weighed in on the first of his innumerable winning mounts, First League was offered for sale. Knocked down to Mr H. Copeland for 120gns, First League never won another race.

Young Thomas never did return to Ayr Academy, happy that his future education lay in the realms of horses and racing. Besides, events on a wider stage threatened to change the world in which Thomas had grown up. On 14 August Great Britain had declared war on Austria-Hungary. One of the casualties was to be Ayr racecourse, requisitioned for military purposes.

A certain giddiness followed the declaration of war. Young and old flocked to enlist, eager to do their bit for King and Country. They would soon show Kaiser Bill what made Britain great. In fact, this war would be over by Christmas. As for the racing programme, with a few exceptions, it continued as before. No invader had set foot on English soil since 1066.

The increasing success of the Applehirst stable led *Ruff's Guide* to include James Burns under 'Principal Trainers and their Employers' for 1914, when the main stable patrons were listed as R. B. Dobell, W. Traill and W. Turnbull. James Burns trained six winners of seven races, while young Thomas increased his tally by four winners from just twenty-seven mounts. Brother James had yet to open his account.

Despite Britain being at war, fighting now on the Western Front and in the Dardanelles, racing continued at home. Early season successes for the Burns father-and-son team at Nottingham and Stockton with Finery, then with Denizulu at Catterick, where Cataract made it a stable double. The duo struck closer to home at Bogside with Dimorphodon and Quack.

Young Thomas registered his first outside win when riding Pericardium to win for Middleham trainer Dobson Peacock at Stockton. The accompanying synopsis in *M'Call's Racing Chronicle* gave an intimation of the young apprentice's developing tactical finesse. "Inside the distance Dan Rodney headed Red Star, but was caught in the last few strides by Pericardium, who got up on the rails and won - length and the same." The following day Thomas rode Fairlight to win for his father, the middle leg of a treble for the Applehirst stable.

Then the awful truth began to emerge. Far from being 'over by Christmas', the war had become bogged down in murderously wasteful trench warfare on the Western Front, in tandem with horrendous losses against the Turks in the Dardanelles. Responding to political pressure, the Jockey Club announced that, as and from 22 May 1915, "Further English racing, Newmarket excepted, is suspended from this date owing to the war."

It was little comfort to the Burns family that James and John were over the age for military service, while James's sons were still too young. As a racing team they were out of business, on the British mainland anyway. Perhaps they contemplated joining the massive exodus of British racing personnel across the Irish Sea. Whether or not, Ireland proved to be their immediate salvation. James Burns answered a call from William Hall Walker, one of his newer owners, to move across to the Curragh of Kildare as his trainer.

Like the majority of the racing fraternity, the Burns family left no written record of their life and times. Thus their reaction to the prospect of making a new life across the Irish Sea can only be imagined in the light of what western Scots knew of Ireland and the Irish. It cannot have been a particularly uplifting image, inevitably linked to the seasonal shiploads of migrant farm labourers recruited from Achill and Mayo to graft in Scottish potato fields under conditions little better than slavery. Until recent times that facet of the Irish diaspora has remained cloaked in silence, a shameful reminder of an impoverished, landless labour force – tattie-hokers.

Chapter Three

Born on Christmas Day 1856, William Hall Walker was a member of the wealthy Lancashire brewing family, Peter Walker & Sons, Warrington. His father, Sir Andrew Barclay Walker, Mayor of Liverpool, had presented the Walker Art Gallery to the Merseyside capital of the northwest. An enthusiastic owner-rider from the time he left Harrow, William Hall Walker registered his colours as early as 1878. He began by racing Galloway ponies, to such effect that his record soon stood at 120 victories from 250 attempts. An all-round sportsman, William Hall Walker turned his hand with equal facility to fencing, deerstalking, polo and yacht racing. Progressively drawn into racing through the National Hunt sphere, Hall Walker realised every Liverpudlian's greatest racing ambition when winning the 1896 Grand National with The Soarer.

WILLIAM HALL WALKER – brought James Burns to the Curragh in 1915.

Turning his attention to flat racing, Hall Walker came to prominence in 1900, when bearers of his 'blue and white check, cerise cap' won almost £9,000. An increasing fascination with thoroughbred breeding and the intricacies of mating complementary bloodlines in appropriate doses had led Hall Walker to purchase a substantial tract of prime limestone pasture on the southern outskirts of Kildare town, an ancient monastic centre bordering the western end of the Curragh. Taking the title from the townland, he named his property Tully Stud. Intent on proving the worth of his stock on the racecourse, Hall Walker brought over John Smith as his private trainer.

Pooh-poohed by many for his insistence on mating his mares by astrological charts, Hall Walker silenced his critics by heading the Irish owners' table in 1903, when five of his representatives won twelve races worth £3,151. James Daly might have exceeded that monetary total the previous year, but prior to that no Irish owner had netted more since Maurice G. Prendergast as long ago as 1820. The principal contributor to Hall Walker's prize fund was juvenile speedster Jean's Folly, bred in Tully by Ayrshire out of Black Cherry. John Smith acted as Hall Walker's private trainer, as he was to do until 1915.

Two years later victories in the 1,000 Guineas and Oaks with homebred Cherry Lass contributed to Hall Walker becoming leading owner in Britain, a title he regained in 1907 when his Witch Elm won the 1,000 Guineas.

Hall Walker's greatest triumph was achieved thorough Minoru, another Tully-bred that he had leased to King Edward VII to register enormously popular victories in the 1909 2,000 Guineas and Derby. Following King Edward's death in 1910 Minoru had reverted to his breeder, who promptly sold him to Russia.

Obstinate in his opinions and prejudices, Hall Walker had chopped and changed his English-based trainers with such frequency as to earn the sobriquet 'Whimsical Walker'. London-born W.T. 'Jack' Robinson, based in Foxhill, had done him proud. In addition to Cherry Lass and Witch Elm, Jack Robinson had credited his

JAMES BURNS -
on his one-eyed hack, Curragh, during WWI.

principal patron with the 1913 St Leger through White Hawk and the Gimcrack Stakes three times in four years with Colonia (1905), Royal Realm (1906) and Lily Rose (1909). Jack had also sent Cherry Lass, Merry Moment and Knight of Tully back to the land of their birth to complete a hat trick in the Anglesey Stakes.

A 1918 interview provided an informative insight into the difficulties of training for Hall Walker. Referring to Night Hawk's St Leger, his owner-breeder had this to say. "I had told him [Robinson] that I wanted Night Hawk specially trained for the Cesarewitch, but when the Doncaster meeting came round I informed him that, as I should be there, I wished my horse to run in the St Leger. Robinson raised the objection that Night Hawk was not fit enough, but I knew the colt required very little work and expected him to win. In order to have the laugh over Robinson I put £50 on for him without telling him. To my utter surprise I got 50/1 to my money."

Besides such vagaries, Hall Walker had begun to show signs of disenchantment with racing and breeding. These were soon to become reality. Nevertheless, James Burns decided to accept the offer to move to Ireland and take over from John Smith, who promptly set up as a public trainer in Rossmore Lodge. However, Burns insisted that he, too, would continue to train in his new location for any of his existing patrons who wished to follow him, in addition to any others who chose to have horses with him. Whether or not James Burns reckoned on having to take on a vast influx of Hall Walker horses from Foxhill is unknown.

In any event, James Burns and his family moved to County Kildare, settling in the Clonree Hotel on the northern edge of the Curragh, close to Lumville Manse, then home to Major Thackeray, resident magistrate for the district. The problem of finding accommodation for eighty-odd horses at short notice has become part of the Burns family folklore. As Tommy was subsequently to tell his son, TP, "They were here there and everywhere, some even in hen houses."

Chapter Four

As England's oldest and closest colony, Ireland was almost equally affected by the turmoil in Europe and the Middle East, already experiencing an intensive recruiting campaign. Those who enlisted had to be trained and hastily, for casualties in France and Belgium were mounting to catastrophic proportions. As early as February 1915 a cryptic notice in the *Irish Racing Calendar* indicated as much. "Permission to abandon Fermoy Meeting was granted owing to the course being in the occupation of the military."

While Fermoy was relatively remote from the Curragh, historic headquarters of Irish racing, the Curragh also contained the largest military camp in Ireland. The railway siding behind the Curragh grandstand might have been created to facilitate transport of racegoers from Kingsbridge Station in Dublin and elsewhere. However, it was also flanked by stabling for one thousand army remounts, awaiting shipment to the battlefields. The Turf Club could not ignore the course of events in English racing, as the Calendar disclosed.

> *"May 26th - A conference between the Stewards and the Members of the Turf Club, for the purpose of considering the continuance of racing in Ireland, was held.*
>
> *The question was fully debated, and the following decision was arrived at –*
>
> *'That racing should be continued in Ireland for the present.'*
>
> *The Stewards and members of the Club came to this conclusion after earnest consideration of the grave effect that the discontinuance of racing would inflict on the horse-breeding industry, to the existence of which the continuance of racing is essential. The Stewards and members further recognise that the conditions which influenced the Jockey Club to place the present restrictions on racing in England do not affect this country. The Members of the Club authorised the Stewards to order the suspension of racing should any intimation be received from the Government to the effect that racing in Ireland interfered in any way with the Public Service."*

That announcement triggered a rush of applications for trainers' licences from English trainers,

J. T. ROGERS (1866-1940) the other WWI newcomer to found a racing dynasty on the Curragh in 1915. TP and his father rode winners for three generations of their Curragh neighbours.

whose livelihoods had otherwise been extinguished. Messrs H. Braime, W.T. Robinson, J. R. Ryan, Thomas Schofield, John Fallon and Leonard A. Cundell formed the first wave to be granted licences to train a maximum of 12 horses apiece 'on the lands of the Turf Club'. These were quickly followed by W. A. M'Kie, J. T. Rogers and J. Burns, subject to similar restrictions.

Inevitably, such sudden proliferation of Curragh trainers brought problems in its wake. The door could not be left open indefinitely. The Calendar of August 20th carried this notice. "The Stewards decided not to grant any further licences to persons to train on their lands at the Curragh." The door had closed.

Fortunately for the latecomers, the Turf Club was content to licence other émigré trainers in different locations, leading *The Irish Field* to observe that Baldoyle, the seaside racecourse north of Dublin, became a training centre almost overnight.

Besides his trainer's licence, James Burns secured a flat licence for his apprentice son Thomas. At the same time a full licence under both codes was issued to one John Burns. While that might seem more than coincidental, there is no recollection in the Burns of Ayr family history of Tommy's brother John ever becoming a jockey. In TP's received wisdom, "Uncle John had too much upstairs to be bothered riding. He was a dealer all his life."

Having received their licences, the Burns team wasted no time in opening their Irish account. On June 30th, in the Harristown Plate, which immediately preceded the Irish Derby, young Tommy Burns got Half Caste home by a head at 6/1. Connections retained their stable stalwart for £130. They followed up with R. B. Dobell's Flying Aero in the aptly-named Red Cross Handicap at Baldoyle. *Racing Up-to-date* recorded, "Deposit fell over the rails and was killed. Crubeen crossed his

TOMMY BURNS – as an apprentice in William Hall Walker's colours.

legs and fell." Crubeen's fall left John Doyle with a partly dislocated neck, which finished the former Irish champion jockey's riding career. Half Caste, Denizulu and Flying Aero continued to advertise both trainer and jockey with further successes. At the season's end young Thomas had ridden 17 winners in his first Irish campaign, a respectable score in the wake of Charlie Hawkins, champion professional with 44 winners. Young Mr W. J. Parkinson, whose father, James J. Parkinson controlled the largest public stable in Europe, headed the overall list with 72 winners.

That successful entrée to the Irish racing scene proved timely, for in November 1915 William Hall Walker startled racing and breeding circles by offering his bloodstock to the Government, provided they would purchase his stud farm at Tully and his racing stables at Russley, close to Lambourn in Berkshire for £75,000 or any less figure at which the properties might be valued.

The circumstances whereby James Burns was to lose his principal employer were recorded in the *Bloodstock Breeders' Review* some years after the event. "The avowed purpose of the proposed gift was to enable the Government to breed stallions that could be used to increase the supply of horses suitable for the Army.

"The war had been in progress fifteen months and the nation's finances were being severely strained; moreover, it was open to doubt whether the stud could be conducted in a way calculated to achieve the aim suggested. It was understood at the time that the Army Council favoured acceptance of the offer, but that the Board of Agriculture took a contrary view. Anyway, the proffered gift was politely declined. Thereupon Colonel Walker entered all his

The handover of the Curragh Camp May 16, 1922. Lt. Gen. O'Connell, on left and Lt. Col. Sir F. Dalrymple, on right with walking stick. (Below) Staff officers at the Water tower

bloodstock in the catalogue of the approaching December sales at Newmarket. Although thoroughbreds were then fetching comparatively poor prices, it was realised that the breeding stock at Tully would be eagerly sought after. Agents in England were, indeed, commissioned by stud masters in distant parts of the world to bid for many of the lots. Meanwhile, Lord Lonsdale and one or two others were busy behind the scenes striving to persuade the Board of Agriculture to reverse their decision. These efforts were successful, and the day before the mares and other thoroughbreds from Tully were to have come under the hammer, Colonel Walker received from the President of the Board of Agriculture a telegram reading: 'Gladly accept your generous offer, and buy your properties at Tully and Russley.'

"And so it came about that the big establishment at Tully was converted into the National Stud. The result of the valuation of the land and buildings there and at Tully was the payment to the vendor of £65,625. Captain Greer (now Sir Henry) valued the bloodstock presented to the nation at £74,000. It consisted of the stallions White Eagle and Royal Realm, thirty mares, ten yearling fillies, twenty foals and eight horses in training, including Night Hawk, Great Sport, and the fillies Dolabella, White Lie, Flash of Steel and Tillywhim."

As to Hall Walker's motives in suddenly disposing of the concern on which he had lavished so much time, effort and expense, the same writer advanced the following surmise. "There is reason for believing that his resolve to close down was to a large extent reached because of apprehensions concerning the political outlook in Ireland. One may, indeed, suppose that when he heard of the Easter rebellion in 1916 he thanked his lucky stars that Tully was off his hands."

William Hall Walker was elevated to the peerage for his gift to the nation, choosing the title Lord Wavertree. He was eventually elected a member of the Jockey Club in 1920 and died in 1933, without a male heir, whereupon the Wavertree peerage became extinct.

Chapter Five

With no prospect of resumption of racing in Britain, James Burns had little choice but to persevere in Ireland. Duly his name appeared in the *Irish Racing Calendar*, November 17th, 1915. "Trainers' licences in accordance with Rule 26, Rules and Orders of the Turf Club were granted to the following - Messrs A. Anthony, H. Beasley, P. Behan, J. Burns (for twenty horses), M. Dawson, John Doyle, James Dunne, J. Fallon (for twelve horses), M. Hanley, J. Hunter, T. Miller, R. A. Mahon, J. J. Parkinson, T. W. Price, M. Reidy, J. T. Rogers (for twenty-five horses), and J. Westlake."

In December *Irish Life* ran its rule over the Curragh, revealing that a Curragh trainer's licence cost £105 per annum, plus £2 per horse (£7 in Newmarket). There were approximately 500 horses in training on the Curragh, hence the Turf Club's guarded acceptance of the English wartime 'invasion'. There was a £1 levy on all outside runners on the Curragh, "but for this sum they may remain three weeks and obtain free stabling. This is to protect the gallops from an invasion of country-trained animals. . . and a judicious move would be to remove those stone posts (a relic of the ancient ages) in favour of wooden ones and those protected by bushes or hurdles; especially might this be done on the race tracks."

By this time conscription had come into force throughout the British mainland. However, the island of Ireland remained the sole exception throughout the European theatre of war to this compulsion, Consequently, there was no echo in the *Irish Racing Calendar* of the following Jockey Club notice, dated December 31st, 1915. "It is requested that any jockey of military age [18-45] who intends to apply for a licence to ride under the Rules of Racing will forward, with his application, a certificate to show that he has already joined

TOMMY BURNS – 1917 cartoon.

JAMES DUNNE – creator of Osborne Lodge, who provided Tommy Burns with his first Irish classic winners on Captive Princess in 1916.

His Majesty's Forces, has attested under the Group System, or has been rejected as unfit or ineligible."

James Burns started his 1916 campaign on a positive note when Simon Ashton won over hurdles at Baldoyle on New Year's Day and had trebled his tally when the momentous events of Easter Week in Dublin led to racing being suspended until June. Resuming where he had left off, James Burns went on to saddle a further twenty winners, while young Thomas continued to impress. *Irish Life* sang the youngster's praises in September. "Burns, the Scottish lightweight, has been riding any amount of winners lately and was really the jockey to follow at the Phoenix Park with three winners on the first day and one on the second. He showed brilliant horsemanship on Courier Belle."

Increasingly in demand by other trainers, Thomas completed a five-timer at the Curragh September meeting, three of those on his father's charges. Most importantly, he opened his classic account on Captive Princess for Osborne Lodge trainer James 'Fairy' Dunne in the Irish Oaks, following up in the second running of the Irish St Leger. Recalling those classic-winning rides fifty years later, Tommy Burns emphasised the virtue of patience in riding the Curragh, observing that frontrunners so often become sitting ducks in the closing stages.

A new name appeared in the 1917 *Irish Racing Calendar*, when young James Burns was officially indentured to his father and namesake. The Burns family have traditionally confined male Christian names to James, John and Thomas, with William in reserve, should the need of another name arise. The new recruit had to wait until the final Curragh meeting of the season to open his account, which he did on Genevieve for owner-trainer J. R. Markey. The youngster drew 5st 9lb on a filly scoring for the first time on her 17th start of the campaign.

Thomas, on the other hand, was flying throughout his best season to date. Highlights included the Irish Oaks on Newmarket raider Golden Maid, trained by Sam Pickering and a second Irish St Leger on Double Scotch, completing a similar Irish St Leger double for 'Fairy' Dunne. Curiously, it was at the very end of the season that James Burns trained his first winner for William Hall Walker when the well-bred Wildwood (White Eagle – Jean's Folly) won at Leopardstown under Thomas.

Unfortunately, it was his riding of Wildwood in the Stand Plate at Leopardstown on April 1918 that cost Thomas his licence for the greater part of the campaign. "The Stewards objected to Wildwood, placed second, on the grounds of foul riding by T. Burns. After hearing the evidence of Capt Tuthill (Judge), C. Aylin and T. Burns they disqualified Wildwood, suspended Burns for the remainder of the meeting, and reported him to the Stewards of the

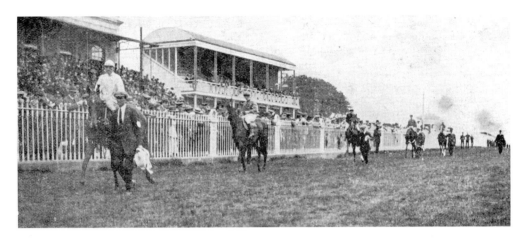

CURRAGH, July 25, 1917 – fillies parading before the Irish Oaks

Turf Club, who withdrew his licence to ride, but restored it to him September 16th."

Thomas returned in time to win the Turf Club Cup at the Curragh on H. G. Keswick's My Land, trained by his father. James junior doubled his score when winning on William Wyllie's The Squire, also trained by his father, at Leopardstown in November. Ten days later, at the eleventh hour of the eleventh day of the eleventh month, the 'war to end all wars' was over.

James Burns reacted quickly to the prospect of racing's resumption across the Irish Sea. Having saddled The Squire to win at Baldoyle on New Year's Day 1919, James Burns returned to Applehirst, Ayr, with his family and string of horses, among them Wildwood. During his spell on the Curragh James Burns had sent out approximately one hundred winners. It was a time of decision for young Thomas, by now firmly established on the Irish racing scene. Thomas decided to make Ireland his base.

While in Ireland James Burns had had another apprentice, George Formby, later to become a celebrated music hall entertainer. George's father had a couple of horses with James in Ireland, but his son failed to win on either. Remarkably, young Formby elected to continue his apprenticeship with Hon George Lambton, then training for Lord Derby in Newmarket. Predictably, that move did nothing to boost his faltering career and he soon drifted out of racing, only to discover his true vocation, on the boards.

Tommy Burns winning the Irish Oaks on Newmarket raider Golden Maid.

Chapter Six

James Burns was soon back among the winners in his native Ayr, signifying his return with a double on his local course in April 1919, both ridden by his apprentice son and namesake. Meanwhile, riding as a freelance in Ireland, Tommy Burns formed a mutually beneficial alliance with Clonsilla trainer Maxwell Arnott.

One of a wealthy Cork mercantile family, that had developed Cork Park as the 'Leopardstown of the south' and then the Phoenix Park racecourse, Maxie Arnott had begun his lengthy career as assistant to Captain Bob Dewhurst in Greenmount, Clonsilla. When Dewhurst transferred his operation to Newmarket in 1904 to concentrate exclusively on the flat, Maxie Arnott had assumed full control of the Clonsilla stable, sending out a steady stream of winners all over Ireland. Like J. J. Parkinson of Maddenstown Lodge on the Curragh, Maxie Arnott would despatch horses to any course, however lowly and remote, in search of that winning bracket, so useful for attracting English customers.

Maxie Arnott shared friend and rival Harry Ussher's predilection for the annual Galway fixture in July, carrying off the featured Galway Plate six times between 1908 with Shady Girl and the indomitable East Galway, successful in 1928 and again in 1930. While never champion trainer, for five years in a row and six in all Maxie Arnott won more races than any other trainer. Any jockey riding regularly for the Greenmount stable could expect plenty of winners, while visiting every course in Ireland.

With such backing Tommy Burns brought his 1919 total to 48, within hailing distance of Joe Canty, who secured the first of his seven Irish titles with 65 winners. With Maxie Arnott supplying the quantity, Tommy won more valuable prizes for such as Fred Grundy and F. F. MacCabe, in addition to carrying off his third Irish St Leger with English raider Cheap Popularity, sent over by Hugh Powney to triumph in the colours of renowned Irish owner-breeder Albert Lowry.

Less than a month previously young James Burns – or "Uncle Jimmy" to TP – travelled to

WAVY STRIPE – bought out of a Limerick Junction seller by James and John Burns in 1918. Wavy Stripe won 3 races for the brothers on their return to Ayr in 1919. Sent back to Ireland in 1920, Wavy Stripe was unbeaten in 6 Curragh starts for trainer Fred Grundy, ridden each time by Tommy Burns.

Catterick Bridge to ride Fairy Lantern, having won on her at Pontefract in July for Malton trainer John Renwick. Unlike Pontefract, Catterick Bridge is a skidpan track. Fairy Lantern came down. James made an adequate physical recovery, sufficient to resume riding, latterly under National Hunt rules. However, those close to Uncle Jimmy reckoned that his mental recuperation was far from complete and almost certainly contributed to his premature death in 1928.

Continued association with the Arnott stable brought Tommy the first of his two Galway Hurdle victories in 1920, on Lord Lascelles' King Eber. Fred Grundy provided three of Tommy's four winners at the Curragh in August, among them that great sprinting mare, Tut Tut, owned by Fred Myerscough, the man who re-established Goffs as a domestic alternative to Tattersalls, then based in Doncaster.

Jimmy's limitations following his dreadful fall at Catterick saw father James calling on Tommy's services with increasing frequency. One such fleeting visit to his home town in July 1920 yielded a treble, two for Middleham maestro Dobson Peacock and the featured Montrose Handicap for his father on Forest Guard, not only the biggest horse that James Burns ever trained but also the best.

Busy riding winners at Tramore when Forest Guard followed up at Stockton in August, Tommy ensured his availability for the Western meeting at Ayr in September, where he and Forest Guard triggered off memorable celebrations when repelling all-comers to land the coveted Ayr Gold Cup, instituted as long ago as 1804. In capturing Scottish racing's greatest prize, James Burns realised his late father's death bed wish. His Irish tally of 46 winners saw Tommy near the top of the list, headed by Michael Beary.

1920 had not been all work and no play. On December 1st, in Dublin's University Church on St Stephen's Green, Thomas Burns married Stella Anastasia Josephine O'Connor of The Abbey, Roscommon, daughter of James and Katherine O'Connor. Nineteen at the time of her marriage, Stella had been sent to Loreto Convent on St Stephen's Green to complete her education. The reception was to have been held in the Shelbourne Hotel. Not only did Stella bring her ravishing good looks, but also a dowry of £10,000, a not inconsiderable sum in 1920.

As to how they met, TP surmised that his vivacious and glamorous mother enjoyed the social whirl into which her brother Gerald, a man about town, had introduced her. Her future husband was equally enamoured of the bright lights and the attraction proved mutual. Gerald would subsequently consolidate the family's racing involvement by marrying Mona, a daughter of the 'Baron' Fleming, Turf Club official, one of the leading lights of Tramore racecourse and bloodstock manager. Tommy Burns could be said to have brokered that marriage, for Mona, Stella's close friend, had recently been jilted by her fiancé and was feeling disconsolate. Tommy suggested that she accompany Stella and himself on a weekend visit to the O'Connor home in Roscommon. There Mona met Gerald.

The newlyweds were reported as setting up home in Yorkshire, as Tommy had agreed to ride for Middleham trainer Dobson Peacock in the forthcoming season. While the intention was always to make their home in Ireland, Tommy and Stella would bide their time, presumably until such time as suitable accommodation became available in the vicinity of the Curragh of Kildare. The reality was somewhat different. They made their first 'home' in the Gresham Hotel, Tommy commuting to Yorkshire.

It wasn't just about accommodation either. On Sunday November 21st 1920, at 9.00am exactly, on Michael Collins' orders, eleven members of British Army Intelligence, otherwise dubbed the 'Cairo Gang' had been shot dead in various locations around Dublin. An almost certainly erroneous casualty was Captain Paddy McCormack, Royal Army Veterinary Corps, gunned down in the Gresham Hotel. Mollie, his wife, was Stella's sister. Collins' subsequent admission, "We have no evidence he was a Secret Service Agent, some of the names were put on by the Dublin Brigade," provided scant solace. If Collins' 'Twelve Apostles' could be wrong once, and with such consequences. . .

By one account, Paddy McCormack had been in the process of being transferred to India. That had necessitated frequent visits to Dublin Castle to complete the requisite paperwork. Observers had interpreted those visits as intelligence reporting missions. Paddy's tragic death threw Tommy and Stella's wedding arrangements into understandable disarray. The planned reception in the Shelbourne Hotel was scrapped, replaced by a quiet gathering in a friend's house.

T. Ryle Dwyer confirmed the issue of Paddy McCormack's fatal misfortune in his recent book, *The Squad*. He had been sitting up in bed in Room 22, reading the paper, when the assassins burst in, shooting him five times. One carried a sledgehammer. Hamar Greenwood subsequently informed the House of Commons that McCormack's body had been hideously disfigured. "The hammer was possibly used as well as the shots to finish off this gallant officer."

The same author cited Collins as personally admitting that Paddy McCormack had been murdered in error. He had in fact been about to leave for Egypt, to take up the position of starter with the racing club out there.

PADDY McCORMACK – assassinated on 'Bloody Sunday' November 21, 1920 on suspicion of being a member of British Intelligence.

That dark period in Irish history created such lasting

WEDDING BELLS – Tommy and Stella were married in muted circumstances on December 1, 1920, following the recent murder of Paddy McCormack, Stella's brother-in-law.

bitterness and division that two generations at least had to go to their eternal reward before the events of that time became acceptable topics for appraisal. Anyone of a certain age educated in Ireland will readily recall that Irish history, as taught in school, ended abruptly in 1916. Befitting his generation, TP remained reticent on the subject of Paddy McCormack's fate and its motivation. Rather would he recall his parents' occasional references to the slain RAVC officer as a man who would have gone on to make a success of his life, had he been spared.

In tandem with his veterinary accomplishments, Paddy McCormack had made a name for himself as competent amateur rider, at a time when the unpaid brethren more than held their own against professionals, particularly Leslie Brabazon over jumps and young Billy Parkinson on the flat. The *Irish Racing Calendar* records Mr P. F. McCormack riding H. C. Bourke's Nellie Mac to victory in a flat race at Limerick in May 1915 and E. Callaghan's Towanda in a similar event at Claremorris in June.

At the time her husband was slain, Mollie had a baby daughter, Gay. Through her subsequent marriage to Johnny Doran, a bank manager in Sligo, Mollie had a second daughter, Jacqueline.

Tommy's traversing of the Irish Sea meant that he had five winners on the board, including the valuable Jubilee Hurdle at Manchester on Phantom Bold, before opening his Irish account for 1921. That he proceeded to do with customary panache, riding Soldennis to victory in the inaugural Irish 2000 Guineas. One of the outstanding Irish flat racers of his era, Soldennis was trained on Maryborough Heath, where 'Shem' Jeffery held the trainer's licence for his employers, the Blakes, pillars of the Turf Club. *Racing-up-to-Date* described Soldennis as winning the Irish Guineas "in a canter." Transferred temporarily to Lord George Dundas's Newmarket stable as a four-year-old, Soldennis justified hot favouritism in the Ayr Gold Cup, one of 24 career victories. His full-sister, Wet Kiss, became the dam of Coronach, winner of the 1926 Derby.

Increasing time spent in England and Scotland yielded another valuable family success when Forest Guard lifted the Gosforth Park Cup at Newcastle. Back on their local course trainer James and rider Tommy combined to win a modest handicap with a mare belonging to Belfast businessman D. W. Barnett. Not even her most fervent admirers could have forecast that a Curragh Pattern Race would subsequently honour her name – Athasi. Repeatedly mated to Blandford, Athasi produced Trigo, (1929 Derby, St Leger and Irish St Leger), Harinero (1933 Irish Derby and Irish St Leger), Primero (1934 Irish Derby and Irish St Leger) and Harina (1935 Imperial Produce Stakes).

When he did return to Ireland and resume riding regularly, Tommy did so as stable jockey to Michael Dawson, master of Rathbride Manor. While Michael Dawson deliberately restricted the number of horses under his care, they tended to include the best in the land. Likewise, Michael Dawson's owners were content to wait until that meticulous trainer advised accordingly. Four training successes in the Irish Derby, to supplement three as a jockey, bore eloquent testimony to Michael Dawson's talents.

Stella Burns could not exercise similar restraint, giving birth to her son James – 'Jimmy' – at her family's home in Roscommon. While delighted to welcome his grandson into the world under his own roof, James O'Connor felt the time had come for his son-in-law to get himself and his young family installed in more appropriate and permanent surroundings than the

Gresham Hotel. As James O'Connor had not minced his words on the subject, Tommy Burns gave the matter his prompt attention.

SOLDENNIS – Outstanding winner of the inaugural Irish 2000 Guineas in 1921, Successful in the 1920 National Produce Stakes, Soldennis won a further 17 races at the Curragh 1921-24, besides winning a Phoenix Park sprint under 11st 1lb. He also won the 1922 Ayr Gold Cup. Tommy Burns rode Soldennis on his 24th and final victory at Manchester in November 1924.

Chapter Seven

Tommy and Stella seized their opportunity when Lumville Manse, just up the road from the Clonree Hotel that had been home to James Burns and his family during the war, was suddenly vacated.

The historic signing of the Treaty between the British Government and the provisional Government of the Irish Free State on 6 December involved the prompt withdrawal of the army of occupation. Nowhere was more effected than County Kildare, with military barracks in Naas, Newbridge, Kildare and the Curragh Camp, with its population of over 7,000. Informed estimates suggested that the forthcoming military withdrawal would remove between £90,000 and £100,000 per month from the local economy.

Among those who predicted a further 'terrible beauty' being born was Major Thackeray, resident magistrate and tenant of Lumville Manse. "I think there is no doubt that the Treaty will be signed and that an immediate and drastic change will take place in this country."

LUMVILLE – as it looked when becoming home to Tommy and Stella Burns in 1922, following the abrupt departure of Major Thackeray, RM.

Accordingly, Major Thackeray relinquished his lease and departed.

Just a few yards up the road Major Percival Henry Compton found himself in a rather worse predicament, for he had signed a five-year lease on Rangers Lodge in 1920. In the aftermath of the Treaty the major petitioned his landlords in Whitehall (Office of Woods). "Owing to the entire change in the state of affairs in this country I should be glad if you would allow me to break the lease I made with you. . . The present position was quite unforeseen when I signed the lease, it being not merely a change of landlord but a change of Government. . .I am sure you will realise that my position in this country would be intolerable, living here after I have been spending the past two years fighting them."

The Office of Woods declined to cancel the lease, whereupon Major Compton packed his bags and walked out on 9 February 1922. By that time Tommy Burns had negotiated his lease with the Office of Woods and occupied Lumville Manse, where he promptly erected a new stable block to the rear of the house. It was a commercial investment, for the location of Lumville Manse, on the very edge of the Curragh, would ensure a constant demand for stable accommodation.

While the house had been built to accommodate the Methodist chaplain to the Curragh Army Camp, it had never actually been occupied in that capacity. Instead, the Wills tobacco family had used it whenever a member happened to be posted to the Curragh. In future the Burns family would refer to their abode simply as 'Lumville'.

TOMMY BURNS in the 'Black, red disc and cap' of Belfast solicitor A. H. Macaulay, who held the trainer's licence in Lumville.

James was followed into this world two years later by Thomas Pascal. Born in Lumville on April 14th 1924. Known as Thomas to distinguish him from his father, Tommy, he became TP from the outset of his racing career. Daughter Stella came next, in October 1925, while John completed the Burns family. Born in September 1929, John was referred to by his mother Stella as "My afterthought". His siblings came to regard the baby of the family as, "spoilt something rotten!"

Tommy's riding career continued to flourish, Michael Dawson providing the bulk of his 26 Irish winners in a year when the racing programme was repeatedly disrupted by the ravages of civil war. Return visits to Scotland yielded winners at Edinburgh and Bogside, as well as across the border at York and Carlisle.

It could all have been very different, as this post-Epsom Derby 1922 cutting from the meticulous Burns family scrapbooks disclosed. "It was distinctly unlucky for T. Burns that the great 'Steve' found himself in a position to accept the mount on Captain Cuttle.

"It may not be generally known that Burns had actually been offered and accepted the mount on Captain Cuttle.

"He went to Beckhampton and rode the colt in his gallop on the Saturday before the race, only to learn a little later that his services would not be required, as Donoghue had decided to take the mount.

"Burns is certainly entitled to sympathy, as such a glorious opportunity is not likely to occur again for a long time."

For many years the telegram booking Tommy Burns for Captain Cuttle was preserved in Lumville as a bitter-sweet reminder: "Terms for riding Captain Cuttle in the Derby - £100 to ride, £1,000 if you win." In fairness to all concerned, Tommy did eventually receive that winner's present, though not without overtures on his behalf.

In later life Tommy would claim that he had been 'robbed' of the mount on Gainsborough, winner of the 1918 Triple Crown because his wartime sojourn in Ireland had rendered him 'politically incorrect'. That was just another element of the myth and legend that surrounded Tommy Burns. After all, who would remember at a distance of time that T. Burns had been under suspension from April until September 1918? In fairness, it was said that James Burns had signed an agreement with Lady James Douglas, Gainsborough's owner, giving her first claim on his son Tommy's services for the 1918 season. Tommy's Leopardstown suspension had effectively nullified that agreement. Ironically, Joe Childs, who came in for the mount on the 1918 Triple Crown winner, was currently serving in the Third Hussars, then stationed in Newbridge. Colonel Goring, his commanding officer, acceded to Lady Douglas's request to grant the irascible jockey leave to ride, should conditions permit. Joe Childs marked his appreciation by donating his 1918 riding fees to regimental funds.

In any case, Tommy Burns could claim to have ridden in both the New Derby Stakes and New St Leger, as the wartime substitutes run at Newmarket were titled. In 1917 Colonel Hall Walker's Kingston Black was sent over to start second favourite for the Irish Derby on his seasonal debut. Ridden by veteran Otto Madden, Kingston Black had refused to jump off, trailing his field throughout. Tommy had ridden outsider Prince Lionel to finish fourth in the colours of Hall Walker's elder brother, John Reid Walker. Tommy got the mount in the New Derby, run on July 31st, in which Kingston Black behaved rather better, finishing sixth to Gay Crusader. Odds-on when winning a Newmarket maiden the following month, Tommy and Kinston Black took on Gay Crusader in the New St Leger, 33/1 outsiders in a field of three. While no match for the Triple Crown winner, Kingston Black did finish second. Other anecdotes would have Tommy Burns riding for three English monarchs, an emperor and even the Kaiser.

In the years that followed Tommy Burns was to become the proverbial living legend, one that he was never averse to embellishing. Falsifying his date of birth to coincide with St Valentine's Day was only the beginning. The 'riding for the Kaiser' story had, after all, some slender connection with the truth. 'Tommy Burns' had indeed ridden for the Kaiser, as this notice from the *British Bloodstock Breeders' Review*, 1913, confirmed.

"November 14th. – T. H. Burns, who was "Tommy" to his familiars, one of the best jockeys of the day, was on this date killed on the railway between New York and Sheepshead Bay, where he was spending the winter recess with his family. He had recently returned from Germany, where he held a retainer from Mr. V. Bennigsen, of Mausbach, and for whom he was have again ridden next season. Born in Canada, Burns was 34 years of age. He rode his first winner in 1895. So rapid was his progress that in 1898 he won 277 of the 973 races in which he rode that year. The following year he had 273 winning mounts. In fourteen seasons on the American Turf (1898-1912 – he was riding in France and Germany in 1907) he had 6,450 mounts and rode 1,333 winners, 1,131 seconds and 1,009 thirds – a very remarkable record. Burns married the daughter of famous jockey James McLaughlin."

If 1922 had been somewhat disappointing by Tommy Burns' now accustomed standards, the following season was to prove very different. Martin Quirke, J. J. Parkinson's stable jockey, had become temporarily disillusioned. For all his success on Maddenstown Lodge runners, Martin became convinced that he had lost the trainer's trust. Learning of the jockey's plight, Michael Dawson inveigled him into riding out for Rathbride Manor, gradually coaxing Martin back into winning form with the prospect of becoming champion.

Jim Parkinson thus needed a stable jockey for a large string, made even larger by the addition of fleets of horses owned by new client John Musker. Tommy Burns filled the bill, notching up 69 winners in Ireland. Highlights included a second Galway Hurdle on Smoke Cloud for his retaining stable and a second Irish 2000 Guineas on Soldumeno, trained, like Soldennis, on Maryborough Heath by S. C. 'Shem' Jeffery. John Musker headed the owners' table with 22 winners of 50 races, while Jim Parkinson broke all records, sending out 60 winners of 134 races. Unfortunately for Tommy, Michael Dawson's promise to Martin Quirke that he would make him champion jockey duly came to pass, with an Irish record 86 winners. Continuing with Jim Parkinson in 1924 yielded 59 Tommy Burns winners, not enough to prevent Joe Canty claiming his second Irish title with 72 successes.

1925 saw Martin Quirke reunited with J. J. Parkinson, but the invincible form of the Dawson and Phillie Behan stables ensured Joe Canty retained his crown, this time with 117 winners, just one less than Gordon Richards' English tally for the season. Admittedly, Joe amassed his total under both codes, whereas Gordon confined his activities to the flat. In the interim Joe Canty had become Michael Dawson's son-in-law, marrying Lena. Tommy Burns might only have managed 26 winners in Ireland and a further 12 in Britain, but he had changed his *modus operandi*.

In April Tommy rode the speedy juvenile, L'Aine, to success at Leopardstown, trained by a newcomer to the ranks of Irish trainers – Peter Tierney. This enormously capable and experienced Scots stableman had come to Ireland and James Burns with the Hall Walker horses in 1915, staying on when his employer returned to Scotland in 1919. Peter Tierney now held

Allets - winner of the 1925 Phoenix '1500' ridden by T. Burns, de facto owner and trainer.

the licence at Lumville. Unfortunately, Peter Tierney's tendency to over-imbibe rendered him a menace at a racemeeting. While it was an open secret that T. Burns, jockey, was also *de facto* trainer, in flagrant contravention of Turf Club rules, an official blind eye could be turned, provided some unfortunate public indiscretion should not oblige the authorities to investigate.

As a form of insurance Tommy had recruited burly, influential Belfast solicitor, Arthur H. Macauley as an owner, who might even be granted a trainer's licence should that need arise.

The newly-formed stable behind Lumville housed another speedy juvenile – Allets – or Stella in reverse. Tommy had spotted this near-black daughter of Athlone at Goff's August Sales, securing her for 700 guineas. At that apparently modest figure the half-sister to Bright Maid still topped the sales that day. Indeed, when the sale ended two days later, only three yearlings – all of them fillies – had sold for more. While Tommy Burns was pleased with his purchase, S. C. Dawson of Cloghran Stud was equally satisfied. Only six months previously he had secured the filly for 200 guineas at the dispersal sale of the late Paddy Cullinan's bloodstock at Carrollstown. Moreover, Athlone was an unknown quantity, this being his first crop. A son of Orby, Athlone had won five Curragh sprints over four seasons

Two educational runs at the Curragh had revealed enough to ensure that Allets started only third favourite for the Phoenix Park 'Fifteen Hundred' in Horse Show Week. Tommy Burns got down to within 1lb of Allets' allocated 8st 3lb. His sacrifice proved worthwhile when he drove the filly home with a head and the same to spare over Joe Canty and future champion Jack Moylan to land the juvenile sprint championship of 1925.

Whether the occasion proved too much for Peter Tierney is unknown, but Allets proved to be the last winner from Lumville credited to him. For the remainder of the season and for seasons to come Lumville runners appeared under the name of A. H. Macauley, officially the owner of Allets.

Transferred to James Burns in Ayr as a three-year-old, Allets won again under Tommy at Hamilton Park. Prior to that, Tommy had ridden Resplendent to finish second in the Oaks at Epsom to Short Story. He kept the mount when H. S. 'Atty' Persse sent her over for the Irish Oaks in July, which she duly won as an even-money favourite should.

Tommy Burns had a much more comfortable follow-up in the 1926 Phoenix Park 'Fifteen Hundred' in which Archway ran out the five-length winner for Crotanstown trainer J. T. 'Jack' Rogers. However, this combination's performance in the Londonderry Plate at Leopardstown later in August caused a degree of official disquiet.

PHOENIX PARK, August 7, 1926 – owner C. Wadia leading in Archway, the second of Tommy Burns' four '1500' winners.

"The Stewards enquired into the starting and running of Archway [1/1F, btn a head] in the above race, and having heard the evidence of Mr D. Ruttledge (the starter), Mr J. T. Rogers (the trainer), T. Burns (the rider) and inspected some of the betting books they failed to find any evidence of wrong doing, but advised Burns to be most careful that his riding in future should leave no loophole for suspicion."

Chapter Eight

When not plying his trade in Ireland, or riding winners regularly in the north of England and Scotland, Tommy Burns remained true to his ancestry – buying and selling horses. To this end he acquired a potential stud farm in Pollardstown, on the northern fringe of the Curragh. Approximately 150 acres in extent, what had been 'Old' Connolly's farm would carry broodmares, young stock and boarders, with the Pond Division rented to cattle grazier Paddy Higgins. The virtual procession of horses through his hands needed accommodation, for many were destined to continue their travels elsewhere.

One that was destined to stay for longer than usual was a chestnut yearling colt by Loch Lomond, acquired at Ballsbridge Sales in 1925 for just 300 guineas. Unraced as a two-year-old, Old Orkney had an introductory outing at the Curragh in April 1927, nominally owned and trained by A. H. Macaulay and ridden by stable apprentice Peter Fitzgerald. In August the same combination lined up for the Moderate Optional Selling Plate at Limerick Junction. Backed in to 3/1 second favourite, Old Orkney landed the gamble with ten lengths to spare.

Actually, the Lumville gamble was not as lucrative as its architects had anticipated. They had quietly backed Old Orkney at SP in Belfast and even further afield. No money must appear on course. Unfortunately, Billy Parkinson, Irish wartime champion jockey and now a fulltime punter, had got wind of Old Orkney's ability. All he needed to learn was the day the horse was fancied. Martin Quirke was riding the favourite, Zorro Pardo, for Parkinsons in the same race. Jack Moylan was to ride Lothian for Churchtown farmer Dan O'Brien. It had no chance. Billy and Jack conferred. If Jack could find out from young Fitzgerald down at the start whether Old Orkney was 'off' and if the answer was affirmative, then Jack was to charge the tapes, break them and continue a furlong up the course before pulling up. The ensuing delay would afford Billy the opportunity to lump all he could on the Lumville runner. When Lothian was seen to charge the tapes Billy's response ensured the 10/1 about Old Orkney swiftly shrank to the 3/1 at which the runaway winner was returned.

Old Orkney was long odds-on when completing a riding treble for Tommy Burns at Leopardstown in September. Entered for the Irish Cesarewitch in October, Old Orkney seemed to have been set a stiff task for a three-year-old under 8st 2lb. It became still more onerous as Tommy put up 2lb overweight. Old Orkney's supporters were undeterred, sending him off clear 2/1 favourite to beat fifteen rivals. The result was never in doubt, Old Orkney coming home a comfortable winner, making it five winners for Tommy Burns over the three-day Curragh meeting.

By that time Old Orkney ran in the colours of J. J. Murphy, who had given £3,000 for the horse. J. J. Murphy was introduced to the Irish racing fraternity as a brother of F. X. Murphy, T. D., and member of the Board of Governors of the Bank of Ireland. He was also reported to "own very large estates in India, where he has a stable of 22 horses, and where he built a racecourse grand stand."

CURRAGH, October 19, 1927 – Old Orkney (T. Burns) cantering winner of the Irish Cesarewitch.

When Old Orkney's name appeared among the entries for the Manchester November Handicap, finale of the English flat season and a traditional gambling medium, the handicapper took a chance, allotting the Irish colt just 7st. Tommy Burns could not possibly do the weight, but Steve Donoghue could get within 1lb of it. Disregarded by English bookmakers and punters alike, Old Orkney was allowed to start at 8/1.

Mr Murphy had every reason to show his appreciation when his horse came home with something in hand. 'Captain Keen' informed his readers: "He won a good sum in bets and he has, I believe, given 'Steve' Donoghue a present of £500 for having ridden the winner."

Mr Murphy's largesse extended further, Stella Burns receiving lavish gifts of jewellery as a memento of that momentous triumph on English soil.

Transferred to Captain Dick Gooch's East Ilsley stable, Old Orkney developed in to one of the prominent stayers of his age. In a memorable duel for the 1929 Ascot Stakes Old Orkney and Freddie Lane defeated the mighty Brown Jack and Steve Donoghue by a short head, eight lengths clear of their field. They renewed rivalry in the Goodwood Cup, in which Old Orkney and Freddie Lane once again triumphed by a short head. As it transpired, those epic encounters had taken their toll. Over succeeding seasons Brown Jack became the most popular flat racer of his era, or any other. Although eclipsed by his great rival, Old Orkney had nonetheless played his part in establishing the Brown Jack legend.

It was all change in Lumville as well, at least in racing terms. Arthur Macaulay did not renew his trainer's licence in 1928, while Tommy Burns caused general surprise when announcing his retirement from the saddle, aged only twenty-eight. He confounded his admirers further by not exchanging his rider's licences for a trainer's ticket.

MANCHESTER, November 26, 1927 – Old Orkney (Steve Donoghue) landing a massive gamble in the last big handicap of the season.

On the domestic front Lumville had accumulated a personnel that was to endure relatively unchanged for decades. Mrs Chevalier – 'Chev' – had joined as housekeeper, having been deserted by her husband, a serving soldier, during the Great War. Housekeeper, cook, lady's maid, confidante and surrogate mother, 'Chev' would run the household for the remainder of her working life. Devoted to her mistress, 'Chev' would brook no nonsense from the master of the house.

Paddy Aspell from Sunnyhill, green-fingered gardener, handyman, general factotum and devoted aide to the mistress of the house, was to spend over half a century in Lumville. His son and namesake would in time become a lynchpin of Sean Mulryan's Ardenode Stud, while grandsons Leighton and Paddy would make their mark as jump jockeys across the Irish Sea.

'Nursey' Melia married the stud groom in Loders' Eyrefield Lodge, a circumstance that led Lumville governess, Miss Almack, to a noteworthy outing in that direction. Matty Almack, her father, was stud groom in the National Stud, as Tully had become through William Hall Walker's wartime gift to the British nation. No doubt reared on the legend of Pretty Polly, the Eyrefield-bred Triple Crown heroine, winner of all but two of her 24 races all of twenty years previously, Miss Almack sallied forth with young Tom to pay their respects to that wonderful old mare, by then retired from stud and living out her days in Eyrefield Lodge.

Bashfully, TP conceded that he hadn't just visited the old mare. Young Tom had pleaded to sit up on her, "on the lawn in front of the house, it was." Considering that she had carried off her fillies' Triple Crown as long ago as 1904, Thomas Pascal Burns can safely claim to be the last man living to have ridden the legendary Pretty Polly.

Chapter Nine

Young Thomas Pascal Burns had commenced his formal education, in a private school in Newbridge, when his father renewed his rider's licences in the latter part of 1928. That abbreviated campaign yielded just one winner, Flower Song for Sir Bryan Mahon and his trainer Fred Grundy at the Phoenix Park in October. The same period brought sadness to the Burns family on either side of the Irish Sea with the premature death of Tommy's younger brother James, who had never made a complete recovery from that fall in Catterick Bridge.

Still disinclined to resume riding in 1929, Tommy Burns took out a trainer's licence, to media acclaim. "The decision of Tommy Burns to relinquish his riding licence and to establish himself as a trainer will win for him the good wishes of his many friends.

   "Burns' friends in racing are numerous, for everyone admires horsemanship of the standard of brilliance which for so many years this accomplished rider has so consistently shown in public.

   "His amazing assertion of strength, and the intensified effort by which he snatched the verdict, virtually on the post, involved him in well-nigh innumerable spectacular finishes, and exalted him to a high plane in popularity.

   "With the disappearance of Burns from among our jockeys, there is rather unpleasantly emphasised a further shrinkage in the number of first-class riders now available for owners. At the moment, we have, in this respect, struck a decidedly lean period. Indeed, it is doubtful if first-class jockeys were ever available in such limited number."

DAPPER DAN –
TP in 1929, aged 4¹/2.

The new trainer opened his account at Ayr in April when Lotus Lass ran out an easy winner of the Doon Selling Plate under Jimmy Doyle and was retained for 200 guineas. Miss Marlhill promptly followed up closer to home, winning the Apprentices' Handicap at the Curragh under Lumville protégé Bernard Curran. Jimmy Doyle then delivered on Flying Top at Leopardstown. Bought in for 230 guineas, Flying Top won a similar event at the Curragh Guineas meeting, becoming the property of J. J. Parkinson for 210 guineas. That was a fruitful meeting for the Lumville team, with Fanatist making a winning debut, Sir Crispen taking the apprentices' event and White Mixture making it three-in-a-row for the stable under John 'Chalk' Doyle. The following day Miss Marlhill made it a first and last race double following Flying Top's success in the opener.

Back at Ayr Jack Mytton, ridden by Jimmy Doyle, dead heated in the Montgomerie Handicap. Nuxford won outright at Manchester, but had to survive an objection, before changing hands for 760 guineas. Miss Marlhill and Bernard Cullen continued their winning run in the race immediately before the Irish Derby. Kopi, the winning favourite in that 1929 Irish Derby, was trained in Newmarket by Walter Earl for Solly Joel. He had been secured as a yearling at Ballsbridge by Tommy Burns for just 50 guineas. Tommy had passed the colt on to Solly Joel, with a contingency of £500 should he win a race.

At the Irish St Leger meeting Tommy used Miss Marlhill to launch another of the Lumville apprentices – Peter Maher. She became the first of hundreds of winners ridden by this accomplished lightweight in a lengthy career spent mostly in England. Over at Lanark Tommy renewed his partnership with Steve Donoghue to land Captain Hardy home in front in a juvenile seller. On the home front the Curragh continued to be a Burns' happy hunting ground, yielding another double at the October meeting with Queen's Park and Roman General, the latter in an amateur event, ridden by Mr Bryan Rogers, son of Crotanstown trainer Jack Rogers. This new pairing promptly followed up with Bonanza at Leopardstown.

What had been a very respectable first season as a trainer had surely laid a solid foundation on which to build. But perhaps it lacked excitement for one so young after his high-flying exploits in the saddle. Besides, betting on horses ridden by others, particularly inexperienced apprentices, was hardly as attractive as holding the fate of those wagers in one's own hands.

There was another aspect to be considered as well – the emergence of several new faces in the trainers' ranks, notably Hon H. G. 'Ginger' Wellesley in Friarstown and Roderic More O'Farrell in Kildangan Castle, bankrolled by the fabulously wealthy Irish tenor, Count John McCormack. The lure was to prove irresistible.

Chapter Ten

Thomas Pascal Burns had graduated to the primary school run by the Presentation Order of nuns in Newbridge, while his elder brother James had been sent away as a boarder to St Gerard's in Bray when their father was granted a flat race jockey's licence for the 1930 season. With the closure of the Lumville stable, Bernard Curran's indentures were transferred to Roderic More O'Ferrall in Kildangan. Peter Maher moved further afield, to Ayr, apprenticed to 'old' James Burns.

Having applied for his riding licence, the 'Scotchman' was duly granted it at the initial Curragh meeting in April, getting his eye in on a couple of unfancied mounts. Such a low profile return was too uncharacteristic to endure.

The jockey's spectacular comeback was described under the banner headline, "Burns signalises his return."

"The Irish One Thousand Guineas was won in a canter by Mr Geoffrey Allen's Star of Egypt. In a way her victory signalised the return to the saddle of the redoubtable jockey T. Burns.

"No matter what can be said about him he is the finest rider of the present day. He possesses the temperament of the genius jockey, and Mr Roderic More O'Ferrall's stable at Kildangan Castle will, with his attributes, score all along the line this season. If this prophecy of mine proves wrong – then talk about surprise."

But the 'Scotchman' – as Tommy Burns had generally come to be known - was always full of surprises. "The announcement that Tommy Burns has severed his connection with the Kildangan stable managed by Mr R. More O'Ferrall caused considerable surprise in Irish racing circles. It was only at the last Curragh meeting that Burns was given a jockey's licence, having a long time previously relinquished his licence as a trainer and transferred the indentures of the clever apprentice, B. Curran, to Mr More O'Ferrall.

"The patrons of the Kildangan establishment include a number of wealthy owners, including Count McCormack. In severing his connection with the stable Burns is forfeiting a very substantial retainer.

STAR OF EGYPT (T. Burns) – Tommy's first Irish 1000 Guineas winner, pictured on Roderic More O'Ferrall's Kildangan gallops in 1930. Owned by Geoffrey Allen, Star of Egypt was the first of six Irish classic winners trained in Kildangan, 1930-1945.

"It is understood that for the present he will ride as a free lance, but his unquestioned ability will no doubt induce some owners to seek his services."

Some owners undoubtedly did just that, but not to any great effect. Racecourse gossip had it as 'gospel truth' that the 'Scotchman' was fit to stop any horse, if it suited his book to do so. Incredibly, for one who was prohibited from betting under the terms of his jockey's licence, the 'Scotchman' actually recorded his wagers during that period in a little ledger still in Lumville. That he soon discontinued this dangerous discipline is perhaps evidence that the balance was rarely in his favour. Gradually and at Nancy More O'Ferrall's instigation, Tommy Burns began to get back on the odd Kildangan runner, though the great majority of Kildangan winners went to Martin Quirke and Bernard Curran. One such 'spare' was on Philip's Fancy at the Curragh in September, the mare's first run since finishing down the field at the Irish Derby meeting.

Kildangan was also represented by the in-form Pitched Battle. Ridden by Joe Canty, Pitched

Battle vied for favouritism, whereas Philip's Fancy was friendless at 20/1. The mare was saddled for the race in defiance of veterinary advice, Joe Cosgrove having treated her both for a knee problem and strained ligaments. Unable to stride out, Philip's Fancy finished down the field. As TP recalled, "She wasn't fit to stride over a straw! But Frankie was a mad gambler and had to find out was the mare worth keeping in training. For all the grandeur of Kildangan, the More-Os had very little ready money. Frankie was always broke, but a very, very nice man. All the gamblers I've known were decent men. And I've known a few!"

"The Stewards of the Turf Club called Mr F. More O'Ferrall (owner), Mr R. More O'Ferrall (trainer), and T. Burns (jockey) before them to explain the running and riding of Philip's Fancy.

"Having heard the explanations, the Stewards postponed their decision for further consideration until the following day (Wednesday), when they again interviewed T. Burns, and withdrew his licence."

It was of scant solace to the beleaguered jockey that he had ridden Count McCormack's Mignonne to victory in the Turf Club Cup before the blow fell. The racing press were incensed, the following being a representative example of the media' response.

"Tommy Burns has had his riding licence withdrawn, the Turf Club Stewards having been dissatisfied with his explanation of his riding of Philip's Fancy in the Kildare Handicap at the Curragh meeting. . .

"It is consoling to realise that our Stewards are watchful, but we cannot refrain from remarking that there have been very many worse cases which have evidently escaped their vigilance, and that they will receive no applause or commendation from the bulk of the Irish racing community for exterminating the most brilliant jockey of the present era for such an offence as that which they have found him guilty of.

"We hold no particular brief for Burns, but we do maintain that the punishment scarcely appears to fit the crime in this case.

COUNT JOHN McCORMACK – entertaining at San Patrizio, his Hollywood home, in 1932. L to R: Lily, Countess McCormack; Cecily Nelson; Maurice McLoughlin, US tennis champion 1912-13: Gwen McCormack; Michael Beary, leading jockey; Edgar Wallace, author, playwright and racehorse owner; Elsworth Vines, US tennis champion 1931-32; Count John McCormack.

LUMVILLE, 1928 – snapshot by Stella of Uncle Billy Burns holding Kitty (TP).

"To put it mildly, Burns has been the victim of circumstances. The Stewards have found him guilty, but they stand alone in their opinion that Burns deserved to have his licence withdrawn for not trying on Philip's Fancy.

"They have never produced a weaker case, and have never had less cause to take away a jockey's licence.

"That they should refuse to open the case when requested is the last word in unfairness. It is almost unbelievable."

The draconian sentence caused a stir across the Irish Sea. Edgar Wallace, respected novelist, playwright and steadfast owner of a long series of moderate racehorses, wrote an open letter to the Stewards of the Turf Club, urging them to reconsider Tommy Burns' ban over his riding of Philip's Fancy. "He has ridden for me and I have always found him to be a straight, decent man."

The protests fell on deaf ears. One of TP's earliest racing memories is of accompanying his father in the car to the railway siding behind the grand stand when racing was taking place on the Curragh and watching from there. As a disqualified person the 'Scotchman' could not set foot on lands under Turf Club control.

As his parents explained to the aggrieved youngster, his father could only bide his time until he received word by the customary circuitous route that he might re-apply for his licence with every prospect of success.

More immediately, the 'Scotchman' had his Pollardstown operation to pre-occupy him. The yard at Lumville was likewise kept busy, used by neighbouring trainer Jack Rogers, always a dealer at heart, to accommodate the stock that he was accustomed to purchase on his regular forays down to Tipperary's Golden Vale. There he relied upon the local scenting skills of the renowned 'Spotter' Ryan to unearth potential racehorses to be purchased, broken and trained and turned over in due course.

By this time young Tom had been joined in the Presentation Convent in Newbridge by his sister Stella, returning home to cut their teeth on Kitty, their favourite pony. As TP recalls, "Kitty was more than just a pony. She was a miniature racehorse." Mother Stella, meanwhile, doted on little John, "my afterthought".

Chapter Eleven

In good time for the 1931 flat season the 'Scotchman' received the welcome news that his application for a jockey's licence would be favourably regarded. He duly applied for and was granted a licence under both codes. The news was enthusiastically received.

"Tommy Burns is back again, the Stewards having granted him his licence for 1931. Thus closes a much discussed incident of the last back-end.

"Burns will be welcomed back to the riding ranks in Ireland, and doubtless he will make his presence felt. Competition looks like being exceptionally keen, with Wing in action again over here and the English light-weight, George Hulme, having arrived to ride for Cecil Brabazon."

In the interim Nancy More O'Ferrall, chatelaine of Kildangan, had made up her mind that her son's stable would best be served by the reinstatement of the 'Scotchman' as stable jockey. This forceful lady formed her opinion not only on Tommy Burns' unquestioned riding ability, but also on his proven capacity to entertain the house parties that filled Kildangan for all the major race meetings. He was socially *de rigueur*, at a time when few flat jockeys were considered to be so. Moreover, Count McCormack, an avowed punter, made it plain that the 'Scotchman' was his favoured jockey.

While Dominic More O'Ferrall actively disliked the racing scene and the social whirl that attended its existence in his Kildangan estate, he deferred to his formidably ambitious wife in such

LUMVILLE, 1930 – Jimmy Burns shows his style on Kitty.

BOGSIDE, 1932 – James Burns, shortly before retiring as a trainer, having, in his own words "made thousands of pounds less than nothing out of racing."

matters. It was Nancy, much more so than her bachelor sons Roderic, Rory and Frankie, who drove the Kildangan stable, ever on the look-out for potential recruits to what was already a wealthy, if raffish collection of patrons. As Jimmy Gorman, travelling head lad for the Kildangan stable once put it to TP, "When the old lady dies they'll all feel the draught!"

Restored to the fold, the 'Scotchman' quickly opened his 1931 score on Count McCormack's Song o' My Heart at the Phoenix Park in April. Equally aware of the need to revive his English connections, he slipped across to Catterick Bridge to land the odds in a lowly seller for Middleham trainer John Drake. Thereafter Kildangan runners kept him busy and while Count McCormack's Beaudelaire could finish only second to Sea Serpent in the Baldoyle Derby and then in the Irish Derby, he did come up trumps in the Irish St Leger.

Millennium provided Tommy with three of his 27 Irish winners in a comeback season marred by the sudden death of his mother in September while accompanying her husband at Bogside races. On the family's return from Ayr, Tommy resumed his winning ways when riding Geoffrey Gilpin's Jackaleen at Listowel and then Tralee.

Christmas in Lumville came perilously close to being spoiled at Leopardstown on St Stephen's Day when Tommy Burns rode the Hon Mrs Brinsley Plunket's Millennium for his retaining stable in the Stand Maiden Hurdle, finishing third.

"The Stewards called T. Burns before them to explain his riding of Millennium in the above race. Having heard evidence, they considered the riding of T. Burns open to grave suspicion, and severely cautioned him as to his future riding."

The 'Scotchman' was thus reminded that he was, in the eyes of officialdom, a marked man. By this time he hardly needed reminding. However, Roderick More O'Ferrall, his principal employer, had also come to the notice of various panels of racecourse stewards and thus to the

DR STRABISMUS – Lady Milbanke's speedy two-year-old contributor of 4 to Tommy 'Scotchman' Burns' 57 winners, making him Irish champion jockey in 1932.

Turf Club. As so often in such cases, it was betting ring intelligence that intensified official scrutiny. Kildangan runners were being backed when recent form said they should not win and doing just that. By contrast, obvious form favourites from the stable frequently ran below general expectations. Those most closely connected seemed to know just when to invest and when to refrain.

For the time being all was well. In 1932 the partnership of trainer and jockey kicked off on a winning note with the speedy Dr Strabismus, successful four times in a row in Lady Milbanke's colours. Smart Aleck won three times for Count McCormack, as did Double Bell in his trainer's livery. Despite their hectic Irish schedule the Kildangan team found time to conquer Chester's turns with Millennium, successful in the Earl of Chester's Handicap at the big May meeting. 'Ginger' Wellesley supplied the 'Scotchman' with numerous country winners, while Cecil Brabazon, Bob Fetherstonhaugh, Geoffrey Gilpin, Hubert Hartigan and Charlie Rogers also contributed to Tommy Burns final Irish total of 57 winners, sufficient to see him crowned champion jockey for the first and only time.

The press gave due prominence to the jockey's triumphant return from exterior banishment in such a short space of time. "Tommy Burns is champion jockey, and he has gained the title through sheer merit. His average is much better than his nearest attendants, Joe Canty and John Doyle. Burns can be compared with the greatest jockeys of this or past eras, and in a voting competition confined to those competent to express an opinion as to which was the best jockey riding in any country at the present time, it would be a close call between Burns, Canty, Richards, Harry Wragg and Beary. I know some trainers who would not hesitate to choose Burns if they had their pick."

However, not all were of that view. Joe Cosgrove was the regular veterinary surgeon in Kildangan in those days. He passed on this anecdote to his nephew, Stan Cosgrove, who succeeded him as veterinarian in Kildangan. Roderic queried Joe Cosgrove one day. "What do they say about my new stable jockey?"

"If you really want to know, they say that if you don't get rid of him soon, McCormack will be singing on the streets of Monasterevan. And you'll be passing round the hat!"

Having seen his son crowned champion jockey in his adoptive country, James Burns relinquished his trainer's licence. Forty-odd years in harness, he had had enough, his decision quite possibly strengthened by the deaths of his son James in 1928 and then his wife in September 1931. Peter Maher, originally apprenticed in Lumville and latterly with 'old' James Burns, returned to Ireland, now indentured to Hon 'Ginger' Wellesley.

While it was written that 'old' James promptly became actively involved in pig dealing, that occupation belonged to his son John. Never afraid to take a punt on his own judgement, John was known to go to Ayr market and buy every porker offered for sale, confident of emerging on the winning side of his ledger.

William, the fourth son of 'old' James, had opened his racecourse account when successful at Catterick in November 1931 on Mardin II, at only his second attempt over fences. In TP's recollection, "Uncle Billy never rode much, too brainy! He married Jessie Duncan, whose family owned the Dalblair Hotel in Ayr. Billy began driving a Rolls Royce. They had no family. When Jessie died, Billy came in for the hotel and promptly sold it."

Chapter Twelve

The general election in Ireland in February 1932 had seen Eamon de Valera's 'slightly constitutional' party – Fianna Fail – come into the political arena and thence into office in Dail Eireann. Curragh trainer Hubert Hartigan was just one of a number of prominent figures in Irish society to declare that he would not continue to live in "Dev's Ireland". He had promptly transferred his stable to Penrith, on the Scottish border. Bringing Joe Canty over when available, Hubert had gotten off the mark at the opening Liverpool meeting in March 1933.

While Tommy Burns had not ridden regularly for Hartigan, the latter's voluntary exile was to prove the forerunner for a substantial racing and breeding exodus triggered by de Valera's decision to withhold Land Annuities guaranteed under the terms of the Free State treaty negotiations. The British government reacted by slapping a 20% *ad valorem* tax on all livestock entering Britain from the Free State. That was soon doubled to a punitive 40%, inducing Irish trainers to follow the exodus of owners and bloodstock alike.

The Dawson brothers – Dick and Sam - transferred champion sire Blandford to England. Stratford and Soldennis, winner of the 1921 Irish 2000 Guineas with Tommy on board, followed suit. Lord Furness abandoned Gilltown Stud in favour of Dorset, while William Barnett moved his stud, including Trigo, to Aston Park in Oxfordshire. The Irish racing and breeding arena faced a crisis.

As those dire consequences of what became known as the Economic War began to take effect, the 'Scotchman'

LUMVILLE, 1936 – Jimmy Burns shows off Manhattan, an Arab racing pony given to the Burns boys by Sir Percy Loraine, "to practise on".

began the defence of his Irish title not in Ireland but across the water. A successful sighting mission with Roderic More O'Ferrall's Cobequid at Haydock Park in February paid off handsomely when Tommy brought Cobequid home six lengths clear in the Gloucestershire Hurdle at the Cheltenham Festival a month later. They completed their hat trick at Baldoyle on St Patrick's Day.

A Phoenix Park treble in April and a succession of winners at practically every Irish meeting led to further classic laurels when the reigning champion brought Spy-Ann home in the Irish 1000 Guineas for Curragh trainer 'Bob' Fetherstonhaugh. While classic success was no longer any novelty to the 'Scotchman', it represented a breakthrough for the 'jumping trainer', forced to leave his family's Westmeath base when the Land Commission had compulsorily acquired much of the land and gallops at Carrick. Relocating to Loughbrown Cottage – where the Curragh Members' car park is today – Bob had gradually adjusted his sights from Irish Grand Nationals to the richer realms of flat racing. The 'Scotchman' took particular pleasure from partnering Bob's first classic winner.

Ten years after being jocked off Captain Cuttle in the Derby, Tommy Burns set out to gain compensation on Kildangan challenger Franz Hals, owned by Count John McCormack. Steve Donoghue, once undisputed king of the Derby, now rode Thrapston, pacemaker for the favourite, Lord Derby's diminutive Hyperion. With Steve carrying out his role to perfection, Tommy Weston drew clear for an easy success on Hyperion, with Tommy Burns a respectable seventh on the Irish contender.

SPY-ANN – winner of the 1933 Irish 1000 Guineas, a 10th Irish classic for T. Burns and the first of nine such victories for trainer Bob Fetherstonhaugh.

They moved up to fourth in the Irish equivalent, well beaten by William Barnett's Harinero. Like Trigo, Harinero was a son of the amazing Athasi, a modest winner for Tommy when trained by his father in Ayr back in 1921.

Thereafter Tommy's season assumed such a low profile that his chances of retaining his title seemed negligible. Nonetheless, with Joe Canty frequently absent riding for Hubert Hartigan, the title remained open. Millennium could still clinch it for the 'Scotchman'. This extraordinary animal initiated his hat trick at Naas on 7 October, making all to win a twelve-furlong hurdle over six flights under 13st. He did the same, now carrying 13st 8lb at Navan five days later. After a three-day break he completed his three-timer at Baldoyle, under 13st 7lb.

Those heroic weight-carrying efforts actually clinched the professional riders' title for Tommy Burns, who finished the year four ahead of Jack Moylan. However – shades of Mr W. J. 'Billy' Parkinson back in 1916 – Mr F. E. 'Eric' McKeever trumped the professionals with a total of 49 winners. Leading amateur for the fifth consecutive time, Eric McKeever turned professional the following year, riding with continued success until killed in a car smash in 1938.

Before the 'Scotchman' had even sat on a winner in 1934 his plans for the campaign were thrown into disarray. Once again it concerned the running and riding of one of Roderic More O'Ferrall's horses. The warning signs appeared in the *Irish Racing Calendar*, 8 January.

Spy-Ann being led in

"The Stewards decided to hold an enquiry into the running of Greek Pie at Leopardstown, December 26th, Baldoyle, January 1st, and Naas, January 6th, but as Mr R. More O'Ferrall, the trainer, had gone abroad for a period, they deferred the enquiry until his return."

The deferred enquiry took place on 12 March. "The Stewards enquired into the running of Greek Pie at Leopardstown December, Baldoyle January and Naas January. Not being satisfied with the explanations of E. M. Quirke (jockey) and Mr R. More O'Ferrall (trainer), the Stewards withdrew E. M. Quirke's licence to ride and warned both Mr R. More O'Ferrall and Quirke off all courses."

While the Kildangan stable was permitted to operate, with head man Jack Murphy holding the trainer's licence, its contribution to Tommy Burns' season would inevitably be diminished.

Nevertheless, he could carry on, unlike the hapless Martin Quirke. To Tommy's surprise the Kildangan team got off to a flying start, providing him with an Easter treble at Mallow.

Fred Clarke, Joe Dawson, Cecil Brabazon and Bob Fetherstonhaugh all helped to maintain Tommy's momentum prior to the Baldoyle Derby. His masterly judgement of pace in producing His Reverence to run down Morny Wing on the odds-on Portugal at the death earned the 'Scotchman' rave notices. It also served to strengthen a working relationship with 'Ginger' Wellesley, whose fortunes were on a sharp upward curve. Other interesting contributors to Tommy's 1934 total were Jas. J. Murphy and Tom Taaffe, for whom he reeled of a hat trick on Woology, owned by eccentric millionaire Harry de Vere Clifton, who ran his horses by astrology. As Harry and the recently deceased Lord Wavertree both hailed from Lancashire this may have been more than just coincidental.

Similar encomiums followed when Tommy got Sir Percy Loraine's Kyloe home by a neck in the Irish 1000 Guineas for Kildangan and deputy trainer Jack Murphy. Kyloe's stamina limitations were ruthlessly exposed in an optimistic foray to Epsom for the Oaks. The partnership could finish only seventh to Light Brocade. A field of six for the Irish Derby saw Tommy Burns in the stands as William Barnett's Primero, yet another son of Athasi, dead heated with Patriot King, each trained in England. Indeed, a year that saw Tommy Burns third in the overall table with 40 winners to W. T. O'Grady's 74, saw three of the five Irish classics exported, Primero having returned to carry off the Irish St Leger.

Chapter Thirteen

What with J. T. Rogers completing the first and only clean sweep of the Irish classics with Museum and Smokeless and Phillie Behan achieving a near-monopoly of the major juvenile contests in 1935, pickings were thin for such as Tommy Burns, not normally associated with either stable. Moreover, reinstated Roderic More O'Ferrall thought it only fair to make amends to Martin Quirke, also recalled from exterior darkness. Compounding Tommy's bleak prospects was Ginger Wellesley's decision to promote Peter Maher, Tommy's erstwhile apprentice in Lumville, to stable jockey.

Tommy duly sought to resurrect his English clientele. As TP observed years later, his father, for all his exuberance, had always displayed a certain distaste for the rigours then associated with frequent traversal of the Irish Sea and its interminable train journeys on the other side. Had he been more accepting of those hardships, he could, in TP's belief, have had his pick of many leading stables throughout the 1930s. As it was he opened his English seasonal account at Chester, landing a 'touch' on Alletsoi for Tern Hill trainer 'Max' Barthropp. That Alletsoi, bred by his rider, had thus become the first winning produce of Allets, victorious in that epic battle for the 1925 Phoenix 'Fifteen Hundred', ridden and effectively trained by one T. Burns, only added to the satisfaction of a Chester double for trainer and jockey completed by Mum in the Ormonde 2-y-o Stakes.

The Burns voyage of rediscovery took in Ripon, where Sarragossa landed the odds for Weyhill trainer Frank Hartigan. A busy book of rides at Royal Ascot yielded one good winner in Black Speck in the Coventry Stakes. Owned by James V. Rank, the colt was trained in Lambourn by Harry Cottrill. While jockeys of the day could not expect to receive a percentage of the prize money as of right, the fact that the Coventry Stakes was worth more (£2,170) than any race in Ireland other than the Irish Derby serves as a stark indicator of the relative penury of Irish racing at that time. Run-of-the-mill races in Ireland in 1935 were worth on average £44 to the winner.

Retracing a once-familiar path to Hamilton Park, near Glasgow, the 'Scotchman' was rewarded with a double, provided by 'Sam' Armstrong and 'Max' Barthropp. Similar success attended

Tommy's return to Lanark in July, followed by a long odds-on winner for J. V. Rank and Noel Cannon at Bogside. Back home Bob Fetherstonhaugh, Cecil Brabazon and latterly Roderic More O'Ferrall were the principal contributors to a sadly diminished total of 14 winners from just 100 mounts, well down the table beneath W. T. O'Grady, who retained his title with 54 successes.

Tommy Burns' travels in 1935 bore dividends the following year. Ginger Wellesley had followed his owners across the Irish Sea, setting up in Newmarket, while English owners and trainers sending raiders over for Irish prizes had the 'Scotchman' fresh in their minds as their desired jockey.

At a more provincial level, a Mallow double on Easter Monday 1936 included Solford, owned and trained by sporting Churchtown farmer Dan O'Brien, a very early portent of a much higher-profile partnership between their respective sons. Just a week later an urgent telegram from Ginger Wellesley summoned the 'Scotchman' to Epsom to renew acquaintance with His Reverence in the City and Suburban Handicap. His journey was handsomely rewarded when making every yard of the running on His Reverence to win that time-honoured event by three lengths, at a most gratifying 100/7.

Steve Donoghue had originally been booked for the mount, only to be carted by His Reverence on the Newmarket gallops. Steve had subsequently volunteered the information

EPSOM, April 22, 1936 – The 'Scotchman' justifying trainer 'Ginger' Wellesley's eleventh-hour summons when making all on His Reverence to land the historic City and Suburban Handicap, first run in 1851.

that his intimate friend Lady Torrington had the proverbial 'good thing' for the City and Suburban in Quai d'Orsay II. On Steve's departure, Ginger had wasted no time in summoning the jockey, whose honesty he had never had cause to doubt when riding for him.

That headline success at Epsom saw Tommy Burns booked for Thankerton in the Two Thousand Guineas, in which he finished third to Pay Up and Mahmoud. At Chester Tommy rode Farranjordan, a rare English runner for Bob Fetherstonhaugh, to a neck success in the Stewards' Stakes. A fleeting return to Ayr was rewarded with a win for Middleham trainer 'Bob' Armstrong on Sandy Grey.

Thankerton's good third in the Guineas gave his rider grounds for optimism that he could be his long-awaited Derby winner. Unhappily, a much-delayed start saw Thankerton kicked and Tommy hit in the mouth by another horse's head. Thoroughly upset, Thankerton charged to the fore at the top of the hill, turning into the straight six lengths clear. Two furlongs out his continued momentum forced Charlie Smirke to give chase on Mahmoud. Close home Thankerton's earlier exertions took their toll. Mahmoud won in record time, with Taj Akbar coming late to deprive Thankerton of second place on the line, thereby giving the Aga Khan an exceptional one-two in the Derby. Tommy's disappointment aside, the result was full of irony, for Smirke had been jocked off the better fancied Taj Akbar in favour of champion jockey Gordon Richards, only to gain the last laugh.

Mrs Shand, Thankerton's owner had so much hoped to become the first woman ever to own an Epsom Derby winner. Her disappointment became double-handed delight just twelve months later when Mrs G. B. Miller and her mother, Mrs Talbot, shared in the Derby success of Mid-day Sun. Curiously, when Mid-day Sun broke that hoodoo on lady owners, his immediate victim was Florence Nagle's Sandsprite.

A treble at Manchester and a further success on His Reverence at Doncaster preceded a trip to Paris to ride Vatellor for Leon Volterra in the Prix du Jockey Club (French Derby) at Chantilly in June. The 'Scotchman' had Steve Donoghue to thank for that booking. Steve, then Volterra's number one, took another ride in the race, assuring his patron that T. Burns was just the man to deputise. As at Epsom, Tommy Burns looked like putting his name on a Derby, until mown down close home by Mieuxé, the outstanding French colt of his generation.

Third in the Guineas, third in the Derby and second in the French equivalent, the 'Scotchman' had yet to open his seasonal account in Ireland when lining up for the Irish Derby on English raider Raeburn, trained at Manton by Joe Lawson and a first Irish runner for owner S.D. Hollingsworth. Joint third favourite of four seemed a fair assessment of Raeburn's chances, and of his rider winning a Derby in whatever jurisdiction.

Riding his customary waiting race over the Curragh's round course, Tommy avoided the three-

CURRAGH, June 24, 1936 – Mrs Sydney Hollingsworth leading in her husband's Raeburn, Tommy Burns' 12th Irish classic success and his sole Irish Derby winner at his 14th attempt, having finished second three times in Ireland's oldest classic.

way scrimmage between the battling leaders two furlongs out. Bringing Raeburn with a long, smooth run on the outside, he appeared to have the race in safe keeping until rammed by the veering favourite, Battle Song. Balancing Raeburn in a flash, Tommy won that final duel by a length and a half. The 'Scotchman' thereby netted the premier Irish classic to complete his nap hand of all five Irish classics, sixteen years after Captive Princess had initiated that process in the Irish Oaks and St Leger.

While the 'Scotchman' appeared to out-wait his rivals in anything other than sprints, he had already begun to impress upon his sons the difference between the straight and round Curragh courses. He maintained that over the straight course one could wait and wait, and then wait some more, picking off the front runners as they came to the end of their tether. Conversely, riding the round course, he contended that it was vital to be on the heels of the leaders turning into what was actually quite a short run-in. Freewheeling downhill into the straight from the round course, front runners got a boost that could carry them to the line. His observations would not be lost on TP.

Having disappointed at York and finished last in the St Leger, Raeburn went into winter quarters with the Ascot Gold Cup as his primary objective in 1937. That event was to assume a far greater significance for his jockey than winning the Irish Derby, were anyone even to suspect.

Tommy Burns doubled his Irish score for 1936 on another classic winner – Lindley – at Baldoyle in July. However, four years had elapsed since Lindley had won the Irish 2000 Guineas. Now an elderly gelding, Lindley was earning his corn in handicaps for owner-trainer Captain C. J. Clibborn. "The old thief," remained vivid in TP's recollection. "The captain went to endless trouble over that horse, hunting him in an effort to sweeten him up. But he still refused to have anything to do with the Curragh. Father won on him again in Galway, mainly because the old so-and-so didn't know where he was."

A Phoenix Park double for Bob Fetherstonhaugh on Fireside and Passage promptly doubled Tommy's Irish score again. Further little Irish winners sandwiched victory on Alletsoi at Bath. Restricted by his minimum weight – 8st 5lb – to the upper half of handicaps and with only Bob Fetherstonhaugh of the Curragh trainers behind him, Tommy Burns was living on scraps.

On Charlie Rogers' recommendation the 'Scotchman' found himself heading to Worcester in

Raeburn - this portrait held pride of place in Lumville for many years.

October 1936 for one of that course's only two flat fixtures of the season. Perhaps determination to justify Rogers' confidence saw Tommy drive Ethland home by a head and the same for Eastbury trainer Donald Snow. The outcome of the modest little Tewkesbury Maiden Plate was to assume a greater significance in the years ahead. The winner carried the 'blue, yellow hoop and cap' of the Hon Dorothy Paget, already famous as the owner of Golden Miller and one of the heaviest punters of the age. Famously averse to members of the opposite sex, 'DP' made an exception for her bloodstock manager Charlie Rogers, dubbing him 'Romeo'.

Married to May Paget, Dorothy's cousin, debonair Donald Snow was regarded as a playboy trainer, until suddenly landed with Dorothy Paget's costly and extensive flat string following her well-publicised break-up with Basil Briscoe over Golden Miller's antics at Aintree. That great horse had simply developed an enduring dislike of the Aintree fences. Prone to punt beyond his means, Donald had Dorothy to thank for averting default and thus retaining his trainer's licence.

By the end of 1936 Tommy Burns had ridden 22 winners in Ireland, a respectable score in the circumstances, if a long way below Ted Gardner, champion for the first and only time with 54 winners to his credit. J. T. Rogers, Gardner's employer, retained his trainers' championship, well ahead of Roderic More O'Ferrall.

Chapter Fourteen

Had it not been for the glittering prospect of Ascot Gold Cup triumph on Raeburn, Tommy Burns might well have retired from the saddle to resume training in Lumville. Besides, as keeper of the best table and cellar on the Curragh, the 'Scotchman' had had to curtail his own intake for most of each year for far too long. Moreover, his sons, James and TP would soon be ready to take his place in the saddle, having long since outgrown the ponies that had formed part of their existence since they had begun to walk. James had completed his academic education and had already attained a physique that strongly indicated that his days on the flat would be numbered.

TP, when not finding outlets for his apparently inexhaustible energy around the Lumville yard, was coming to the end of his time at Newbridge College, together with Con, son of trainer Michael C. Collins, and Robert 'Brud' Fetherstonhaugh, Bob's boy. TP's appetite for the life of a jockey was due to a degree to an understandable desire to emulate his father. Stella Burns raised no objection to her younger son carrying on what had become an established Burns family calling, provided he complete his formal education. Just in case.

TP had further, more contemporary role models to whet his desire. Peter Maher, apprenticed to the 'Scotchman' back in 1929, was heading swiftly towards the top ten in Britain. Wally Wing, Morny Wing's son, even closer to TP in age, had been crowned champion apprentice in Britain in 1936, with 37 winners to his credit. When quizzed by the great Gordon Richards on Morny's preference to remain riding in Ireland for small beer, the youngster had replied that his father wouldn't have been able to compete against either Gordon or himself.

For the present it was business as before when the 'Scotchman' rode the juvenile Sedan to win at the opening Phoenix Park meeting for old allies Fred Myerscough and trainer Fred Grundy. Golden Lancer, last in Raeburn's Irish Derby, carried Tommy to an easier assignment when winning a Tramore maiden for trainer Oliver Slocock. Bob Fetherstonhaugh's Spion Hill put Tommy among the winners at the Irish 2000 Guineas meeting.

Meanwhile Raeburn's public preparation for the Ascot Gold Cup had concluded with a promising fifth in the Yorkshire Cup. In contrast to previous years, Tommy Burns had only one mount over the four-day Royal Ascot meeting. Nonetheless, if he could win that Gold Cup, his faltering fortunes must surely improve. Precipitation started firm favourite, despite money for Cecil and Fearless Fox, making a quick reappearance having won the Ascot Vase two days previously. If that seemed a stiff question, Jack Jarvis, his trainer, had accomplished that very double with Golden Myth back in 1922. Raeburn was easy in the market at 100/6.

Precipitation and Cecil led into the straight for the final time, with the race clearly between them and finished in that order. Raeburn, travelling in fourth place, suddenly lost his action, veering left and right before Tommy could pull him up. He immediately dismounted, realising that his Irish Derby winner had broken down badly. Raeburn's erratic path had undoubtedly caused interference to Fearless Fox. If that were not sufficiently disastrous, worse soon followed. In the light of subsequent events, it seems appropriate to let trainer Jack (later Sir Jack) Jarvis, one of the principals, give his version first in this extract from his autobiography, *They're Off*, published in 1969.

"It gives me little pleasure to recall the unfortunate repercussions of that race. It had seemed to me that Fearless Fox got a very rough passage and I was genuinely under the impression that a certain jockey was less concerned with winning the race than with roughing up Fearless Fox, who had paint from the rails on his flank when he returned to the paddock. In those days trainers were allowed in the jockeys' changing room and I was talking about the race to Eph Smith when Bill Rickaby came in and corroborated what Smith had told me, saying that he had pulled out from behind Fearless Fox as he thought Fearless Fox was going to be brought down.

"Now I have never been accused of being a vindictive man but I admit to possessing a temper, the combustion point of which is fairly low. Of course I was quite wrong to do it and I regret still the words I used, but I could not restrain myself from tearing a considerable strip off the

LUMVILLE, 1938 – TP with Bill Tindall, head man for many years

51

jockey I deemed to have offended. I certainly should not have used the expression 'Irish Bastard', particularly as the jockey in question was born in Scotland. I was just beginning to cool off and dismiss the whole incident from my mind when I was sent for by the Stewards. I thought they were enquiring into incidents during the race, but to my surprise and annoyance I was in fact 'on the mat' for my remarks to the jockey and was duly fined £25 by Lord Hamilton. Of course nowadays the situation would be very different as the camera patrol would provide incontrovertible evidence.

Nor did this sorry business end with my fine. I was sued for slander by the aggrieved jockey, who was represented by the formidable Sir Patrick Hastings, KC., while Sir Norman Birkett KC (later Lord Birkett) appeared for me. Eventually the case was settled out of court. I have exchanged words with the jockey concerned since then, but the likelihood of our ever becoming friends can be regarded as slender."

In three carefully worded paragraphs, published posthumously, Sir John Layton Jarvis (1887-1968) summarised and dismissed a *cause célèbre*, destined to achieve headlines not only across the Irish Sea, but also across the Atlantic. T. Burns, a jockey based in Ireland, had initiated legal proceedings against one of the most prominent trainers in Britain. Moreover, that trainer's prominence was largely due to the patronage of one of the towering personalities of the time – Albert Edward Harry Meyer Archibald Primrose, 6th Earl of Rosebery.

David might have got lucky when upsetting the odds on Goliath, but the likelihood of T. Burns doing similar was so remote that Stella Burns foresaw the ruination of her husband, family and household. In TP's recollection, "My poor mother wasn't cut out for that sort of pressure. She suffered dreadfully under the strain, the continual press intrusion. God only knows how many novenas she completed, how many candles she lit."

Before that particular cat could be set amongst the pigeons the 1937 Irish Derby threatened to produce an almighty upset, when the 'Scotchman' appeared to have stolen a march on his friend and rival Steve Donoghue. Then in his final season, Donoghue rode Phideas, the odds-on favourite for Sir Victor Sassoon and Jack Rogers. The 'Scotchman' rode William Barnett's English raider, Senor. Inside the final furlong the 'Scotchman' seemed to have stolen the prize, until Donoghue extricated Phideas in the nick of time to snatch the spoils.

However, the affable but permanently impecunious Steve Donoghue sensed a way of putting money in his friend's pocket. He advised the 'Scotchman' to institute legal proceedings against Jack Jarvis, his Ascot assailant, arguing that Rosebery's resources would ensure a handsome settlement. Such feckless advice was quite in character, as the 'Scotchman' should have instantly perceived. There was another potential problem. Steve's evidence looked like being crucial. But Steve was retiring to commence training and could not afford to prejudice his future career.

Moreover, Tommy Burns' racecourse luck was currently right out. Beaten a short head in the Ulster Derby, he went down by half a length in the Irish Oaks, by a length in the Irish St Leger and a neck in the Irish Cambridgeshire. Six further winners completed his dismal season in Ireland. Fleeting visits to Bogside in July and September yielded winners for Malton trainer Walter Easterby and enthusiastic owner Lord Peter Milton, heir to the Fitzwilliam fortunes.

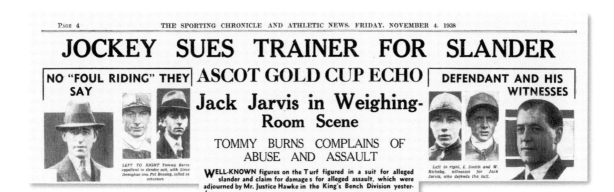

Chapter Fifteen

Having engaged Sir Patrick Hastings KC to represent him in his forthcoming case against Jack Jarvis in a special jury action in the Kings Bench Division, Tommy Burns acted on legal advice in not renewing his jockey's licence for 1938. The damage to his riding career directly due to Jarvis's defamation of his character would form a central plank of his case. To the world at large the 'Scotchman' declared that he had retired to resume training once more "to give the boys a chance." The boys in question were his sons James and Thomas P., both now apprenticed to their father in Lumville. Duly, the *Irish Racing Calendar* recorded the issue of Curragh trainers' licences to Messrs T. Burns, R. E. Hope and Emanuel Parkinson.

TP was soon in action, able as he was to draw 6st 9lb on J. A. 'Gus' Mangan's charge, Modest Sunny, in the Madrid Plate at the Curragh, the oldest race continuously recorded in the *Irish Racing Calendar*, inaugurated in 1813. Modest Sunny might have failed to outrun his name, but owner P. McCavana made it a day to remember for his young jockey when pressing a second riding fee into his hand. "The riding fee was £3. Here was another £3. I thought I was made up!"

In years to come received wisdom would hold that TP 'still has his communion money', in that bantering way we bear out Dr Johnson's observation. "The Irish are a fair people; - they never speak well of each other." Without refuting the charge, TP emphasises the mass unemployment and economic depression in Ireland at the time. Each weekday morning in Newbridge gangs of 'corner boys', as they were known, would quietly converge at Bank corner, Neeson's corner and Coffey's corner in the vague hope of getting a day's casual employment. And if no such offers materialised, they had one another for company, exchanging words with passers-by and eking out their paltry supply of shared cigarettes.

Although by his own admission far from a literary buff, TP would readily endorse another of Dr Johnson's maxims. "There are few ways in which a man can be more innocently employed than in getting money."

T. Burns, trainer, reopened his Curragh account when Lucky Range scored at the Irish 2000 Guineas meeting under Jack Moylan, following up with Fred Myerscough's Tetra Nell at the 1000 Guineas fixture. Meanwhile, TP got plenty of racecourse experience. Motlibai – "a useless filly" – for trainer Bob Fetherstonhaugh at Naas, was one such mount. Her significance, in TP's recollection, lay in her being the first animal put into training in Ireland by HH Aga Khan III.

It was at the Irish Derby meeting that the Burns boys generated the headline 'In Father's Footsteps'.

"Tommy Burns, the ex-jockey, who is now a trainer, will have very happy recollections of the meeting, for his two sons, Tommy and James, who are apprenticed to himself, each rode a winner. Tommy just steered Prudent Rose to victory in the Apprentices' Plate, and James, on Kilglass, rode strongly to snatch a sensational victory in the Welter Plate.

"In each instance these very promising boys revealed in marked degree good judgement, coupled with a strength and determination in getting the utmost out of their mounts. Their many friends will hope that in the near future they will be emulating the brilliant jockey-ship of their father."

The Burns brothers' extraordinary double – each riding his first winner on the same card – was all the more remarkable in that both rode for outside stables. Prudent Rose was trained by Tim Redmond for George Hannon, his brother-in-law, from his Green Road base, round the corner from Lumville. Kilglass, James's winner, was trained at the Kildare end of the Curragh by James Canty. W. J. Kelly, the winning owner, was popularly known as 'Trousers' Kelly, reflecting the success of his gentleman's outfitters business in Dublin.

TP followed up at the Phoenix Park in September, when Brush, trained in Lumville for Fred Myerscough obliged at 10/1. "Tommy Burns was all smiles when his charge, Brush, won the Terenure Plate and he had good

IT WAS A BURNS DAY AT THE CURRAGH
TOMMY'S TWO SONS RIDE THEIR FIRST WINNERS
Young Jockeys Who Look Like Carrying On Family Tradition
Following Father's Footsteps

No wonder Tommy Burns, famous Irish ex-jockey, looks happy. His two sons—James (left) and Tommy (right)—rode their first winners at The Curragh yesterday.

PHOENIX PARK, September 24, 1938 – TP doubling his score, getting Brush home by a length from Raki (Reg Cartwright).

reason to be pleased, for his little son, Tommy, had given an exhibition of how to win without the whip. He promises to become one of the 'best horses' in his father's stable if he continues to ride like this."

Winning trainer 'Scotchman' Burns accompanying Fred Myerscough's Brush to the winner's enclosure.

Macross, owned and trained by Tom Taaffe, completed TP's first season haul at Leopardstown in October. "Macross led all the way in the mile and a half handicap, ably ridden by Tommy Burns, junr., whose style is reminiscent of that of his talented 'dad,' whose tuition is invaluable. Of course, the youngster has a long, long way to go before he can hope to compare with such an artist, but he appears to be an apt pupil."

In contrast to a satisfactory season for TP, his father's finances became ever more precarious, with legal costs mounting daily as his case against Jack Jarvis drew near to hearing. Indeed, it looked at one stage as though Tommy would have to withdraw his case through lack of funding to continue. Fred Myerscough and Arthur Macaulay came to the rescue, each advancing £500 in Tommy's hour of need.

The case duly opened on November 3rd 1938, when Sir Patrick Hastings KC. addressed the court, outlining his client's grievance. "Whilst Burns was in the weighing room after the race, Mr Jarvis, who appears to be a man of somewhat odd temper, rushed into the room, took Burns by the neck and hit him with his umbrella. He called him most

CURRAGH, Irish Derby Day, June 22, 1938 – (L to R) Jimmy, Stella, Tommy Burns, Darby Rogers and Arthur Macaulay.

offensive names – I won't mention them as they appear to be more suitable to language used by Mr Jarvis than to this court. . . Burns, like all jockeys, was in a difficult position because, dependent for their livelihood on the friendship of trainers, it was difficult to give evidence against them. But Burns found Mr Jarvis' words too much for him to keep quiet and he went straight to Weatherbys to put a complaint before the Stewards of the Jockey Club. Mr Jarvis

denied the allegations and said that Burns had interfered with his horse, Fearless Fox. Mr Jarvis and his jockey Eph Smith gave evidence, and the Stewards fined Mr Jarvis – a substantial way of marking their view of his behaviour in the weighing room."

Giving his evidence, T. Burns, plaintiff, stated: "As I put my saddle on the floor of the weighing room Jarvis came up to me, took me by the left shoulder, accused me of deliberately interfering with Fearless Fox, called me an ill-bred Irish - - - - and said, 'Do you think you can come over to this country and interfere with my horses? I have a good mind to knock your - - - - head off.'

On the second day of the hearing, before Jack Jarvis could be called to give his evidence, Sir Norman Birkett KC, counsel for the defence, requested an adjournment. Jack Jarvis was noted in earnest discussion with Lord Rosebery, his principal patron. When the hearing resumed, Sir Norman Birkett addressed the court. "Mr Jarvis has agreed to pay

Stella Burns with a dapper young TP by the Phoenix Park parade ring.

TOMMY BURNS CASE

"Substantial Damages" For Former Jockey

ACTION SETTLED

SETTLEMENT WAS ANNOUNCED IN THE KING'S BENCH DIVISION, LONDON, TO-DAY OF THE ACTION FOR SLANDER BROUGHT BY MR. TOMMY BURNS, THE FORMER JOCKEY, AND NOW TRAINER AT THE CURRAGH, AGAINST MR. JOHN LAYTON JARVIS, THE NEWMARKET TRAINER.

Consultation between counsel took place following a close conversation in Court between the Earl of Rosebery and Mr. Jarvis and Mr. Norman Birkett, K.C., representing the trainer.

Afterwards Mr. Birkett announced the settlement, and said that the terms were satisfactory to both parties. "Mr. Jarvis," he declared, "has agreed to pay a substantial sum of damages to Mr. Burns and the full costs of the action." The charge of foul riding, counsel added, was withdrawn unreservedly.

Mr. Justice Hawke, approving the settlement, congratulated the parties. Jarvis, he said, had been very frank, and Burns had not emulated Oliver Twist by asking for more.

substantial damages to Mr Burns and the full costs of the action."

Mr Justice Chawke declared that Mr Jarvis deserved to be congratulated on his frankness, adding, "There is no shame in withdrawing when you have made a mistake." The judge further commended the plaintiff for exercising restraint. "He has not behaved like Oliver Twist, in looking for more."

The result of an action that Tommy Burns simply could not afford to lose brought an avalanche of congratulatory letters and telegrams. It was indeed an epic victory for the underdog, albeit in a most ill-advised action. Of all the letters of congratulation, one only found its way into Stella Burns' scrapbook, underlining its significance to her and her family.

Gorsewood,
Hook Heath,
Woking.
Woking 4

Dear Burns,

Ascot 1937 will for ever be a memorable day for us both. My horse Raeburn suffered a severe injury which terminated a promising racing career.

You were accused of the most despicable act that it is possible for any jockey to perform.

I never gave credence to these reports and I was delighted to see that you have been completely vindicated, for which please accept my hearty congratulations.

I enclose latest photograph of Raeburn which speaks for itself

Yours sincerely,

S.D. Hollingsworth

Chapter Sixteen

The Irish racing reporters were quick to mark the significance of Tommy Burns' victory. "A second 'T. Burns' looks like being required for the number boards at next year's flat meetings.

"Tommy senr. is resuming his career as a jockey and his son, T. Burns jnr., will, no doubt, be riding frequently in opposition to his dad.

"It is possible that young Tommy will have his indentures transferred to an English trainer, in which case the same necessity will arise because the 'old man' (not so much of the 'old' please) expects to ride a lot on the other side in 1939."

Tommy Burns duly took out a flat jockey's licence for 1939, though not before he had trained Steve Donoghue's Take Time to land the Leinster Leader Handicap Hurdle at Naas in January under Joe Parkinson. Not surprisingly, Tommy Burns' switching of roles was too much for the *Irish Racing Calendar* to catalogue. In consequence he did not appear as a trainer in the annual volume for 1939, despite being officially listed as trainer of Take Time in the weekly issue of that publication. Young Jimmy Burns, apprenticed now to Bob Fetherstonhaugh, was already almost too heavy for any future on the flat. Consequently he took out a jump jockey's licence for the first half of the year. Meanwhile, TP continued his apprenticeship over in England with Steve Donoghue, who had set up as a trainer in Blewbury, Berkshire,

BLEWBURY – Steve Donoghue imparting his immense experience to young TP on the gallops.

Patsy Thomas and Steve introducing Gardenia to the starting gate.

with Dick McCormick as his head man. Paddy Hayden, formerly with Jack Ruttle in New Abbey, Kilcullen, filled the travelling head lad role. "The Boss probably reckoned that Steve's popularity would get me off the ground, even if Steve couldn't train for toffee."

Incredibly, the 'Scotchman' once again marked his return to the saddle by opening his seasonal account with an Irish classic triumph, this time in the 2000 Guineas, on William Barnett's Cornfield. Sent over from Middleham by F. 'Sam' Armstrong, Cornfield was by Trigo and thus a grandson of Athasi, modestly successful when trained by James Burns and ridden by Tommy all those years before. Three days later T. Burns jun – as TP was styled in Britain – bade fair to follow up at Haydock Park on Plutarch. Having ridden like a man possessed to get his mount home by a head, TP incurred the stewards' displeasure. Plutarch was adjudged to have bored into Metalwork and was disqualified.

Ten days later, T. Burns jun made amends when getting Fooled Again home at Hamilton Park for Malton trainer Charles Elsey. "This son of Derby winner April the Fifth was admirably handled by T. P. Burns, son of the well-known Irish jockey Tommy Burns, who rode Chorus Boy in the same race. It was young Burns's first winner in Britain."

Gardenia continued to keep the youngster to the fore, winning juvenile sellers at Worcester, Folkestone and Haydock for Steve and fun-loving owner G. W. Roll. "Gordon Roll had suddenly come into a lot of money. He was mad to get into horses, so he approached Steve, as so many did on account of Steve's popularity. Old Steve was like a magnet to men and women alike. But there were no horses to be got in England with the threat of war. They'd been turned away or put down. So Steve and his lady friend 'Tommy' Thomas, headed to the Curragh and J. J. Parkinson. The old senator never had less than a hundred horses, and all of them for sale, at a price. The senator would turn you upside down for money. In the finish Steve bought seven in a package deal. Gardenia was the runt of the litter, an insignificant little thing. Turned out the best of the lot."

But it was TP's performance on Braydore at Wolverhampton that drew the rave reviews. "Brilliant riding by the young apprentice, T. P. Burns, when winning the Ruckley Handicap on Braydore, was a feature at Wolverhampton yesterday. His finish to beat M. Beary on the favourite, Poetic Licence was remarkably strong."

"I will make a confident prophecy, and that is that the next apprentice to hit the high spots will be little T. P. Burns – son of the famous Tommy – who is apprenticed to Steve Donoghue. I understand that there is another brother who is also a promising horseman.

"By the way, if you want to annoy the Burns family call them Irish. Despite the fact that they have lived at the Curragh for years they are Scots and they will thank you to remember it."

"Make no mistake about it, little 'T.P.' has come to stay and how he will be in demand when the nursery season begins!"

Developments on the European mainland meant that the 1939 'nursery season' was effectively stillborn. "The Folkestone Meeting arranged for September 1 and 2 and all other Jockey Club fixtures after that were abandoned owing to the outbreak of war."

When a limited programme of flat racing in Britain recommenced in mid-October, it was confined to Newmarket and Newbury in the south, with the north restricted to Stockton and Thirsk. Sent back across the Irish Sea with numerous Irish lads too young to be called up for active service, TP found himself the subject of a curious 'lease' arrangement. His indentures continued to be held by Steve Donoghue, but he could meanwhile avail of his precious 5lb apprentice allowance under the control of Colonel Arthur J. Blake, who trained on Maryborough Heath. Having ridden three winners in 1938, TP doubled that score in 1939 when successful on Over Yonder for J. J. Parkinson at the Curragh in September.

That curious lease arrangement was convoluted further by the condition whereby TP was apprenticed to Colonel Blake, but managed by Bert Kerr. Legendary bloodstock agent Bert Kerr had founded Kerr & Co in 1920, buying 20 classic winners and three Grand National

Bert Kerr and Steve Donoghue.

winners in a career that would last until his death in 1973. He had started up his own stable in Summerseat, Clonee in 1939, while fifteen years earlier he had played for Ireland in the 1924 Olympic Games as an amateur footballer. That same year he had captained the Irish eleven that defeated the United States at Dalymount Park. His colours – red and black – were taken from his football club, Bohemians. It was, to say the least, an unusual arrangement, sixty years before jockeys' agents came into existence.

While TP could chafe at this untimely disruption of his fledgling career, his father had even greater reason to regret it. He had enjoyed an English bonanza, beginning with Triguero in the Dee Stakes at Chester. Royal Ascot yielded the Ribblesdale Stakes on Ombro for Cecil Boyd-Rochfort, while Wheatland carried him to victory in the Sandringham Foal Stakes at Sandown, Gordon Stakes at Goodwood and Breeders' St Leger at Derby, to name but a few of his more notable winners in 1939. On the home scene he had ridden Eyrefield, the juvenile champion, to a runaway success in the Phoenix Park 'Fifteen Hundred' for Bryan Rogers, who had made a brilliant start on taking over from his father, J. T. Rogers.

In the aftermath of that 'Fifteen Hundred' success, a curious story emerged. It was said that the 'Scotchman' had been so heavily indebted to the ring that he had agreed to stop Eyrefield, quite in keeping with his reputation. This could be said to explain why the debutante was so easy in the market, when, if reports of her ability were correct, she should have been hot favourite. As she continued to drift, only one punter appeared ignorant of the situation. A scruffy old man mooched up and down the line, backing Eyrefield with 'readies'.

When Eyrefield subsequently bolted in at 6/1, the shabby old man repeated his tour of the ring, collecting wads of cash. Where appropriate, the old-timer peeled off quantities of high value notes, handing them back to bemused bookmakers with a murmured, "That's the Scotchman's debt cleared, I believe."

The curious stop-go nature of the so-called 'phoney war' led to a resumption of racing in Britain in 1940. Anxious to take full advantage of that reprieve – however temporary – Steve Donoghue sent for TP once more. They kicked off at Nottingham in April, where Roisterer II won comfortably without attracting any bid. In Ireland Tommy Burns' opening success on Abrupt at the Curragh in April highlighted the surreal state of the war. Abrupt was trained by J. T. Rogers, who had returned to the helm in Crotanstown following Bryan's call up for

PHOENIX PARK, August 12, 1939 – Eyrefield (T. Burns) belying her SP in the Phoenix '1500', to the consternation of several bookmakers.

military service since the start of the flat season.

Another to answer the call the arms was TP's brother Jimmy, whose riding career seemed to have stalled. Tired of being chivvied by his father for his apparent indolence, Jimmy enlisted with the Royal Air Force, eventually becoming a rear gunner in a Lancaster bomber – 'tail-end Charlie'. Jimmy's interest in aviation had been ignited through his association with the Barthropp family, who in turn were related to the Rogers of Crotanstown. All three families – Barthropp, Burns and Rogers - were to lose sons on active duty with the RAF.

On June 5th at Limerick Junction Tommy Burns rode what proved to be the last winner saddled by J. T. Rogers, who suffered a fatal heart attack on the road back to the Curragh. Darby Rogers, Bryan's brother returned from England to fill the breach in Crotanstown, becoming the third member of his family to hold the licence in the same stable in one season when Tommy brought Bold Maid home in front for him just seven days later.

Across the water TP and his employer struck a purple patch in mid-June, initiated by Sir Victor Sassoon's Jolly at Gatwick. "Jolly is a big horse for a boy to ride, but T. P. Burns handled him like a little workman. It was Burns' fourteenth winning mount."

They made it a Gatwick double the following day with Harar, in the colours of wealthy American Mrs L. D. Beaumont, then resident in Cap d'Antibes. Steve went on to make it three when Charlie Elliott won the finale on Kallias II. It proved to be the absolute finale for racing at Gatwick. The adjoining aerodrome, opened in 1936, had been requisitioned for RAF use in

September 1939. During September 1940, at the height of the Battle of Britain, four enemy aircraft were shot down over the course, which was then annexed by the Air Ministry, marking the end of its life as a racecourse.

Two days later Steve and TP struck again when No Wonder obliged at Wolverhampton in the colours of Steve's companion, 'Tommy' Thomas. Colombella made it a Wolverhampton double the very next day. TP was on a roll. "I'd have gone right to the top, if only for the bloody war!"

TP had got the best out of it, for Wolverhampton proved to be the final meeting in Britain. "The Stewards of the Jockey Club, after consultation with His Majesty's Government, gave notice on June 19 that all meetings under their Rules had been cancelled until further notice." Once more TP packed his bags and caught the boat to Ireland, faced with starting again from scratch. Still only fifteen, he had no problems with his weight. It was simply a matter of getting on horses with live chances.

Amongst those to whom TP bade farewell in the Blewbury stable that time were his compatriots Tommy Cusack and Eddie Reavey. Tommy had been apprenticed to J. J. Parkinson in Maddenstown before transferring to Steve Donoghue. After the war Tommy would come to the fore as one of the leading jump jockeys in England, winning the 1954 Cheltenham Gold Cup on Four Ten for Cheltenham trainer John Roberts. "A lanky lad. Good rider. Rode at the buckle end, like all the Maddenstown men. Went into the horse transport business afterwards."

Eddie Reavey, son of a Northern Irish punter, moved on to join struggling trainer called Noel Murless, then based in 'Black Hambleton' atop Sutton Bank, seven miles east of Thirsk in North Yorkshire. "Noel had terrible horses, 7st 7lb in the worst of handicaps. But they won more than their share and Eddie used stick me in for the rides when I went back again after the war. Eddie wound up back down in East Hendred, training near where we'd started together with Steve. He had that really good sprinter – Polyfoto."

While his father's roller coaster career was on a high through association with Darby Rogers, TP struggled to get rides, never mind winners. Although the influx of English jockeys was nothing like 1915, Michael Beary, Herbert Holmes and apprentice George Wells were making their presence felt. But the biggest predator in such a small pond was unquestionably Charlie Smirke. Not alone had he carried off the Irish Derby and Oaks on English raiders, but he had joined forces with Ginger Wellesley to devastating effect. From Baldoyle to Ballinrobe, Down Royal to Tramore, Osborne Lodge raiders proved invincible. Another redundant jockey to cross the Irish Sea was Athy native P. J. Prendergast, whose experience in Australia was destined to have a profound impact on Irish flat racing in the post-war decades. Down on his luck, he would survive on his wits and his innate ability.

Chapter Seventeen

The breakthrough came at Limerick Junction in August 1940, when Slightly Slow belied his name to win the Croker Cup for Hubert Hartigan, who had also opted to return to Ireland, regardless of the unchanged political situation that had prompted his departure in 1932. Throughout the rest of that extended flat season in Ireland TP kept his name to the fore on winners for Maxie Arnott, Harry Ussher, Joe Dawson and Colonel Blake. However, the winner that was to prove the most significant was Columbia, trained by Charlie Rogers and owned by Dorothy Paget. The virtual cessation of flat racing in England saw the eccentric millionairess transfer fleets of flat horses and jumpers across the Irish Sea. Desperate to find

CURRAGH, June 12, 1940 – seven days after riding J. T. Rogers' final winner, the 'Scotchman' continues the Crotanstown stable's tradition on Bold Maid, trained by 'Darby' Rogers, his late father's successor

PHOENIX PARK – May 1941 – TP returning on Fair Crystal, successful twice in five days on trainer W. J. 'Rasher' Byrne's local course.

accommodation for such numbers of horses, 'Romeo' persuaded his principal patron to purchase Ballymacoll Stud, to the west of Dublin, between Dunboyne and Maynooth.

Yet another recall by Steve Donoghue at the beginning of the 1941 flat season proved short-lived. TP returned to ride a quick Phoenix Park double for Castleknock trainer W. J. 'Rasher' Byrne on Fair Crystal, successful on Saturday May 3rd and again four days later. On each occasion the runner-up was trained by Hon 'Ginger' Wellesley, who tried his best to have those results amended in his favour, as the *Irish Racing Calendar* recorded.

"Mr H. G. Wellesley (trainer of Grand Inquisitor) objected to Fair Crystal being declared the winner of the above race and also of the Laidlaw Plate on May 3rd, on the grounds that the apprentice's licence or temporary apprentice's licence granted to T. P. Burns (rider of Fair Crystal) was not published in the subsequent Calendar. Objection overruled, and Mr Wellesley fined 25 sovs for lodging such a frivolous objection."

A regular supply of winners from Charlie Rogers and Bert Kerr's various trainers included First House for trainer Paddy Beary in the race before the 'Scotchman' rode Uvira to victory in the Irish Oaks for Ginger Wellesley. Charlie Smirke's call-up had reopened that door. Colonel Blake might have captured the Irish 1000 Guineas with Milady Rose and the Irish Derby with Sol Oriens, but they were entrusted to George Wells, former English apprentice champion before transferring to Hubert Hartigan on the latter's return to Ireland.

His inexperience also cost TP the ride on Fair Crystal, winner of the coveted Phoenix 'Fifteen Hundred' giving the 'Scotchman' his fourth success in the Horse Show Week showpiece. "They thought he might have got too strong for me to handle, being four months older by then. There was no horse the Old Man couldn't hold. He had small hands for a jockey. But he was like elastic and wonderfully strong with it."

Nevertheless, TP's dogged pursuit of his profession saw him ride out his claim on Mikado for Charlie Rogers. "That was how it was – 40 winners and you lost your 5lb allowance." As TP went on to win the very next race, on Balbriggan for J. J. Parkinson, the loss of his claim proved less traumatic than was so often the case. He had the Leopardstown stewards to thank for that swift transition. "Once I couldn't claim, the Parkinsons wanted to take me off and put up Morny Wing. The stewards refused permission. Worked out anyway!"

That autumn T. P. Burns rode his first major winner when getting the grey Mill Boy home in the Irish Cambridgeshire for trainer Joe Dawson of Rathbride Manor, in the colours of Joe's widowed mother, Mrs Michael Dawson. Ironically, TP's first major win was at the immediate expense of Joe Canty, foiled by a head in a characteristic late swoop on Abbot of Hainault.

CURRAGH, July 23, 1941 – trainer H. G. 'Ginger' Wellesley leading in Sir Thomas Dixon's Uvira (T. Burns), cantering winner of the Irish Oaks

"Joe Dawson was a gambler, like his brother-in-law, Joe Canty. Riding for gamblers brings its own sort of pressure. Poor Joe died very soon afterwards. He would probably have made a success of training, for he had a lot of get up and go about him."

TP could all too easily recall his wartime routine. "After riding out on the Curragh, I'd take the bicycle on the train to Portlaoise – Maryborough in those days – cycle out to Blake's on the heath, ride as many lots as required, get back on the bike and pedal home to the Curragh. Fit? Of course we were fit!"

The Maryborough Heath horses got pretty fit too. "The runners for the Curragh on a Saturday would set off on the previous Thursday, led, not ridden. It didn't seem to do them any harm, except for one two-year-old. I could win on him at the Phoenix Park or Leopardstown, which he reached by train. But the 20-mile walk to the Curragh flattened him."

A very much longer train journey south had been necessary to ride a piece of work on Astrometer for Churchtown owner-trainer Dan O'Brien. Astrometer was on an attractive mark in the Irish Cesarewitch. While Dan held the licence, his son Vincent made it plain that he gave the instructions. All seemed in order, until Charlie Rogers sought to engage TP for Dorothy Paget's Martin Griffin, twice successful that season, but over a mile. The 'Scotchman' was in no doubt as to his son's course of action, pointing out that Charlie had been very loyal to TP. If TP let Charlie down on this occasion – win or lose – TP did not deserve the trainer's continued support. Bobby Hardwidge rode Astrometer to a short head success from the

'Scotchman', while TP finished in the ruck on Martin Griffin.

Well, TP might have missed out on the Irish 'autumn double', but 22 winners still made it a very solid season. Moreover, to have got the mount on an Irish Cambridgeshire winner so soon after riding out his claim, "I must have been doing something right."

'Doing something right' also involved a tricky balancing strategy for the youngster. It was vital that TP's acknowledged ability to ride winners, inherited from his high-profile father, should not be tainted by any suspicion that TP rode horses to suit his father's ends. Not only did TP have to convince the racing fraternity that he did not bet, but that his mounts ran on their merits in every instance. In an era when winning 'unwanted' was as reprehensible as getting beaten when the money was down, that required a strength of character beyond the maturity and experience of many youngsters making their way in a world where suspicion was ever-present.

Another to demonstrate early signs of uncommon ability was trainer Paddy Prendergast. He kick started his fabulous career with Spratstown in a Naas bumper, following up in a similar event at Leopardstown at Christmas. Students of such matters had already noted the remarkable improvement in W. J. Kelly's runners from Palmerstown during P. J. Prendergast's brief employment there.

LEOPARDSTOWN, September 6, 1941 – TP riding out his claim in style on Dorothy Paget's Mikado, trained by C. A. 'Charlie' Rogers.

Without leaving Ireland in 1942 TP added another 20 winners to his score, the majority for Charlie Rogers and Dorothy Paget. Astronomic at Limerick Junction was an exception, owned and trained by Dan O'Brien, but effectively managed by Dan's son Vincent. By Vesington Star out of Golden Meter, Astronomic was a full-brother to the two horses that were lifting the small Churchtown stable to a degree of prominence – Astrometer and Astrologer. The former had already won the 1941 Irish Cesarewitch, ridden by Bobby Hardwidge when TP had elected to remain loyal to Charlie Rogers. Ironically, when Astrometer went on

CURRAGH, October 4, 1941 – the grey Mill Boy (T.P.Burns) winning the Irish Cambridgeshire by a head from Abbot of Hainault (Joe Canty).

to repeat that success in 1943, he did so for Charlie Rogers and Dorothy Paget. Astrologer's 1943 Cambridgeshire completed that unique full-brothers' autumn double.

Stella Burns, TP's sister, became the latest member of her family to write her name into racing's records when her Lucca Prince won the Ladies' Cup at the annual Punchestown meeting, ridden by Mr P. P. Hogan. Nominally trained by Tommy Nugent, Lucca Prince had earned his qualifying hunter's certificate with the Kildares, ridden by TP. By the relatively obscure Lucca, the six-year-old Burns family favourite was out of Greenogue Princess. Winner of a point-to-point when ridden by Tom Dreaper, Greenogue Princess went on to breed no less than twelve individual winners, subsequently achieving racing immortality as the granddam of Arkle.

Although Lucca Prince was well fancied at only 5/1, his path may have been eased by the fact that Lovely Cottage, third in this instance, had already competed unsuccessfully three races earlier. Only a five-year-old, Lovely Cottage went on to win the 1946 Grand National. Sadly, Lucca Prince met his end during a subsequent qualifying hunt, as TP recalled. "The meet was round Christmas time, from the Red House. We met this drain wrong, going too slow. He caught his hind legs on the edge of the far bank. Broke his back."

Dorothy Paget dominated wartime racing in Ireland through sheer force of numbers, making her leading owner numerically virtually throughout what was euphemistically termed the 'Emergency'. However, at the upper end of the scale a new force had emerged in Joe McGrath,

PUNCHESTOWN, April 29, 1942 – Miss Stella Burns leading in her Lucca Prince, winner of the Ladies' Cup, a fourth success at the two-day meeting for amateur champion Mr P. P. 'Pat' Hogan. Stella's colours had previously belonged to Arthur Macaulay.

fabulously wealthy through the spectacular worldwide success of the Irish Hospital Sweepstakes, which he had done so much to instigate in 1930. Employing Michael C. Collins as his trainer and manager, Joe McGrath had invested heavily in the best bloodstock that money could buy when the threat of renewed hostilities in Europe had given him the opportunity to do so. Recruiting Morny Wing as stable jockey in Conyngham Lodge, McGrath and Collins had gone straight to the top, notably through the exploits of Windsor Slipper. Unbeaten as a two-year-old in 1941, Windsor Slipper retained his record unblemished in three starts in 1942, carrying off the Irish Triple Crown. Only the second animal ever to do so, Windsor Slipper remains the last to achieve that distinction.

Strangely, despite his massive investment in bloodstock and his employment of Michael Collins as his trainer, Joe McGrath had been very slow to retain a top-flight jockey. As John Burns recalled, matters came to a head at Leopardstown one day, when Michael Collins had once again to enter the jockeys' changing room with McGrath's colours in his hand, in search of a suitable rider. That was commonplace not only then but right up into the 1960s, when journeymen and aspiring jockeys could travel to any Irish meeting reasonably confident of picking up at least one 'spare'.

On this occasion Collins threw the colours at the 'Scotchman'. He was already engaged in the race. Wing was available. The McGrath horse duly won, whereupon Michael Collins insisted that Joe McGrath make more concrete riding arrangements. Morny Wing was made an offer that Colonel Blake, to his credit, advised him to accept, for he could not match it. Wing became champion jockey in Ireland from 1941 to 1945. It could so easily have been different.

Perhaps not. Of the top three – Canty, Burns and Wing – Canty and Burns were known to ride to their own agendas. Wing was not known as a betting man. Instead, Morny Wing had his hand-picked 'twelve apostles', who had an agreed amount on for him and whatever they fancied for themselves whenever he gave them the office.

PHOENIX PARK, June 19, 1943 – TP stretchered off the course by St John's Ambulance volunteers.
The 'Scotchman' (2nd right) leaves the scene with Aubrey Brabazon (right).

Arguably this powerful new alliance in Conyngham Lodge impinged more upon the 'Scotchman' than on his son, still far too young to be considered for one of the top jobs in a racing arena that had traditionally deferred to guile and experience rather than trust in youthful flair and dash. Unfortunately for young TP, George Wells' friendship with Dorothy Paget's entrenched jump jockey saw the Englishman usurp that plentiful supply of flat winners in the Paget livery. However, apparent loss was soon to turn into agreeable gain, for Colonel Blake began to use his 'borrowed' apprentice more frequently, thereby boosting TP's seasonal total into double figures. Moreover, at a time when such introductions were infinitely more important than they appear today, the youngster began to win races in the colours of Arthur Blake's coterie of patrician owners. The Heath had always and ever been essentially a private stable, run by and for the Blake family and their invited acquaintances. The experience was to prove invaluable. "You learned how to conduct yourself with such owners, to know your place. My father had never conformed in that regard. Called the lords and ladies by their first names. Some would take it. Many did not."

The 1943 season also led to TP's first brush with officialdom, at Baldoyle in August. "The Stewards enquired into a complaint by Mr P. F. Cannon (Starter) against T. P. Burns for impertinence and disobedience at the Start. Having interviewed Mr P. F. Cannon and T. P. Burns the Stewards reported Burns to the Stewards of the Turf Club.

"The Stewards of the Turf Club met at the Curragh on Saturday, August 28th, to investigate the above report. Having interviewed Mr Cannon, who spoke well of Burns' previous behaviour, and heard the explanation of Burns, who expressed great regret, the Stewards decided to caution him, and pointed out to him if it had not been for Mr Cannon's evidence a more serious view would have been taken of the case."

TP could recall the incident without hesitation. "He was an old pig of a horse. No intention of lining up with the others. I called him an old bastard. Frank Cannon thought I was referring to him. Cannon could be prickly too."

Inevitably, as TP began to stretch, so did his weight begin to climb. From doing 6st 7lb at the outset of his career, he was now wasting to do 7st 9lb. Ironically, the 'Scotchman' simultaneously got down to his lightest for many years to land the 1943 Irish Lincolnshire for Cecil Brabazon on Foam Crest under 8st 1lb. He did likewise to take the historic Madrids on Wykehamist for Roderic More O'Ferrall. Sacrifices were necessary, for in the game of musical chairs that racing has ever been the 'Scotchman' had been displaced on Fred Myerscough's runners by his old rival Joe Canty. While such vagaries were part of the jockey's life, on this occasion it meant missing the rides on the apparent successor to Windsor Slipper – The Phoenix.

Bred by 'Toby' Wellesley and trained by his owner in Dundrum, The Phoenix had progressed from juvenile champion to outstanding classic colt, running away with the Irish 2000 Guineas and Derby, only to surrender the Irish Triple Crown, for which he appeared a certainty, to John Oxx's Solferino, ridden by Jackie Power, likewise a Wellesley protégé.

Therein lay another irony. Solferino belonged to a wealthy Scots gambler, James McVey, long acquainted with the Burns family in Ayr. McVey owned the Hilltown Stud, Clonsilla, where Rosewell held court. John Oxx was stud groom. When approached by McVey about the possibility of training a few for him, the 'Scotchman' had declared that somebody as incurably suspicious as McVey would be better advised to set up his own trainer. Thus did John Oxx move from stud groom in Clonsilla to racehorse trainer on the Curragh. Solferino's Irish St Leger defeat of The Phoenix moved Paddy Prendergast to christen John Oxx 'Merlin', while Astrologer's Irish Cambridgeshire simply confirmed the wisdom of 'Scotchman' Burns' advice. Admittedly, McVey's choice and promotion of John Oxx underpinned the success of that formula.

Chapter Eighteen

With so many Irish men and women serving in the British armed forces and returning on leave, even the rigorous Irish press and radio censorship could not disguise the sense that something momentous was on the cards in 1944. The tide had turned. It was only a question of when the Allies made a final, decisive assault upon the European mainland. One who shared that optimism was rear gunner James Burns. Having had the good fortune to survive one tour of duty, he was confident of coming through a second dice with death in that most vulnerable of positions.

Corkman Jimmy Eddery took the opposite view, slipping back across the Irish Sea AWOL, in military parlance. Intercession at the highest level safeguarded him in 'neutral southern Ireland', where he resumed his riding career with immediate success. Joining forces with Ginger Wellesley, who had likewise abbreviated his military role, Jimmy dead heated in the 1944 Irish 2000 Guineas on Good Morning. TP had a close-up view of that struggle between Jimmy and Jack Moylan on Slide On, beaten a length into third on Pacifier. He had opened his seasonal account in the previous race, putting up overweight on Oola at 7st 10lb.

JIMMY BURNS, rear gunner, RAF

Jimmy Eddery's was just one new face in Irish weighing rooms, for both Aubrey Brabazon of Rangers Lodge and Martin Molony from Limerick had thrust their way to the fore. Admittedly it was difficult to categorise either. Each had made an impression over jumps, but was light enough to ride on the flat. Aubrey had already won the Galway Plate on St Martin and Swindon Glory, while young Molony had enthralled a few and horrified many more when bringing Knight's Crest with a devastating run to rob the idolised Prince Regent of the recent Irish Grand National.

While never short of rides, TP failed to add to his score until after young Vincent O'Brien had advertised his training talents by pulling off the elusive Irish autumn double, whereby Drybob divided the spoils in the Cambridgeshire and Good Days captured the Cesarewitch by a neck at 20/1. TP doubled his 1944 score on Abbot of Hainault at Leopardstown in November. Trained by Jimmy Canty, Abbot of Hainault carried the increasingly familiar red and black of bloodstock agent Bert Kerr, who also acted as TP's agent-cum-manager in Ireland on behalf of Steve Donoghue.

Still officially indentured to Steve Donoghue, even though he had long since ridden out his apprentice claim, TP had no option but to respond to his master's summons to return to Blewbury for the 1945 season. "Another popular lightweight, T. P. Burns, has gone back to Steve Donoghue to whom he was originally apprenticed. He is a top-class rider, one of the nicest mannered youngsters one could wish to meet. Somehow or another he never 'got going' over here, and his ability merited a good deal more patronage than he received. 'Steve' will provide him with the necessary opportunities and the association is sure to be a happy one."

It was to prove a brief association. Steve Donoghue died on March 23rd. "I was there when he left for London on the train in the afternoon, going to visit people called Bennett. He got a heart attack that night in their London flat and was dead before morning."

Never really enamoured of training, Steve had suffered the loss of his younger son and namesake, shot down over the North Sea in December 1941. Ethel, Steve's estranged second wife, had died in February 1942 after taking an overdose of sleeping tablets. On top of those personal tragedies, Steve had struggled with an ongoing problem of financing the keep of a large number of Marcel Boussac's horses entrusted to his care, without any prospect of payment until the war was over. While not only the English racing community, but the public at large mourned the most popular racing idol since Fred Archer, TP returned home once more, his indentures now held outright by Colonel Blake.

He was no sooner home than tragedy struck the Burns family. Scarcely a week before VE-day and the cessation of hostilities, rear gunner James Burns was reported 'missing in action' when his Lancaster was shot down over German territory. There were no survivors.

In June 1945 T. P. Burns 'came out of his time', licensed henceforth as a full jockey. In a season plagued by health problems brought on by excessive wasting, TP rode just two winners, both at the Curragh in Bert Kerr's colours. "Nobody else would even give me a ride! Bert Kerr was a great man to give fellows a leg up. In so many other ways he was ahead of his time."

TP came close to following his English mentor to the grave that very autumn. Returning to Lumville from riding at the Phoenix Park, he complained of a stomach pain. The 'Scotchman' was unperturbed. "He's eaten something that didn't agree with him. He'll get over it."

Evening turned into night and the pain grew worse. Eventually, Tommy Burns acquiesced to

1940s – the Lumville string picking grass after exercise.

Stella's growing concern, sending for Dr Joe Roantree. The good doctor diagnosed appendicitis. TP was immediately brought round to the neighbouring Drogheda Memorial Hospital, where surgeon Dominic Cannon operated successfully. Another hour's delay and TP would have joined his brother James, for in those days a ruptured appendix was almost invariably fatal.

TP's lengthy recuperation fuelled rumours that he had become yet another of the mounting victims of Tuberculosis. TB, for short, was then epidemic in Ireland, equivalent to earlier plague, from which few, if any, recovered. Dr Noel Browne would confront this scourge to lasting effect, but his hour had yet to come.

Written off through perceived terminal illness, T. P. Burns, jockey, needed to resurrect his stalled career. His continued existence might be reasonably assured, but his livelihood was not. Hughie McGovern, a punting cattleman, friendly with both the 'Scotchman' and Martin Quirke, threw the youngster a lifeline. 'Bert' Bullock, Yorkshire trainer, needed a jockey he could trust, preferably a young outsider. He had been 'put away' by too many of the pre-war jockeys' brigade, then firmly in control of northern flat racing.

Bertram Bullock, then training on an old estate near Ripon, within a mile or so of Bobby Renton's powerful Bishopton stable, was a brother of William 'Billy' Bullock, forever famous as the rider of Signorinetta, successful in both the Derby and the Oaks of 1908. The previous season, as stable jockey to Richard 'Boss' Croker in Glencairn, he had won the Irish Derby on Orby, consolation for having been stood down at Epsom, where Johnny Reiff had ridden the first-ever winner of the Derby trained in Ireland. Remarkably, Billy Bullock was still riding the

1940s – TP with Barney Gallivan, who held the trainer's licence for the Lumville stable.

odd winner for Charles Elsey forty years later.

Formerly head man to that great jumping trainer Tom Coulthwaite, Bert Bullock had made his own name when turning out Harmachis to win the 1938 Stewards' Cup at Goodwood. Owned and trained in Ireland by Fred Clarke, Harmachis had been recommended by the 'Scotchman' and Martin Quirke, each of whom had ridden the colt to win in Ireland. Also successful in sprints at Doncaster, Newcastle and York, Harmachis had put his trainer on the map. Kilbelin, a more recent purchase through the same channel, continued the good work post-war, destined to win the 1947 Ayr Gold Cup.

Jack Fairfax-Blakeborough informed his readers of this new alliance. "T. P. Burns, son of Tommy Burns, is riding this season for B. Bullock, the Ripon trainer. Young Burns is the fourth or fifth generation of his family – like Bullock himself – to be associated with the Turf.

"Young T. P. Burns' grandfather, Thomas Burns, was a horse dealer and trainer at Ayr, and in some legal proceedings in Scotland told the judge that he had made 'thousands of pounds less than nothing out of racing.'"

Thus did TP's telephone number change from Curragh 6 to Skelton-on-Ure 1. "He paid me £1,000 to go over. But that was the only good part of it. Mind you, I wised up very fast while I was there. Had to!" It was also surmised that Bert might have had designs on TP as a son-in-law, a topic on which he became dismissive.

Having landed a gamble at Chester for Darby Rogers on Greek Star, a McGrath cast-off, the 'Scotchman' summoned TP home. "You're at nothing there. Get yourself home and back to work." 'Work' involved playing an active part in the running of the Lumville stable, reopened again, this time under the titular control of Barney Gallivan. Proprietor of an exclusive grocery and bar on Newbridge's Main Street, close to Cosgrove's Pharmacy, Barney was close friends with the Mastersons, successful owner-breeders from the Moat of Arschull, where they produced such as Rattle Up, Rattle Along, Knight Commander and Carnalea.

Renewed training commitments cost the 'Scotchman' any role in Darby Rogers' marvellous 1946 campaign, supplanted by Morny Wing, whose fabulous spell as first jockey to Joe McGrath had come to an end, displaced by Jimmy Eddery. However, Tommy Burns had a live classic candidate for the following season in Grand Weather, successful in the Anglesey and Beresford Stakes for Toby Wellesley's Osborne Lodge stable. Ginger Wellesley had departed to continue training in the Phoenix Park.

Chapter Nineteen

Grand Weather duly provided the 'Scotchman' with his fourth Irish 2000 Guineas triumph and his eighteenth Irish classic in all since opening his score on Captive Princess thirty-one years previously. At the opposite end of the scale in age and experience, Martin Molony, the phenomenally successful jump jockey, won the Irish Oaks on Desert Drive, defeating the 'Scotchman' on Isabelline by less than a length, with TP down the field on long-shot Merry Ann. Happily for TP, the Lumville stable had got him back on the map with dual winner High Grass, supplemented by winners for Barney Nugent, Michael Dawson and Cecil Brabazon. TP also rode Morning Wings, a half-sister to Grand Weather, to win at the Phoenix Park, only to yield the mount to Joe Canty when that promising juvenile followed up in the National Produce Stakes

Unfortunately, the upsurge in the Burns' racing fortunes was counter-pointed by domestic worries. Having lost one son and come within an hour of losing a second one, the 'Scotchman' now had to contend with the prospect of losing his wife. Stella was diagnosed as suffering from the dreaded tuberculosis. TP recalled being shown her x-rays. "I couldn't believe the cavities they showed in the poor woman's lungs. How could she survive?"

But Stella would survive, not least due to the tireless ministrations of her loyal 'Chev'. "God bless her, 'Chev' never left Mother's side for twelve months and brought her through that terrible time. Hard to believe, even all these years later."

CURRAGH, 1947 – 'Toby' Wellesley watching (L to R) 'Scotchman', Jimmy Eddery and TP in a gallop.

OSBORNE LODGE, 1947 – TP leading the Wellesley string back from the Curragh gallops.

Gay McCormack, Mollie's elder daughter and Stella's niece, was less fortunate, succumbing to the same insidious disease that carried off so many in post-war Ireland.

During the latter part of 1947 TP spent his spare time riding out for neighbouring trainer Cecil Brabazon. Beau Sabreur was his particular responsibility. Despite only two runs, the youngster had convinced his experienced trainer that he was a colt of immense potential, if he could be cured of his delight in dropping his riders and galloping loose all over the Curragh. "He was a handful and old Cecil never stopping telling me not to let him get rid of me because he thought so much of him."

Before the next flat season opened another Burns put his name on the winning sheet. This time it was John, Stella's "little afterthought," who rode Sea Count to victory at the Tara Harriers point-to-point. Bigger in stature than his father or brother, John was to ride as an amateur for years to come.

TP's perseverance was rewarded with the mount on Beau Sabreur on his seasonal debut in the Tetrarch Stakes at the Curragh in April 1948. Easy to back, Beau Sabreur lived up to his promise, slamming a good field to establish himself as a live Guineas candidate. "Barney Macnaughton got very excited, demanding that the best jockey available be booked. I wouldn't know half enough for such a key role. They looked here, there and everywhere before they asked my father."

Cool as a cucumber, the 'Scotchman' waited and waited, before pouncing to win by a length with an unknown amount in hand. TP got his consolation prize when winning on Beauford for the same connections. Indeed, Cecil Brabazon made amends in the best way possible, for

CURRAGH, April 3, 1948 – TP going down to the start on Beau Sabreur, unexpected winner of the Tetrarch Stakes on his seasonal debut.

all TP's remaining wins that season were for the Rangers Lodge stable. One such was Fanny's Way, successful in the race preceding the Irish St Leger, in which the 'Scotchman' got Beau Sabreur home by a short head from Nathoo, winner of the Irish Derby in Beau Sabreur's enforced absence. The colt entrusted to TP to sort out was voted champion of his year in Ireland.

At the end of 1948 Martin Molony had run away with the riding honours, with 87 winners. Aubrey Brabazon a modest second. Both rode on the flat, over hurdles and over fences. TP had eight flat winners to his credit. Deciding that was the way to go, TP took out a National Hunt licence. The 'Scotchman' was cautionary. "Don't think you won't get knocks. You will. Don't ride bad horses and don't try to play the hero. Nobody respects the bravest man in the cemetery!"

If the leading three names in the 1948 trainers' table looked familiar – Hubert Hartigan, Cecil Brabazon and Darby Rogers – there was a new name on their heels. P. J. Prendergast had burst to the fore with 20 winners of 33 races, a truly remarkable achievement for one who had started from nothing during the darkest years of the war. While it was not yet significant, not even noteworthy, 'Darkie' Prendergast had shown a preference for employing Australian jockeys. Imported by Bert Kerr, both Billy Turtle and Ted Fordyce had attracted Paddy Prendergast's patronage. Not that anybody saw any particular relevance at the time. After all, 'Darkie' had spent time Down Under. Hadn't Kevin, his son, been born there?

Leopardstown, Christmas 1948, was a milestone in a new career for T. P. Burns, jump jockey, when Balladier, owned by recently widowed Mrs J. J. Parkinson and trained in Maddenstown

LEOPARDSTOWN, December 27, 1948 – TP returning on Balladier, his first winner under NH Rules. Trained by Emmanuel Parkinson, Balladier carried the famous 'White, red spots and cap', then registered to recently widowed Mrs J. J. Parkinson. Tony Sweeney, the owner's grandson, pictured 3rd from right.

by her son Emmanuel, won the Glencairn Selling Hurdle at 5/4. The partnership promptly followed up at Baldoyle on New Year's Day 1949. Paddy Power, whose father Patsy had been head man in Maddenstown for decades, recalled that those two victories induced very different reactions from Balladier's trainer, 'Manzer'.

'Manzer' had worked out a programme for the useful but chronically unsound Balladier on seeing TP school the horse successfully over a few flights in Connolly's Bottoms, as the Curragh schooling grounds were traditionally known. Should Balladier oblige at Leopardstown, he was then to have two 'easy' runs, as a prelude to another 'touch' at Mullingar. Paddy became privy to the first part of this plan, having been drafted in as a last-minute replacement to lead the horse up at Leopardstown. Balladier's regular attendant had celebrated Christmas Eve well rather than wisely, injuring himself while attempting to negotiate the unforgiving stile that lay in wait between the nearby pub and his Maddenstown abode.

When the first part of the plan duly materialised at Leopardstown, Paddy led Balladier back to the winner's enclosure. As instructed, he promptly removed the bandages from Balladier's dodgy front legs, giving any potential bidder every opportunity to note the winner's scar-lined tendons. At the subsequent auction Balladier failed to attract a bid. So far, so good. Now for Baldoyle, and that 'easy' run under a 7lb penalty for the Leopardstown success. Even the bookmakers seemed to know that Balladier would not be winning that day, cheerfully offering 6/1, but finding no takers. Leading Balladier up once more, Paddy innocently wished TP all the best in his bid for a quick follow-up.

Perhaps Paddy's parting shot implied a last-minute change of strategy. TP remained vague on the subject. At all events, riding a perfectly judged race, TP brought little Balladier home fully ten lengths clear of his seventeen rivals. Paddy brought the winner back to a very different reception to that which greeted him at Leopardstown. 'Manzer' made his feelings very plain. Essentially, T. P. Burns would never ride another horse trained by Emmanuel Parkinson. Jimmy Mullane was in the saddle when Balladier made a swift reappearance at Naas seven days later, now shouldering a 14lb penalty, finishing down the field. Not that TP was sentenced to

LEOPARDSTOWN, May 11, 1949 – Sadler's Wells (TP) leading Arden Link (Brendan O'Neill) and Bright Cherry (Eddie Newman). Arden Link (rec 21lb) won narrowly from Sadler's Wells with Bright Cherry (rec 26lb) well back in third.

watch from the stands. He happily took the mount on Larry Byrne's Jack o' Down, albeit unplaced, but a riding fee nonetheless.

Any prospect of reconciliation between trainer and jockey receded to vanishing point as Balladier went on to finish second in his next three races. On the last of those 'Manzer' resorted to lodging an objection to Balladier's Phoenix Park conqueror, Trebuh, on grounds of "crossing at the last hurdle," to no avail.

Having ridden a little over hurdles, Paddy Power went on to become a teacher and also the popular and long-serving TD for South Kildare, occasionally reminding his fellow-TDs that while some of them might have led in a winner, he was surely the only TD who could claim to have led one up.

To improve his technique TP began riding work and schooling for Dan Moore in Old Fairyhouse. Dan signified his approval by putting TP up on Sadler's Wells in the 1949 Irish Grand National at Fairyhouse, just across the road from the Moore stable. They finished fifth. Reverting to his original metier, TP rode Beau Sabreur to win a King's Plate at the Curragh and three days later opened his chasing account when successful on Sadler's Wells at Naas. That was more like it.

By the end of that first year mixing it TP had 29 jumping winners, second only to Martin Molony in that sphere, in addition to a further 8 winners on the flat, where Morny Wing took

FAIRYHOUSE, April 11, 1950 – Bright Cherry (TP) clear-cut winner of the Easter Chase, led in by Alison and June Baker.

the honours for the final time in a long career now nearing its close. Highlights included a Kerry National on Sadler's Wells and a Munster National on Confucius for trainer Henry Harty. The Galway Plate was one to elude TP's grasp. Sadler's Wells started co-favourite with Binghamstown, ridden by Aubrey Brabazon. "I was just hacking on the heels of the leaders. Sadler's had such class. Then they died in front of me. I had no choice but to go for my race. Once he hit the front he started to idle. I was there to be shot at. But I didn't need to be beaten by a huntsman!"

The 'hunstman' in question was Harry Freeman-Jackson, a claiming amateur, riding his own horse, Result. As Sadler's Wells downed tools, impervious to his rider's frantic urgings, Harry drove Result past the leader to snatch victory by half a length, with Colin Bell and Green Dolphin in a dead heat for third place just a length further back. While no professional ever enjoyed being bested by 'a bloody amateur', Harry Freeman-Jackson was no 'Tom Soldier'. Before moving to Ireland Harry had trained and ridden his wife Dorothy's Hoilo to win the coveted Foxhunters

Cup at Cheltenham in 1946. Besides his exploits on Result and Sam Brownthorn (second in the 1954 Irish Grand National), Harry hunted the Duhallows for decades, in addition to representing Ireland on four successive Olympic Games three-day event teams. Harry was subsequently *chef d'équipe* to the Irish team that won the world championships at Badminton in 1966, in which his daughter Virginia played a vital role, riding Sam Weller.

TEAM LUMVILLE – L to R: John, TP, Stella and their parents

Sentimentally, TP's special wins were achieved on Bright Cherry at Navan and Baldoyle. Trained by Tom Dreaper, this free-running chestnut mare was out of Greenogue Princess and thus a half-sister to the ill-fated Lucca Prince.

However, TP's campaign came to a temporary halt in November, through a fall from Glennameade in the Independent Cup Chase at Leopardstown. "It was known as a bogey race because the winner of the Independent Cup rarely did anything afterwards. Not that Glennameade was ever going to win it, or any other race. He was a useless bastard. I had him up there in contention when he fell. Half the field must have trampled over me."

That fall incurred the first of a series of back injuries that would necessitate TP riding with a back brace over obstacles. "You could call it a corset. The doctors advised me to wear it. So I did. I came out of that fall a shorter man. Could never get the same crouch again. More upright."

Body protectors eventually became compulsory equipment, though not for another fifty years.

Chapter Twenty

Aflying start to 1950 saw TP with thirteen winners on the board before March was out. One of the more exotic was Solar, trained by Paddy Beary for Prince Aly Khan, infinitely better known for his espousal of the flat. Another significant success was also over hurdles, this time for new trainer J. M. 'Mickey' Rogers, son of Darby and grandson of old J. T. 'Jack' Rogers. He had set out his stall in Stepaside, high on the hill above the Curragh's military cemetery, alongside the Walshestown Road.

That flying start met with a temporary reverse when TP set out on Barney VI for his first and only attempt at the Grand National. The 'Scotchman' had mixed feelings. He had proposed to do likewise on Max – a far better chaser - thirty years before, only to heed the voices of reason. TP and his 100/1 shot got as far as Becher's Brook.

CURRAGH, April 1, 1950 – Knock Hard (TP) landing another O'Brien stable gamble in the Irish Lincolnshire Handicap. The 'Scotchman' won the race for second place on Secret Service.

April 1st, All Fools' Day, saw the Curragh bookmakers the butt of a very serious prank, in which TP played a key role. Rising young trainer Vincent O'Brien, had come a long way in a relatively short period since his autumn double six years previously. He had won the Cheltenham Gold Cup twice with Cottage Rake. His hat trick bid had been postponed when the final day of the Cheltenham festival had been deferred. Vincent and Aubrey Brabazon had also teamed up to win the Champion Hurdle twice with Hatton's Grace.

Knock Hard did not yet warrant such an exalted reputation. True, Harry Keogh's

Owner Harry Keogh leading in Knock Hard, with trainer Vincent O'Brien clearly recognisable on left of picture. Knock Hard went on to win the 1953 Cheltenham Gold Cup.

handsome chestnut had won his bumper, when trained by Willie O'Grady. Transferred to Vincent O'Brien's Churchtown stable, Knock Hard had made it a quick double over fences, at Leopardstown and Baldoyle, the latter just two weeks before the Irish Lincoln. Such strange credentials, together with a hefty 8st 12lb on his back, saw Knock Hard open at 6/1 for the first major handicap of the Irish flat season.

An avalanche of money forced Knock Hard in to 2/1 favourite, with hardly a shilling for his 24 opponents. The bookies could only brace themselves for a painful settling day. TP had the favourite six lengths in front after three furlongs, steadying his margin to five lengths as Knock Hard stormed over the line. The 'Scotchman' won the race for second place on Signal Service. There was only one winner.

TP recalled Knock Hard with respect and affection. "He was a class horse. An Irish Lincoln and a Cheltenham Gold Cup. Yes, Cottage Rake won an Irish Cesarewitch along with his three Gold Cups. Hatton's Grace won the Irish Cesarewitch twice. Arkle would probably have won it too, as was intended. But Knock Hard had the speed to win over a mile. He was really a flat horse that was turned to chasing."

Bright Cherry's all-the-way success in the Easter Chase at Fairyhouse was the other notable victory in TP's haul of 40 winners under both codes for 1950. Brother John added one more to the family total when riding Laurel Hill to win a Roscommon bumper for colourful owner-trainer Mickey Gleeson of Knocknagarm. As to the Irish jockeys' championship, Martin Molony had long since made that his monopoly, this time with 116 winners to his credit.

However, this year's championship contained a foreign ingredient. Paddy Prendergast, champion trainer with 30 winners of 54 races and £25,764 – more than double any previous money won in one year – had employed an Australian as stable jockey. J. W. 'Jackie' Thompson, star of the Sydney circuit, had agreed to come to Ireland for the

Tom Perry, trainer turned cartoonist, is inspired by the Irish Lincoln result.

1950 season, departing as champion flat jockey with an Irish Derby to his credit on Dark Warrior. Despite Darkie's pleadings, Jackie Thompson refused to return. His wife could not endure the prospect of another Irish 'summer'. She may have been right, for Jackie was still riding the Sydney circuit thirty years later. Nonetheless, the seed had been sown.

Under the spell of the Cheltenham Festival ever since seeing Prince Regent win the 1946 Gold Cup, TP got his first taste of action round Prestbury Park in 1951 when sixth on Danny Morgan's Prince Boudoir in the race he was to make pretty much his own, the Gloucestershire Hurdle. Mixing metiers with ever-increasing success, TP rode a two-year-old winner at the Curragh for Eamon Delany as a warm-up to scoring over banks at Punchestown on P. J. Coonan's Rathcoffey Pride in the Bishopscourt Cup. Miss Steel enabled TP to complete his haul of provincial 'Nationals' when successful in the Ulster version at Downpatrick for Dan Moore and Frankie Svedjar.

While TP was heading for his best season to date, Martin Molony had put his name on the jockey's title for the sixth year running when both travelled to Thurles on Tuesday, September 18th for a typical run-of-the-mill day's racing. Martin duly won the first, sat out the second and rode Bursary, odds-on favourite for the third event, the Munster Chase. Deaf to the observation that Bursary had carried Martin to an easy success at Tralee six days earlier, TP

PUNCHESTOWN, April 25, 1951 – P. J. Coonan leading in his Rathcoffey's Pride (TP), ready winner of the Bishopscourt Cup, the race that means more than any other to sporting farmers in the Kildare Hunt country.

remains adamant. "Bursary was a bad horse. Martin was too brave. He rode them all like they were champions. But brilliant. A brief but brilliant career. How wise he was not to come back. He went out at the very top and he deserves to be remembered as such. His secret? Martin was great at clicking horses off, saving their energy until it was needed."

Happily, the country's prayers that Martin Molony would not become the 'bravest man in the cemetery' were answered. Meanwhile, TP went on to win the first chase run over the new Wexford racecourse on Kilbelin Gap for Joe Osborne. Half an hour previously John Burns initiated a curious fraternal double when winning the first maiden hurdle contested at the new Bettyville venue.

Ten days later TP completed his Limerick Junction double on Ahaburn for Vincent O'Brien, odds-on favourite in the Knocklong Hurdle. An intermittent 'bleeder', Ahaburn was ever the subject of stewards' scrutiny. "The Stewards called Mr M. V. O'Brien, trainer of Mr J. A. Wood's Ahaburn, winner of this race, before them to explain the difference in the horse's running in the race as compared with its running in previous races. Having interviewed Mr O'Brien and heard his explanation the Stewards accepted same."

DOWNPATRICK, May 30, 1951 – TP completing his series of provincial 'Nationals' when winning the Ulster National on Miss Steel, trained by Dan Moore for WWII Czech resistance fighter pilot Frankie Svedjar.

TP's first treble – at Clonmel in

*GALWAY, July 31, 1952 – Warrenscourt Lad (TP) beating Cloncaw (Brian Cooper) and
Cool Water (P.J.Doyle) in a driving finish for the Galway Hurdle*

November – contributed to a total that saw only Martin Molony and Jimmy Mullane ride a greater number of winners. The 'Scotchman' continued to defy his years with a dozen successes in the saddle, while the Lumville stable also enjoyed a good year with several well-supported winners credited to 'B.Gallivan'.

A retainer to ride for Barney Macnaughton in 1952 saw TP team up with rising trainer John Oxx on the flat, while continuing to increase his seasonal tally to top the half-century for the first time. Highlights included a hard-fought Galway Hurdle victory on Warrenscourt Lad, at the immediate expense of Brian Cooper on Cloncaw. Warrenscourt Lad was owned and trained privately in west Cork by D. J. Duggan. An undertaker by profession, 'Dinny' Duggan employed Mick Farrissey, formerly head man to Jack Lombard, to train his horses. That Galway Hurdle was Warrenscourt Lad's seventh success of a lengthy and honourable career that yielded a further eleven victories, the last of them as an eleven-year-old in a flat race. Two races later TP teamed up with Lumville runner Coastward to land a flat handicap. The 'Scotchman' invariably laid horses out for Galway. "The strong betting market was the draw, and apart from the Plate and the Hurdle the competition wasn't all that strong, in those days anyway. That's changed now, they tell me."

Northern Gleam was another notable winner, in the Beresford Plate (Stakes since 1955). Trained by Darby Rogers, Northern Gleam had put herself firmly in the classic picture for the following season. It was in the December gloom at Navan that TP rode Noreast, trained by schoolmate Con Collins, to win over fences, en route to wrapping another successful campaign that had yielded 52 winners.

Mrs D. J. Duggan leading in her husband's winner.
TP's Galway Hurdle success followed his father's victories on King Eber (1920) and Holy Fooks (1923).

Chapter Twenty One

New Year's Day 1953 at Baldoyle augured well. Noreast, on the back of his recent Navan win, was sent off joint-favourite for the handicap chase. He came down, giving TP further serious back injuries. He never rode over fences again. At least one who 'went round' with TP over fences thought that a wise decision. "He used to go into flat race finish mode before he got to the last. The rest of us would be hooking them up, making sure they'd get over it. God help him, but nobody ever told him what he was doing wrong. Why would we?"

Sidelined for four months, TP had returned to ride three winners before the Irish 1000 Guineas. Under the terms of his retainer from the Macnaughton family TP rode Beau Co Co, an outsider in the market headed by her stable companion, Banri an Oir, ridden by Jackie Power in the colours of H.E. the President, Sean T. O'Kelly. The 'Scotchman' took over on the strongly fancied Northern Gleam.

After Banri an Oir had made the early running Beau Co Co and Northern Gleam moved into contention. Two furlongs from home Beau Co Co hit the front. The ensuing drama was graphically portrayed in the *Irish Horse*. "Meanwhile, Northern Gleam, doing all she could although obviously hating the [firm] ground, was inching nearer with every unhappy stride, but her supporters, appraising the distance separating the leader from the finishing line, were not optimistic. Steadily, however, the gap was being narrowed. Then, inside the last 150 yards, came the reward for such perseverance. Beau Co Co, who had been ridden with perfect judgement to take advantage of everything the run of the race had offered, was obviously

CURRAGH, May 14, 1953 – The 'Scotchman' gets Northern Gleam (right) up in the final strides to best Beau Co Co (TP) in the Irish 1000 Guineas, completing his tally of 21 Irish classics, commenced on Captive Princess back in 1916

weakening. Gallantly as she fought back she could not summon up another ounce of reserve.

"Tommy Burns, with no less than 41 years' race-riding experience behind him, probably appreciated the predicament of his son on the fading leader, moments before it became apparent to onlookers. He picked up Northern Gleam for the final thrust, nosed her in front a few feet from the post and drove her past the judge a neck to the good. An exhilarating piece of jockeyship by an accomplished artist, and a revelation of that inexplicable sympathy which always exists between horse and horseman. Thirty-seven years ago Burns had his first classic success on Captive Princess, the winner of the Irish St Leger in 1916."

'Scotchman' Burns assuring Lady Bury, owner of Northern Gleam, 'Youth really is wasted on the young'.

Northern Gleam proved to be the last of 21 Irish classic winners ridden by Tommy 'Scotchman' Burns, a total bettered only by Morny Wing, who had retired in 1949 with 23 to his credit. The ageless 'Scotchman' went on to ride another nine winners in Ireland in 1953, besides landing a touch at Ayr on Upadee at the big Ayr Western Meeting in September. Ironically, the 'Scotchman' brought off that stroke on home ground by upsetting an odds-on shot owned by Lord Rosebery and trained by Jack Jarvis. Rosebery had long come to regard the Western Meeting as an end-of-season bonanza. Jack Jarvis invariably sent up a strong team to gratify his principal patron. They had already won four races over the three days and Niccolette was regarded as a certainty in the final race of the meeting. Back from the shadows came the "Irish bastard" to spoil the script, albeit by just a neck.

Bought as a yearling for 300 guineas on behalf of Dublin motor assembler Tommy McCairns, Upadee had already run up a Curragh three-timer, 'trained B. Gallivan'. The slender filly was ridden each time by apprentice Andy Kelly, who recalled that his instructions were simplicity itself. "Get her down to the start, point her in the right direction and she'll do the rest."

Of course that was all very well when the filly was supposed to win. But there was no earthly sense in bringing her to Ayr on the back of a hat trick. Upadee would be no price. She needed a 'duck egg' in front of her name. Navan in August was the chosen venue, There could be no question of the 'Scotchman' carrying out this task, being a marked man. It fell to TP to do the necessary. "Six furlongs up Navan. And Upadee was at her peak. I never had a more difficult job in my life. But I managed to find enough trouble. We finished on top of the first four and nothing was said."

TP bounced back from that narrow defeat on Beau Co Co to ride more winners in Ireland than anyone bar Pat Taaffe and Liam Ward. An increasing number of TP's winners were coming from John Tonson-Rye's Cork stable, which also provided John Burns with the last of his five winners that year.

The early weeks of 1954 gave little hint of what lay in store for TP and other members of the Burns family. He had ridden just one domestic winner when opening his English hurdling account on Knockabout for Vincent O'Brien at Newbury in February. Owned by Hugh Stanley, Knockabout was on a sighting mission for the Gloucestershire Hurdle, a race now targeted by Vincent and his punting owners as an ideal gambling medium. The best of his younger horses were laid out for it, often twelve months ahead. Vincent had drawn first blood with Cockatoo two years previously, ridden by his younger brother, Mr A. S. 'Phonsie' O'Brien.

As was often the case, the 1954 Gloucestershire Hurdle was run in two divisions. The Ballydoyle team collected in the first division when Stroller justified favouritism under Pat Taaffe. Knockabout and TP were sent off hot favourite to make it an O'Brien double in the second division, only to be beaten a head by the French-trained Tasmin, ridden by René Emery. Despite typical English prejudice against French jockeys, TP held René Emery in some regard, "A fair jockey. Don't take him too cheap."

TP's luck changed the very next day, when Bryan Marshall was incapacitated before the Spa Hurdle in which the O'Brien stable had Lucky Dome. TP had ridden this versatile performer to victory in the Ulster Cesarewitch at Downpatrick five months previously. Not only did Lucky Dome run out an easy three-length winner of the Spa Hurdle, he did so at the immediate expense of René Emery on the favourite, Spring Corn. Having availed of what he considered a very generous 100/8, owner John A. Wood showed his appreciation. In TP's estimation, "John Wood was a generous owner. You were never forgotten."

Dermot O'Brien, Vincent's brother, assistant and handicap expert, recounted the episode to Raymond Smith in *Vincent O'Brien – the Master of Ballydoyle*. "On form it did not seem worthwhile sending Lucky Dome to Cheltenham, but John A. Wood, who loved to have a runner at the Festival, told Vincent to let him take his chance. Bryan Marshall had a bad fall and was stood down. I said to Vincent, 'T. P. Burns has no ride. Let's book him,' and that was how TP came to be on him that day. Lucky Dome won easily and, of course, the Stewards may have felt they had every reason to ask questions about that unplaced run in the hurdle race at

WINNING TEAM – trainer John Oxx, TP and Norman Macnaughton, by whom TP was retained. They shared many successes with such as Beau Co Co, Beau Joyau, Beau Sire, Beau Sejour and Mrs Macnaughton's Belle Cobeau.

CHAPTER TWENTY ONE

Baldoyle."

The O'Brien stable went on to land another gamble when Pat Taaffe brought Quare Times home in front in the National Hunt Chase to make the 1954 Cheltenham Festival one for bookmakers to forget. However, the O'Brien runners were coming under increasing official scrutiny, win or lose, as the *Irish Racing Calendar* duly recorded on April 2nd, 1954.

"The Stewards of the I.N.H.S. committee called Mr M. V. O'Brien before them on 22nd March to explain the inconsistent running of four horses trained by him – Royal Tan, Lucky Dome, Early Mist and Knock Hard.

"The following witnesses were examined – Mr D. D. Bulger and Mr T. J. Hurley (Stewards' Secretaries in Ireland), P. J. Doyle, T. P. Burns, P. Taaffe, E. J. Kennedy, Mr A. S. O'Brien, Mr D. O'Brien, Mr J. R. Rogers, Mr M. H. Keogh, and the hearing was adjourned until March 31st, when the following witnesses were examined – Rear Admiral H. B. Jacomb, Lt-Col J. M. Christian (Stewards' Secretaries to the N.H. Committee in England), Bryan Marshall and Mr J. A. S. Wood.

DOWNPATRICK, October 28, 1953 – TP enjoys a sauntering success in the Ulster Cesarewitch on Lucky Dome – "so dependable when the money was down " – trained by Vincent O'Brien for generous owner John A. Wood. They followed up in the Spa Hurdle at the 1954 Cheltenham Festival.

"The Stewards of the I.N.H.S. Committee could not accept Mr M. V. O'Brien's explanations, and when considering what action to take had before them the fact that Mr M. V. O'Brien had been warned and cautioned on several previous occasions as to the running of his horses.

"The Stewards under Rules 16 (ii) and 104 (vii) withdrew his licence to train for three calendar months from April 2nd, 1954"

Vincent O'Brien duly issued the following statement. "I attended an Inquiry of the Irish National Hunt Stewards on 22 March and today. I was asked to explain the inconsistent running of four horses trained by me, viz: Royal Tan, Lucky Dome, Early Mist and Knock Hard.

"Today the Stewards gave me their decision that they could not accept my explanations and withdrew my licence to train for three calendar months from April 2.

"I am completely in the dark as to what, if any, offence I am alleged to have been guilty.

"No suggestion was made against the manner in which the horses were ridden in any of their races. In fact no specific charge of any kind in respect of the running of any of the horses in any of their races has been made."

Temporarily deprived of one source of winners, TP went on to ride his fair share for John Oxx, Willie O'Grady and Kevin Bell, with whom he had been to junior school in Newbridge years before. Meanwhile the 'Scotchman', alias 'B. Gallivan' gave Upadee a few quiet runs in preparation for what was to be Tommy Burns' farewell to the saddle – at Royal Ascot.

As the filly continued to please in her work, the 'Scotchman' alerted his aged father and all his punting cronies round Ayr that something was afoot. Knowing that his career was at its end, the 'Scotchman' undertook those three stopping missions. TP still had his future to safeguard. In between her races Upadee was partnered exclusively by Stella, TP's sister, who quickly developed a bond of affection for this utterly genuine filly, making due allowance for her one consistent quirk. "She would go out on to the Curragh like an old sheep. But there was one point at which she simply had to stop every single morning, gaze left, gaze right, reassure herself that all was exactly as she had seen it previously, and then go on about the business of the day."

Sadly, James Burns would not live to see the day, dying at his Applehirst home on June 11th, aged eighty. The *Irish Field* paid due tribute. "The death occurred on 11th inst of Mr James Burns, of Applehirst, Ayr, the outstanding Scottish racehorse trainer of his day. He was the father of Tommy Burns, the Irish jockey, and grandfather of T. P. Burns,

"In his time Mr Burns trained about 500 winners, notably Forest Guard (Ayr Gold Cup), Wildwood (Ayrshire Handicap) and Beech Hill (Ayrshire Handicap). He believed in putting up a first-class jockey when he fancied a horse, and those who rode for him included Sir Gordon Richards, Steve Donoghue, Bernard Carslake, Tommy Weston and Vic Smyth.

"During the first World War Mr Burns trained in Ireland, and had eighty horses under his charge. For a few years while he was in Ireland, George Formby, the comedian, was apprenticed to him."

Four days later, in the Queen Anne Stakes at Royal Ascot, Upadee left her recent Irish form a long way behind when the 'Scotchman' rode her to overturn Big Berry, the favourite, ridden by teenaged phenomenon Lester Piggott, by three-quarters of a length. Upadee was returned at 100/6. Possibly prompted by the recent sensational withdrawal of Vincent O'Brien's licence for the perceived inconsistent running of his horses, the stewards sent for trainer B. Gallivan. Their summons was in vain, for Barney Gallivan was otherwise engaged, overseeing his business in Newbridge. In his absence Upadee had been saddled by Denis 'Dinny' Quirke, Martin's brother, former lightweight jockey for Lord Derby in France and sometime trainer.

ROYAL ASCOT, June 15, 1954 – 'Scotchman' Burns signing off on 42 years' race riding in style, with Upadee in the opening Queen Anne Stakes, overturning Lester Piggott on 3/1 favourite Big Berry. The 'Scotchman' had bought Upadee as a yearling for 300gns, training her to win 5 races for Tommy McCairns. Absentee Newbridge grocer and publican Barney Gallivan appeared in the record books as winning trainer for the final time.

The *Racing Calendar* revealed that three enquiries into Upadee's apparent improvement in form had left the Ascot stewards none the wiser. Even though the six-month ban on Lester Piggott had subsequently dominated the Royal Ascot headlines, the Stewards of the Turf Club felt compelled to instigate their own enquiry into the 'Upadee affair.' The outcome was revealed in the *Irish Racing Calendar*, June 25th 1954.

"The Stewards of the Turf Club and the I.N.H.S. Committee interviewed Mr B. Gallivan (trainer) and T. Burns (jockey and authorised agent for the trainer) at the Curragh on Wednesday, 23rd June, with regard to the Notice in the Racing Calendar relative to the running of Upadee in the Queen Anne Stakes at Ascot on Tuesday, 15th June. They noted that Mr Gallivan was not present at Ascot and that T. Burns (authorised agent) had no explanation to offer when interviewed by the Stewards of the Meeting. The Stewards of the Turf Club and the I.N.H.S. Committee heard evidence from Mr T. McCairns (owner), Mr Gallivan, T. Burns, Major R. Turner (Handicapper) and Mr D. D. Bulger (Stewards' Secretary). They considered that Mr Gallivan had not been exercising adequate supervision over the horses in his stable and withdrew his licence to train under Rule 102 (vi) Rules of Racing and Rule (vii) I.N.H.S. Rules.

"(N.B. – A person whose licence is withdrawn under Rule 102(vi) Rules of Racing, and Rule(vii) I.N.H.S. Rules is not a disqualified person)."

The same edition of the *Irish Racing Calendar* contained the terse announcement: "Thomas Burns has relinquished his licence to ride." In his 43-year career in the saddle the 'Scotchman' claimed to have ridden over 2,000 winners on the flat, and 100-plus over jumps. The latter figure is probably closer to reality, while the 21 Irish classics remains beyond dispute.

While the Ascot stewards let it be known, through unofficial channels, that Mr Gallivan's presence on the day would have enabled them to accept his explanation, whatever it might have been, the general hilarity among the Irish contingent that greeted Barney's summons to the stewards' room had compelled them to pursue the matter.

Happily distanced from all the Ascot fall-out, TP continued to mount his challenge for his first Irish jockeys' championship, fuelled principally by John Oxx, Kevin Bell, Willie O'Grady and the reinstated Vincent O'Brien. His was a campaign of quantity rather than quality, amassing small winners at almost every meeting. Notable among those 'run-of-the-mill' winners was Roddy Owen. TP rode the future Cheltenham Gold Cup winner to score over hurdles at Navan for trainer Danny Morgan in the colours of Lord Fingall. TP's recollection of Roddy Owen – "not a natural jumper" – would be echoed by others over the seasons ahead.

As 1954 drew to a close, veteran racing journalist T. E. Healy filed his summary of the racing year in Ireland for the *Bloodstock Breeders' Review*. "In so far as I can trace, the first dead heat for the jockeys' championship is that between James Eddery (chief jockey for Seamus McGrath's stables) and T. P. Burns (who held a retainer from Mr N. S. Macnaughton and others). Eddery has ridden both on the flat and over hurdles in most previous years but during the past season he rode solely on the flat. T. P. Burns, following his usual custom, rode under both rules. Each had 48 winners, and closely pressing them in third place is P. Powell junior with 47 wins, and in fourth place is Pat Taaffe with 43 wins. Powell rides on the flat and over hurdles, but Pat Taaffe is exclusively a jumping jockey. A. Woods did best of the apprentices, and Mr D. A. C. Auld topped the Corinthians."

While publishers have always and ever put pressure on contributors to file in good time, in this instance that practice misfired. TP rode a further brace of winners in December to claim the title outright, with a total of 50 winners from 329 rides in Ireland. Curiously, the traditional method of calculating Irish racing statistics on a calendar year basis yielded the anomalous situation whereby TP was crowned overall champion, although Jimmy Eddery headed the flat category, Pat Taaffe doing likewise over jumps.

Chapter Twenty Two

TP's defence of his crown began quietly, with just one winner in Ireland before heading to Cheltenham in March. However, Ilyric's Leopardstown success in January was to prove significant. Traditionally, proceedings at the Cheltenham Festival opened with the Birdlip Selling Hurdle, carried over this year, as Tuesday was snowed off, its card transferred to the Wednesday and Thursday's card abandoned except for the Gold Cup. TP rode Ahaburn, trained by Vincent O'Brien for John A. Wood. "Ahaburn was a regular bleeder and consequently an old rogue. But if you let him warm into his race without hustling him, he'd do the rest."

Ridden accordingly, Ahaburn duly delivered at 2/1, giving John Wood his best ever start to his annual joust with the Cheltenham bookies. The race carried a winner's prize of £462, less than half the 950 guineas that it cost a jubilant John Wood to retain Ahaburn at the subsequent auction. An hour later TP rode the race of his life on Stroller in the Champion Hurdle, only to be beaten a head by Fred Winter on Clair Soleil. Their spectacular duel so moved the stewards that Lord Willoughby de Broke, chairman of the National Hunt Committee summoned both jockeys to congratulate them on the finest finish for a Champion Hurdle any of the panel was ever likely to witness.

Foiled in the Champion Hurdle, Vincent made amends in the first division of his favoured Gloucestershire Hurdle with Vindore, ridden by his brother 'Phonsie'. TP was entrusted with the second division on Ilyric. Although recalled by his rider as "an old bastard," Bob Mulrooney's horse delivered on the day, thereby enabling TP to emulate the 'Scotchman', successful in the 1933 Gloucestershire Hurdle on Roderic More O'Ferrall's Cobequid.

CHELTENHAM, March 9, 1955 – Ahaburn (TP) hugging the rails when level with Chasseur (Tim Brookshaw) over the last. Three lengths clear at the line, Ahaburn got punting owner John A. Wood off to his best-ever Cheltenham start.

Illyric Being led in after winning Gloucester Hurdle.

CHELTENHAM, March 10, 1955 – Illyric (TP) led in by owner Bob Mulrooney having justified favouritism in the Gloucestershire Hurdle, Division II. Vincent O'Brien had earlier taken Division I with Vindore (Mr A. S. O'Brien).

Back home TP set about retaining his title with a steady stream of winners, among them the Tetrarch Plate on Bright Night for trainer Kevin Bell and his brother-in-law Morny Wing and the Blandford Plate on Nile Bird for J. M. 'Mickey' Rogers. An unexpected contributor to TP's second Irish jockeys' title was Reinstated. George Robinson's charge had been beaten fair and square by Ballyknock in the Irish Cesarewitch. However, rumours that all was not as it appeared in relationship to the ownership of Ballyknock prompted an enquiry by the Stewards of the Turf Club, resulting in the disqualification of Ballyknock, whereby the Irish Cesarewitch was awarded to Reinstated. That brought TP's annual total to 55 winners from 330 mounts in Ireland. Once again TP was overall champion without heading either category, as Jimmy Eddery rode more flat winners than any other, as did Pat Taaffe in the jumping sphere.

On the domestic front TP found time to purchase a parcel of land to the east of Stepaside, flanking the unsurfaced laneway leading to Athgarvan. He acquired the site, with space for a couple of paddocks in a circuitous way. "It was only a corner of a big farm owned by two spinster sisters, who refused to sell off their land piecemeal. It had to be all or nothing and Paddy Cox was their 'said man'. I more or less put it out of my mind, until Paddy came to me, saying he had agreed to buy the whole farm and would I be interested in taking the bit I wanted off him. Cash was scarce at that time and he knew I had some. So we came to an arrangement."

There he began to build the bungalow, which he named 'Landfall' at his mother's suggestion. At the time there were no essential services whatsoever in that corner of the Curragh, obliging TP to pay Kildare County Council and the ESB to provide same. "Getting the road out from Walshestown tarred cost me more than it did to build the house!"

Stroller & Clair Soleil jumping last hurdle in Champion Hurdle. Cheltenham

Still adrift over the last, Stroller (TP) ran favourite Clair Soleil (Fred Winter) to a head in a gripping finish.

99

Firmly ensconced as Vincent O'Brien's hurdle jockey, with 'Toss' Taaffe riding the Ballydoyle chasers, TP had made a speedier start to defending his title before the 1956 Cheltenham Festival came round. Gloucestershire Hurdle contenders had come successfully through their preliminaries at Gowran Park and Naas respectively, while Stroller had demonstrated his well-being in the Rose of Lancaster Hurdle at Manchester.

Stroller duly started favourite to avenge his narrow defeat in the 1955 Champion Hurdle, only to hit the deck at the third last. As TP ruefully recalled, "He was brought down by a swinging hurdle. The only fall I ever had from one of Vincent's. And I rode hundreds for him.

"Vincent wasn't going to allow the big gambles at Cheltenham to go astray because his challengers could not jump. He took infinite patience in teaching them. One of the greatest attributes of all Vincent O'Brien-trained horses in National Hunt races, especially hurdle races was that they could jump. They would invariably gain that vital length in jumping. . . It was a pleasure to ride for him, as he was a true professional himself, always."

The Gloucestershire Hurdle aspirants made up for that reverse in style the next day, each sent off favourite. Boys Hurrah won in Michael Sheehan's colours at 9/4, while Pelargos carried Vincent's own colours to an even more convincing success in the second division at 7/4. On the final day Vincent ran both Stroller and Lucky Dome in the concluding Spa Hurdle. TP rode Lucky Dome, with English hurdles ace Harry Sprague on Stroller. TP's premonition that he was on the wrong one proved well founded as Harry Sprague used all his formidable powers of persuasion to propel Stroller home by a short head from Bobby Patton's Kilkilogue, ridden by Paddy Crotty. TP finished third, two lengths adrift on Lucky Dome.

CHELTENHAM, March 7, 1956 – Boys Hurrah (TP) pinging the last to justify favouritism in the Gloucestershire Hurdle, Division I. His closest pursuers, Bowsprit (Jack Dowdeswell) (centre) and Camugliano (Rene Emery) finished second and third respectively.

Back home TP's title came under increasing threat from Liam Ward and 'Toss' Taaffe, whose mounting scores on the flat and over jumps respectively looked likely to be greater than TP's customary combined total could exceed. Throughout the flat season TP enjoyed an excellent run in HE the President's blue and gold livery – he was the only jockey ever to receive a presidential retainer – winning on Sail Anair and Gorm Abu for John Oxx and Fanai Tire for Colonel Blake. The last-named enabled TP to complete a Leopardstown double initiated on a classy juvenile trained by Vincent O'Brien for a new American patron, John McShain. The elegant chestnut colt went by the name of Ballymoss.

As 1956 drew to its close Liam Ward appeared certain to depose TP as Irish champion jockey, with 'Toss' Taaffe a close second, though 'Toss' was still in with a shout when Liam's flat season ended in November. Unlike the majority of his rivals, who mixed *métiers*, Liam Ward did once ride a winner over hurdles, but declined to repeat the experience. However, champion or ex-champion, TP still had at least one very important mission to accomplish. It centred round a lowly maiden plate at Manchester, on the final day of the English flat season. The medium was a once-raced filly called Gladness.

Owned and bred by Leamington Spa stud farmer Sidney McGregor, famous as the breeder of 1932 Derby winner April the Fifth, Gladness had run just once in the backend of her juvenile year. Superficial injuries sustained in a collision with a stationary van in the yard at Ballydoyle had kept her off the course until the 1956 flat season was almost over. However, she had run out such a clearcut winner of a demanding trial at Gowran Park as to be considered a virtual certainty for a maiden. Manchester was identified as the venue.

In the greatest secrecy Gladness was shipped to Manchester, though not to the racecourse stables. TP went over to ride Floor Show to win for Paddy Sleator on the Thursday, ostensibly

CURRAGH, May 10, 1956 – Gorm Abu (TP), three lengths clear of dead heaters Bruletta (Gerry Cooney) and Derita (Herbie Holmes) in the Bann Maiden Stakes.

flying back to Ireland that night. Thus it came as a surprise when Gladness was declared for the Broughton Maiden Plate on the Friday, to be ridden by T. P. Burns. Warily, the bookies priced Gladness up at 11/10. To their horror, price turned out to be irrelevant. It was simply a matter of how much O'Brien's punters could get on. Dermot O'Brien provided Raymond Smith with this vignette. "There was this Irish punter standing under William Hill's pitch and when he saw me coming he put two and two together and moved in quickly to get his bet on before I got on. I said to William Hill's representative, 'The best odds to £1,000,' and he replied, 'You have evens to £200.'"

By the time the field was coming under orders John Wood could be seen patrolling up and down the line of bookies, entreating any of them to lay him to his last thousand. There were no takers. TP enjoyed the proverbial 'armchair ride'. Turning in sixth, he sent Gladness into the lead two furlongs out, winning by five lengths. Hit hard by Gladness, the bookies were on

TP congratulated by winning owner H.E. the President of Ireland, Sean T. O'Kelly. TP had a retainer to ride the Presidential runners, all products of the Irish National Stud.

their knees after the following race, in which Fuel, trained by Cecil Brabazon and ridden by his son Aubrey, was backed at every price from 8/1 to 5/4 before running out an equally facile winner.

By the time racing in Ireland went into pre-Christmas recess at Mullingar on December 15th Liam Ward seemed certain of his first Irish jockeys' title, having ridden 64 winners. 'Toss' Taaffe had 62 to his credit, while TP trailed this pair on 51, out of the running. Set to ride two winners over Christmas to share the title and three to gain it outright, 'Toss' Taaffe made the title his own with a St Stephen's Day treble at Leopardstown, all trained by Vincent O'Brien. Going down with his colours still flying, TP replied with a double. 'Toss' travelled down to Limerick the following day, where he put clear blue water between himself and his closest rival when riding yet another treble.

If TP had to forfeit his title, he could hardly have asked for it to be taken from him in more spectacular style. Moreover, he could console himself in the realisation that the foundation of 'Toss' Taaffe's solitary championship had been provided by Vincent O'Brien's steeplechasers. Ballymoss and Gladness promised to bring the steeplechasing era in Ballydoyle to a close. After all, Vincent O'Brien could be said to have scaled those heights, again and again. His Grand National hat trick with Early Mist, Royal Tan and Quare Times was unlikely ever to be equalled. Cottage Rake had likewise provided Vincent with a Gold Cup hat trick. Knock Hard had won him a fourth Gold Cup, while closer to home Alberoni had carried off the Irish Grand National and the Galway Plate. It was time to focus on the richer pickings of the flat.

Vincent had already demonstrated his ability to adapt to the rarified atmosphere of 'proper' racing. Quite apart from those handicap successes with Hatton's Grace, Cottage Rake and Knock Hard, he had won an Irish Derby with Chamier in 1953 and a Beresford Stakes with Barfelt six years previously. It was simply a matter of finding owners with money to spend.

How often had Vincent taken TP into his confidence about the daunting overhead that Ballydoyle constituted, with four men employed fulltime just on the gallops? Moreover, for one who believed that nothing was too good or too expensive for his horses if it made that vital difference to their performance, owners who queried items such as glucose on their monthly accounts had now fulfilled their role. TP was a willing accomplice. "What do I think drove Vincent O'Brien in those days? Money. You have to realise that Vincent started out with nothing, nothing at all. The family farm had gone to his older half-brothers. He had nothing but ability and ambition. To get to the top was going to take money. He didn't have any, so it had to be got somehow, anyhow."

Chapter Twenty Three

The steeplechasers might almost have had their day in Ballydoyle, but those Gloucestershire Hurdle hotpots held their place in the scheme of things, and with good reason. The stable needed to bet to survive and the 'Gloucester' was its proven metier for doing just that. Moreover, the massive Saffron Tartan promised to excel. Sent to Vincent to train as an unbroken store, Saffron Tartan had simply outgrown his strength, a great big, ungainly creature. Yet Vincent had discerned something of immense potential lurking deep within his massive frame.

The shambling store was lucky to have been born at all. His dam, Kellsboro' Witch, might have been a half-sister to Grand National winner Kellsboro' Jack. Nevertheless, her sometime owner, Maurice Springfield MFH, recalled her as "a holy terror, both in the hunting field and on the racecourse." She had won just once, at Hethersett in 1936, when her solitary rival fell. Even then she had taken fifteen minutes to complete, refusing at every fence at least once. Maurice Springfield always insisted that, had his hounds been short of food when he returned with Kellsboro' Witch that same night, he would not have seen the pack go hungry. All those years later her strapping son's potential was ready to be tapped.

A pensive Vincent O'Brien in conference with Col G.R. Westmacott, part-owner of Saffron Tartan, and TP.

Odds-on to make a winning debut in a Naas bumper in February 1957, Saffron Tartan duly sauntered home under 'Phonsie' O'Brien. Two weeks later TP rode him to an equally impressive hurdles debut at Baldoyle, also odds-on. That completed the big horse's public preparation for his Gloucestershire Hurdle challenge. Vincent had others to run at the Cheltenham Festival, but over fences. TP had just one ride over the three days, the one that mattered.

Put in at even money, Saffron Tartan was immediately plunged upon, starting once again odds-on. TP had already ridden three winners of this most competitive of novice hurdles and knew what was involved. 'Saffron' made it look so easy, as TP confirmed. "He was the best of them all, the finest novice that ever left the stable. He had the rest of them stone cold from the top of the hill and beat Predominate as if he was a selling plater."

A decent hurdler and already a formidable stayer on the flat, Predominate went on to become a tremendous public favourite in the tradition of Brown Jack, Old Orkney and Trelawny, winning 14 flat races in his lengthy career. The Predominate Stakes at Goodwood, a recognised Derby trial, was instituted in his honour. 'Saffron' had to be every bit as special as TP held him to be. "Saffron Tartan was unbeatable until he went wrong of his wind and a very nice ride for all his size and bulk. Moved like a flat racer. Vincent always said he could have won a Lincoln if necessary. I didn't say it to anyone except Vincent, but up the Cheltenham hill that day I thought Saffron's wind sounded very coarse. . ."

That mission accomplished, Vincent switched his focus to the flat, running both Gladness and

CURRAGH, June 26, 1957 – Before – Ballymoss might have been odds-on for the Irish Derby, following his good second to Crepello at Epsom, but Vincent still had instructions to impart to his attentive jockey.

Ballymoss in the Trigo Stakes at Leopardstown in May. With TP in the saddle, Gladness started odds-on favourite to improve on her second in the Irish Lincoln, in which she had carried 10st. The firm ground was all against Sidney McGregor's mare, but in favour of Ballymoss, winner by a neck under Jackie Power at 20/1.

TP recounted the sequel to that mixed result, apropos Ballymoss going for the Derby. "There'd been discussion between the Boss, Dermot and me whether Ballymoss should take his chance, for the Trigo had, at least, put him in the picture. In a mixed gallop on the Curragh I rode Ballymoss. I'd been associated with him from day one. There were three or four of Paddy Prendergast's horses, and two of the McGraths' and we galloped one mile three furlongs on the inside of the course. The Derby gallop we call it. Ballymoss didn't just beat them. . . he trotted over them! We were all amazed. It was then confirmed that he would take his chance at Epsom."

After – Ballymoss cruising home, well clear of Hindu Festival (Rae Johnstone) and Valentine Slipper (Paddy Powell). TP thus emulated the 'Scotchman', successful in the 1936 Irish Derby on Raeburn.

As no Irish-trained horse had ever won the Derby until Orby in 1907 and none had done so in the interim, Ballymoss was disregarded in the ante-post market, until some support saw his odds trimmed from 100/1 to 33/1. Of course, the Irish colt had no chance against the favourite Crepello, already an impressive winner of the Two Thousand Guineas and a firm 6/4 shot to give Lester Piggott his second Derby success.

"Why did his price come down like that? Well, Vincent said after the trial that he couldn't send a hundred-to-one shot over for the Derby. The owner wouldn't be impressed. So he got a few of his punters like Mick Sheehan together and their money dropped the price very quick."

Simultaneously, Michael O'Hehir, Ireland's outstanding sports broadcaster, advised Peter O'Sullevan, his English equivalent, to have an interest in Ballymoss, terrific each way value at 100/1. Peter, who regularly carried out commissions for Vincent, duly rang to enquire whether the trainer wished to be 'on'. Vincent demurred, saying that while he wouldn't put Peter off Ballymoss, a slight interruption in the horse's preparation might have left him a little short in his work. The concerted interest in Ballymoss from two 'informed sources' had the desired effect.

The 1957 Derby was not exactly a reprise of Thankerton and the 'Scotchman' twenty-one years previously, but there were echoes in TP's post-race account. "I was about fourth coming down the hill and had a grand run through on Ballymoss, though squeezed a little for room by Palor entering the straight. I took the lead about two furlongs from home and then thought that I should win. Crepello passed me about a furlong out and went two-and-a-half lengths ahead, but then started to look about him and we reduced his lead a little, though I would say he won cheekily."

From second in the Derby at their first attempt, trainer and jockey switched their sights to Tramore to win a maiden hurdle with Colonel Westmacott's Ballybrittas and thence to Mallow to collect a juvenile plate with John McShain's Strong Rage, before heading to the Curragh, where the Irish Derby appeared a formality for Ballymoss. And so it proved. Sent off long odds-on, Ballymoss carried TP to an effortless four-length victory over Hindu Festival and Rae Johnstone.

A steady succession of country winners, including a treble at Limerick Junction – the scene of Vincent's first training success – edged the trainer towards his first Irish title and TP towards his third, before they headed to York in August, where Ballymoss contested the Great Voltigeur stakes, a traditional St Leger trial. No Irish-trained horse had ever won the oldest of the English classics, at least outright. Russborough had dead heated with the mighty Voltigeur in 1850, only going under by a length in the run-off.

Nor did Ballymoss look any more likely to become the first Irish-trained St Leger winner, beaten four lengths by the northern long-shot Brioche, ridden by Australian Edgar Britt. Excuses were made for Ballymoss, particularly the dead and sticky going that rain can so quickly induce on the Knavesmire. In TP's belief, "Ballymoss was a top-class colt with plenty of gears, provided the ground was good to firm or better."

On Vincent's advice John McShain had not crossed the Atlantic to witness Ballymoss at Epsom. However, he and his wife did make the trip to Doncaster, only to be greeted by steady rainfall. By that time Peter O'Sullevan had invested £1,100 each way on Vincent's behalf. The bets would have to stand. As connections admitted afterwards, the continual rain made for a somewhat cheerless lunch. From sharing favouritism with Brioche, Ballymoss drifted out to 8/1, his chances diminishing in the drizzle. On the credit side, there was no Crepello to beat and Vincent had left something to work on since

DONCASTER, September 11, 1957 – A very pensive TP going on Ballymoss, bidding to become the first Irish-trained winner of the oldest classic. Following him is Court Harwell (Scobie Breasley).

After – Ballymoss making history, a length clear of Court Harwell, with Brioche (Eddie Hide) a close third.

York. As the runners came into line, the sun broke through.

In the event there was little cause for worry, as TP subsequently recounted to the assembled reporters. "Ballymoss is a free-running horse and I did not want to get him too well away. We were only cantering all through the race. Approaching the turn he was pulling so hard that I let him move up to fourth or fifth place and passed Tenterhooks about two furlongs from home. . . I never had the slightest doubt after turning into the straight that we would win. He was not tiring at the end. The ground was good, with the horses just cutting into the surface. . . but of course when one wins as easily as that, the going usually seems good, but it might be different for those under pressure."

In addition to TP's post-race resume, the *Bloodstock Breeders' Review* also described the scene after Ballymoss's historic victory. "Returning to the saddling enclosure, Burns had to wait at the entrance until the beaming Mrs McShain arrived to lead him in. Horse and owners received a mighty ovation from the sporting Yorkshire crowd, to which were added the vociferous voices of O'Brien's many associates and friends who had travelled over from Ireland in the hopes of witnessing the first-ever St Leger victory of an Irish-trained horse. Mr and Mrs McShain, who had flown from the United States only the previous morning, had not come to Epsom for the Derby as Vincent O'Brien had thought that Ballymoss was not then quite at his peak, having missed a few days' work owing to a poisoned foot; they had, however, seen his victory at the Curragh. Mr McShain, head of a large firm of builders whose constructions include Washington's Pentagon, lives in Philadelphia and maintains in the United States a large string of horses which run under the nom de course of Barclay Stable – hence the white jacket with red 'B' front and back of his racing colours."

Peter O'Sullevan summed it all up so succinctly in his *Horse Racing Heroes*, published almost half a century later. "Appropriately, the infinitely dependable TP Burns rode Vincent's first English classic winner."

Those lucky colours were to the fore again a week later when TP guided Gladness to a smooth win in the Leinster Handicap at the Curragh, her first run since Leopardstown in May and her first in the McShain livery. Gladness was aimed for the Prix de l'Arc de Triomphe and Ballymoss for the Champion Stakes at Newmarket, prior to the Washington International at Laurel Park, Maryland. For Vincent O'Brien and T. P. Burns the world had become their oyster.

It didn't quite work out that way. Gladness got very upset during the preliminaries in Paris and ran no race at all in finishing a disappointing eleventh behind Oroso. Ballymoss, upset after kicking the rails in the parade ring, ran far too freely at Newmarket, beating only one home, well adrift of Rose

TP urges his St Leger winner to accompany owner's wife Mary McShain into the winner's enclosure.

Royale and Jean Massard. His intended trip to Maryland was promptly cancelled. However, Gladness ended her season on a winning note with a bloodless victory under TP in the Irish Champion Stakes at the Curragh. Both would remain in training, with every prospect of carrying their jockey to even greater triumphs in 1958.

Despite his dramatic breakthrough from jumping to the heights of the flat, Vincent had to give best to Seamus McGrath in the Irish trainers' table. By contrast, TP's combined total of 56 winners in Ireland sufficed to see him crowned champion jockey for the third time in four years. Liam Ward was leading flat jockey for the third time with 47 winners, while 'Toss' Taaffe headed the jumping table with 37 winners to his credit.

Chapter Twenty Four

Before Ballymoss and Gladness were due to reappear in 1958 there was that all-important business of the Gloucestershire Hurdle to be resolved. On this occasion Vincent selected Prudent King and Admiral Stuart as his preferred weapons. Prudent King satisfied trainer and jockey when winning his maiden hurdle at Gowran Park. Admiral Stuart took two preparatory races, finishing second each time. He wasn't the bravest of horses of TP's now considerable acquaintance.

While TP had an agreement to ride on the flat and over hurdles for the Ballydoyle stable, he never sought a retainer. Nor had one been proffered. "The arrangement suited both Vincent and myself. With Vincent you always got what was due to you, never less and never more. And in fairness to him, if owners proved ungenerous or forgetful, he would do what he could to correct their ways. In one particular case he declared that he would have to turn the man upside down and shake him to see if any money fell out of his pockets, for he had tried and failed by any other means.

"As to being easy or difficult to ride for, I never had any problems. Once you had gained his confidence, Vincent would simply say, 'You know him better than I do. Ride him as you think best.' Other jockeys found Vincent overly demanding in his orders. With me, if something went wrong, he would put it behind him and concentrate on retrieving any losses next time."

They took a number of hurdlers to the 1958 Cheltenham Festival, though without any real confidence in Dunnock, Pelargos or the ageing

CHELTENHAM, March 12, 1958 – hot favourite Admiral Stuart (TP) (left) drawing level with Flaming Star (Arthur Freeman) en route to comfortable success in Division I of the Gloucestershire Hurdle. TP and Vincent completed yet another Gloucestershire Hurdle double with Prudent King.

Stroller. Everything depended on the Gloucestershire Hurdle contenders. Clem Magnier's double on the opening day with Top Twenty and Springsilver gave the Irish punters ample ammunition to plunge on Admiral Stuart in the first division of the 'Gloucester'. Mrs T. V. Ryan's seasoned seven-year-old was sent off 6/5 favourite, the layers going 6/1 bar one. Threading his way quietly through his rivals, TP hit the front at the last to win comfortably by three lengths, without Admiral Stuart's suspect mettle being put to the test.

"That was the only ride Vincent ever actually praised me over. 'You rode him well, Tommy. He's a very slow horse.' Otherwise, you had simply done what was expected of you. Nothing needed to be said. But if you made a bags of it, he might say in his quiet way, 'You've ridden better races than that, Tommy.' Anyway, you'd know quick enough by his manner."

Tom Dreaper and 'Toss' Taaffe then bagged a quick double with the full-brothers Fortria and Sentina. As a consequence, Anson opened a short-priced favourite to make it a Dreaper-Taaffe treble in the second division of the Gloucestershire Hurdle. Anson drifted rapidly in the face of a gamble on Dan Moore's Cusack, ridden by Aubrey Brabazon. The O'Brien supporters took full advantage, helping themselves liberally to Prudent King at 4/1 in to 3/1. This time TP had to work a little harder, only shaking off Magical Approach and Mick Bachelor close home to win by half a length. In three years out of four Vincent O'Brien had carried off both divisions of the Gloucestershire Hurdle, with TP in the saddle on five of those six winners. Saffron Tartan had brought TP's total to six.

Now on their way to a record eight wins at a Cheltenham Festival, the Irish suffered a rare reverse in the opening Spa Hurdle on the final day. Stroller was backed in from 7/2 to 9/4 clear favourite. The form book recorded TP's mount as "never going well, always behind." Neither trainer nor jockey were particularly dismayed, Stroller owed neither of them anything whatsoever. Winner of a 1954 Gloucestershire Hurdle for Vincent and owner 'Mincemeat Joe' Griffin, Stroller belonged to

Gladness in oils - a present from John McShain

Blaney Hamilton when TP rode him to win at Liverpool and Manchester later that year. Sold once more within the stable, he continued to win carrying the colours of Harry Lane, made famous by Teal, winner of the 1952 Grand National.

The reigning Irish champion jockey returned to his realm to win the Athasi Stakes at the Curragh on Minou, for Darby Rogers and owner H. F. Mumford-Smith. As the only jockey ever to receive a presidential retainer, TP piloted Tula Riona to victory for John Oxx at Dundalk and then did likewise for the 'Scotchman' in a flat race at Kilbeggan with Maranboy, owned by film director John Huston. Further afield TP rode Ballymoss to finish second to HM Queen Elizabeth's Doutelle in the Ormonde Stakes at Chester on his seasonal reappearance. The following Sunday TP finished second again, this time on Gladness, beaten a length by Scot in Prix du Cadran on soft ground at Longchamp. Both stable stars had wintered well and their prospects looked excellent.

Meanwhile, there were lesser lights to ride on the home front, such as Michael Sheehan's Boys Hurrah, likewise trained by Vincent O'Brien, second favourite for the Tipperary Cup at Clonmel on May 22nd. The notice in the *Irish Racing Calendar* was quite explicit. "The Stewards enquired into the falls in this race of Mrs B. Farquhar's Cloncahir and Mr M. J. Sheehan's Boys Hurrah. Having interviewed D. Auld (rider of Cloncahir) and P. Hughes, who rode in the race the Stewards were of the opinion that Cloncahir slipped up and brought down Boys Hurrah. They were unable to interview T. P. Burns (rider of Boys Hurrah) owing to his injuries."

Hospitalised for ten weeks with serious spinal injuries and a fractured breastbone, TP could only follow in frustration the fortunes of 'his' plum mounts. On June 5th Ballymoss swept to a smooth success in the Coronation Cup at Epsom with Australian ace 'Scobie' Breasley in the saddle. Two weeks Later Lester Piggott listened inattentively to Vincent's detailed instructions before piloting Gladness to an historic Irish-trained Ascot Gold Cup triumph. The following month Scobie and Ballymoss enjoyed an even easier win at Sandown Park in the Eclipse Stakes. They continued their imperious progress in the King George VI & Queen Elizabeth Stakes at Ascot just seven days later.

CLONMEL, October 16, 1958 – John Burns returns on Fenian, winning favourite of the Lee Maiden Plate for owner-trainer John Tonson-Rye.

On July 31st Gladness and Piggott took over centre stage when beating three opponents in the Goodwood Cup. Three weeks later they carried off the Ebor Handicap – the richest race of its kind in

Europe – in such fashion that bookmaker William Hill declared it the finest handicap performance he had ever witnessed. As a sometime Black & Tan, Hill regretted aloud that he had not taken the opportunity to have the winning trainer shot.

Gladness had finished her seasonal campaign before TP was fit to resume riding. But Ballymoss had not. He was aimed for the Prix de l'Arc de Triomphe, in a bid to become the first Irish-trained winner of the European all-aged championship. TP had been his partner when Ballymoss had made history twelve months previously in the St Leger, but not this time. He had made his comeback on one of Vincent's at the Curragh on August 30th. However, there was never really any question of Scobie Breasley being taken off, unbeaten as he was on Ballymoss in three of Britain's most prestigious races.

Once again Ballymoss had to overcome rain-softened going to become Ireland's first 'Arc' winner when galloping on strongly to prove himself a true champion of Europe. As such Ballymoss and Breasley went off hot favourite for the Washington D. C. International at Maryland on Veterans' Day (November 11th). Starting stalls were discarded in deference to the visiting runners. Instead, a walk-in start resulted in six recalls. After a very rough race the home-trained Tudor Era ran out a comfortable winner, with Ballymoss a head behind Sailor's Guide in third. Following an objection by Howard Grant, rider of the Australian runner-up, the stewards reversed the first two placings.

Far removed from all that globe-trotting, TP had got back in winning vein after five months when successful at Naas on El Toro for Vincent and Cork owner Tim Hallinan. Clearly Vincent's confidence in his jockey remained undiminished by his accident and prolonged absence. As TP recalled, "They went for a right touch at 6/1."

A further handful of domestic winners brought TP's 1958 total to 19, supplemented by the Mince Pie Selling Hurdle at Liverpool in December for trainer Willie O'Grady on Tansy, promptly sold for 300 guineas. A new name appeared at the top of the Irish jockeys' table – G. W. 'Willie' Robinson. Like TP, Willie headed neither the flat division (Liam Ward) nor the jumpers (Bobby Beasley). TP's eclipse was easy to understand, whereas Vincent's plunge down the Irish trainers' standings – from second to fourteenth – was hard to reconcile with his overseas triumphs.

The year was at its close when Vincent brought TP into his office in Ballydoyle.

"What about next year, Tommy? How about a retainer?"

"No thanks, Vincent. After that bad fall I'm not going to push myself. There'll be plenty of rides going round. Let it swing."

Chapter Twenty Five

Courts Appeal had become TP's final winner in 1958 when successful in a Leopardstown maiden hurdle over Christmas. He would not appear again before the Cheltenham Festival and that Gloucestershire Hurdle ten weeks hence. York Fair, likewise owned by John McShain, joined that 'Gloucester' shortlist when successful in his maiden hurdle at Naas in January. When Prudent King and TP ran the odds-on Fare Time to less than a length at Sandown in February he joined the raiding party, bound for the Champion Hurdle.

CHELTENHAM, March 4, 1959 – York Fair (TP) clear over the last in Division I of the Gloucestershire Hurdle to give Vincent O'Brien his 10th and final victory in the race. TP shared in 7 of those in just five seasons.

It was Fare Time that found the greater improvement, running on much too strongly up the hill to beat Ivy Green and Prudent King in the 1959 Champion Hurdle. Happily, York Fair and TP encountered no such opposition when cruising home a comfortable winner of the first division of the 'Gloucester'. Courts Appeal duly went off hot favourite to complete the double in the second division. Having pulled too hard for his own good, Courts Appeal – "gutless bastard, wouldn't battle" - found nothing up that punishing hill, beaten six lengths by Clem Magnier's indestructible Albergo. With ten divisions of the Gloucestershire Hurdle and twenty-two Cheltenham Festival winners to his credit, Vincent O'Brien bade farewell to the crucible he had so often made his own.

Despite his incredible Cheltenham record, Vincent left Prestbury Park in 1959 a frustrated man. He had nursed Saffron Tartan back from illness to such effect that he had arrived in Cheltenham hot favourite for the Gold Cup, successful in his last three chases. He was heard to cough on the morning of the Gold Cup, leaving Vincent with no choice but to withdraw him. TP could recall the drama. "It was common knowledge in the racecourse stables that 'Saffron' was coughing his guts out. But who was going to break the bad news to Vincent? Luckily, he heard the horse himself when he coughed at exercise that morning. Nobody was more relieved than 'Toss' Taaffe. You don't want to be on a sick horse that's hot favourite for a Gold Cup."

While Vincent's withdrawal from the jumping game was well and truly signposted, his riding arrangements on the flat for the 1959 season came as a surprise to many. Garnet Bougoure, an Australian then riding in Singapore, had been retained as first jockey to the Ballydoyle stable. Subsequently it would transpire that Vincent had made overtures to Scobie Breasley in response to owners' pressure to appoint an 'international' stable jockey, befitting Ballydoyle's dramatically enhanced profile.

Scobie had been too long at the top of the tree in England, with established retainers firmly in place, to contemplate moving to Ireland. He had recommended 'Garnie' Bougoure, who had consulted an atlas and then Jim Marsh, Irish-born veterinary officer to the Singapore Jockey Club, before accepting the post. Simultaneously, fashionable English apprentice Wally Swinburn signed up as first jockey to Paddy Prendergast's powerful Rossmore Lodge stable. Another door had closed.

"Yes, the news leaked out through the lads in Ballydoyle. I said nothing, just kept on going down to ride work when I'd be asked. My old man was very good with advice in those matters. 'Just keep doing what you're doing. These things have a way of working out. You'll see.' I used wonder sometimes why he so seldom heeded his own counsel. Anyway, I stayed on the party list in Ballydoyle!"

Far from feeling sorry for himself, TP revived earlier connections, among them Charlie Weld, for whom he promptly won on Farney Fox. Garnie Bougoure opened his Irish account at the initial Curragh meeting, scoring a quick double on Ross Sea and El Toro, both in the colours of C. Mahlon Kline, a new American patron of the Ballydoyle stable. As founder of what later became GlaxoSmithKline, this wealthy bachelor with a dry sense of humour fitted Vincent's

'desirable owner' profile. Both colts were intended runners in the Irish 2000 Guineas, in which it was generally assumed that TP would ride whichever Bougoure discarded. When the stable jockey was nominated to partner Ross Sea the market followed suit, making Bougoure's mount second favourite, with El Toro an easy-to-back 100/9.

CURRAGH, May 13, 1959 – El Toro (TP) repelling a strong overseas challenge to give Vincent O'Brien the first of his five Irish 2000 Guineas victories. English raider Red Ross (Charlie Smirke) finished second, with French colt Vallauris (George Moore) third.

In TP's recollection, El Toro was always going to be his ride in the Guineas. "The lads in the yard never stopped assuring me. 'You ride the little chestnut. He's yours.' And so I did."

Biding his time as his father had so often demonstrated with such success over the stiff Curragh mile, TP let others make play before sending El Toro about his business in the final furlong for an impressive success. Ross Sea finished fifth. It was just the headline winner TP needed to retrieve any lost momentum. Dick McCormick put him up on Gigi to win the Phoenix Park 'Fifteen Hundred' for Laurie Gardner. TP's association with Dick McCormick harked back to his earliest days in Blewbury with Steve Donoghue, who had paid this tribute to his righthand man. "As soon as I decided to take out a trainer's licence I asked Dick to come and help me, as I consider he knows more about feeding horses than any man in the country."

By the time TP completed his score at the Leopardstown Christmas meeting on Paddy Sleator's Sangre Grande, he had 48 Irish winners on the board, one less than Garnie Bougoure and only four behind Liam Ward, outright champion for the first time.

News that Wally Swinburn would not be returning to ride for Paddy Prendergast in 1960 was tempered by the disclosure that Paddy had secured his own Australian contract rider – Ron Hutchinson. The bobbing lightweight came recommended by Jackie Thompson, Paddy's original Aussie, all of ten years previously. If that were not enough, Seamus McGrath then revealed that he had secured the services of yet another Aussie – Bill Williamson. With the

PHOENIX PARK, August 8, 1959 – Gigi (TP) (far side) beating Nice Guy (Wally Swinburn) and Arodstown Boy (Liam Ward) to land the coveted Phoenix '1500'.

three leading flat stables in Ireland all employing Australians, opportunities at the higher levels were becoming severely limited. And should this vogue for Australian stable jockeys become widespread. . .

Bill Williamson's engagement to ride for Glencairn raised another issue. TP had never ridden for the McGraths. Could there be any particular reason why one of the most widely respected jockeys on the Irish scene had never been handed the 'Green, red seams and cap'?

"I can tell you exactly. It was all over one race, at the Curragh, the first meeting of the year [1951]. Eamon Delany had a sharpish two-year-old, Black Eagle. I'd ridden him a few pieces of work on the beach up at Laytown and he could go. We'd give him a run. See what he'd do. He had a nice introduction at Naas. Learned from it. In those days 'Daddy' [Joe] McGrath was betting big. When he bet, he expected to win. The McGraths ran Stella Aurata in that Curragh race, first time out. Bobby Quinlan rode him. They backed him from 6/1 to 'no offer'.

"Stella Aurata went on to be one of the best of his year. But that day he came up the straight like a snipe. Leery bastard. Still beat me a length. As I was walking back to weigh in, Dan Bulger, the stipendiary steward, rushed up to me. 'Burns. You'll object!' Not knowing what to think, I did as I was told."

The sky fell in.

The *Irish Racing Calendar* duly recorded the drama following the Boyne Plate (Division II). "Stella Aurata won by a length from Black Eagle, 5 lengths away Lion's Claw was third, Trafalgar was placed fourth.

"The Stewards enquired into the objection lodged by T. P. Burns (rider of Black Eagle) against Stella Aurata being declared the winner of the race on the grounds of crossing twice and lying on him in the last two furlongs. Having heard the evidence of T. P. Burns, R. Quinlan (rider of Stella Aurata) and John Power (who rode in the race), also of Mr F. F. Tuthill (Judge), the Stewards sustained the objection, disqualified Stella Aurata and awarded the race to Black Eagle. Lion's Claw was placed second and Trafalgar third."

"Oh, I got the race all right. Once I lodged my objection the stewards had no hesitation in throwing out the winner. But 'Daddy' McGrath never forgave me. Black Eagle was maybe the most expensive winner I ever rode."

John Burns, TP's brother, *aide de camp*, chauffeur and constant companion for many years, put that episode into perspective, at least in his belief. John contended that in those days before patrol cameras, stewards and officials concentrated almost exclusively on non-triers. Interference in running, unless it amounted to foul riding, was left to aggrieved jockeys to avenge in their own fashion. On that basis, had TP not objected to the winner on grounds of

Major Laurie Gardner leading Gigi in. Winning trainer Dick McCormick (right) had been Steve Donoghue's head man in Blewbury when TP became apprenticed to Steve 20 years before.

interference costing him the race, no official action would have been thought necessary. However, once that fateful objection was lodged, the Curragh stewards simply had no option other than to disqualify the winner.

A stewards' apologist might have attempted to explain the unthinkable. Joe McGrath was not a man to be crossed. Whoever coined the phrase, "The English never remember, the Irish never forget," could well have had Joseph McGrath in mind. His wealth as co-founder of the Irish Hospitals' Sweepstakes had enabled him to invest in racing and breeding on a scale never previously known in Ireland. In an earlier life his roles in the war of independence and the subsequent civil war had earned him a fearsome reputation. His very size and stature exuded menace. A scapegoat was essential. "What else could the chaps do? Of course it was most unfortunate. Burns really should have considered his position before putting a gun to the stewards' heads, so to speak. Such a sensible bloke, normally. Never been known to have a bet, unlike his old man. So it wasn't about money. Quite, quite extraordinary."

Half a century later the magnitude of TP's hasty objection and the havoc that it wrought is difficult to comprehend. In a country still riven by civil war allegiances, on top of pre-1916 social structures, racing was still run by the Anglo-Irish ascendancy, or its remnants. Although impoverished by changed circumstances, the 'Old Guard' continued to run Irish racing as they had done since time immemorial. The country might not have been theirs any longer to do with as they pleased. *Droit de seigneur* might have been consigned to the past. But on the racecourse their writ still ran. The same men who administered Irish racing had lived through a sea change, encapsulated in one seismic shift of popular opinion.

In the early months of World War I Irishmen who had not joined the stampede to enlist could expect to be given the white feather – symbol of cowardice. By the time the survivors returned, four years later, having done their bit for the 'freedom of small nations', they found themselves ostracised by the same society that had driven them to enlist in the beginning. From patriots they had become traitors to a subsequent struggle and its resultant martyrdom. True, there had been notable and heroic casualties closer to home. One who had survived and thrived through the tumultuous evolution of the Irish Free State was one Joe McGrath. Within weeks the English press would have to grapple with the appalling actuality of Joe McGrath – 'IRA gunman' – winning the Derby with his home-bred Arctic Prince. Fortunately, Arctic Prince was trained and ridden by Englishmen.

At this distance of time it would be intriguing to identify the hapless stewards on duty at that Curragh meeting, Wednesday, April 18th, 1951. While such detail was edited out of the annual volumes of the *Irish Racing Calendar*, it did appear in the weekly sheet editions. Curiously, recourse to the weekly issues revealed that those details were religiously included for every meeting in Ireland, except the Curragh.

Chapter Twenty Six

Hobdayed since that Cheltenham fiasco, Saffron Tartan had also changed stables, symbolic termination of Vincent O'Brien's fabled jumping career. 'Saffron' had been sent to Epsom trainer Don Butchers. A leading jump jockey in England between the wars, Don Butchers had achieved a rare double on a fleeting visit to Ireland in 1938, winning the Galway Plate on Symaethis and the Galway Hurdle on Serpolette. Since beginning to train in 1946, Don Butchers had gained a reputation as a master at bringing horses back after injury or ailment. His chosen path with Saffron Tartan was over hurdles. Hence TP renewed an old partnership to ride 'Saffron' to victory in the Champion Hurdle Trial at Birmingham in February 1960. The duo started almost favourite for the Champion Hurdle. But age and infirmity had dimmed Saffron Tartan's once devastating turn of foot. They finished a good third to Another Flash and Albergo. In any case, to TP, Cheltenham without Vincent and his army of punters was akin to Hamlet without the Prince.

Back home TP continued to ride work in Ballydoyle, picking up winners where and when he could. One of those came his way in bizarre circumstances. Vincent ran three in the Ballysax Maiden Plate at the Curragh on April 20th. Chamour, odds-on under Garnie Bougoure, duly obliged, with TP second on Timobriol. Back then four winners each day were post-race sampled for sweat and saliva. Chamour was among those sampled that day.

Friday, May 13th 1960 became 'Black Friday' for many of the racing fraternity. First came news of Prince Aly Khan's death in a Paris car smash. Then the second bombshell. "The stewards of the Turf Club met at the Registry Office, 25 Merrion Square, Dublin on Friday, May 13th to hear Mr M. V. O'Brien's explanation of the presence of a drug or stimulant in the samples of saliva and sweat taken from Chamour, trained by him, after the colt had won the Ballysax Maiden Plate at the Curragh on April 20th.

"The Stewards of the Turf Club, having heard the evidence of Mr F. Clarke, M.R.C.V.S., Mr T. J. Hurley, M.R.C.V.S., Lt-General P. A. Mulcahy, Mr A. O'Connor, Mrs L. M. Mundy, F.R.I.C., F.P.S., Professor Baxter, M.R.C.V.S., M.I. Biol, Mr M. V. O'Brien, Mr D. O'Brien,

G. Bougoure, D. Egan, C. Stack, M. Connolly, E. O'Sullivan, C. Maher, R. Delahunty, Mr J. S. M. Cosgrove, M.R.C.V.S., Mr R. P. C. Griffin, M.R.C.V.S., Mr W. Freeman, M.R.C.V.S., Mr P. Connolly, Mr P. Farrell and Sgt. Johnson, were satisfied that a drug or stimulant had been administered to Chamour for the purpose of affecting his speed and/or stamina in the race. The Stewards of the Turf Club accordingly withdrew Mr O'Brien's licence to train under Rule 102(v) Rules of Racing and declared him a disqualified person under that Rule and uner Rule 178, from May 13th, 1960 until November 30th, 1961. They also disqualified Chamour from the Ballysax Maiden Plate, Curragh and ordered the Stakes to be forfeited under Rule 178 and ordered that Timobriol be placed first and Cassieme second (on disqualification of Dillycar): no third placed.

"At the conclusion of the case, when Mr O'Brien had been informed of the decision of the Stewards, he was warned by them that none of the horses under his care could fulfil their engagements unless and until they had been transferred to another licensed trainer or trainers.

"Mr O'Brien was further informed that such transfers should be notified to the Registry Office in the normal way and that the Stewards, when satisfied that the transfers had actually taken place, would immediately issue instructions to the Keeper of the Match Book to allow such horse or horses to fulfil their engagements."

The following week's *Irish Racing Calendar* revealed an amendment to that draconian sentence. A. S. 'Phonsie' O'Brien had been granted permission to deputise in his brother's enforced banishment from Ballydoyle, taking charge of the 68 inmates. TP continued to ride work, though the promoted Timobriol was to be his only winner from Ballydoyle in a tumultuous season that saw Chamour win the Irish Derby, triggering riotous demonstrations, and 'Phonsie' crowned champion trainer.

TP kept picking up winners, among them the rapidly improving Farney Fox. He remained a bit player once again when the unwelcome spotlight of officialdom swung on to a Lumville representative, involving another 'cast of thousands'.

"The Stewards of the Irish National Hunt Steeplechase Committee and the Stewards of the Turf Club (Hon W. E. Wylie, Q.C. acting for Mr Jos. McGrath and Lieut-General P. A. Mulcahy acting for Major Victor McCalmont) met at the Registry Office, 25 Merrion Square, Dublin, on July 22nd to enquire into the running and riding of Rising Spring in the Marino Handicap Hurdle at Baldoyle Meeting on July 13th, which matter had been referred to them by the Stewards of Baldoyle.

"They heard the evidence of Mr D. D. Bulger and Mr T. J. Hurley (Stewards' Secretaries), Capt L. M. Magee (Handicapper), Mr T. Burns (trainer of Rising Spring), J. Devine (rider of the horse), Mr P. J. Prendergast (part owner of the horse), R. Hutchinson and P. Taaffe and

BIRMINGHAM, September 26, 1960 – Joe Malone leading Farney Fox (TP) out as favourite to win the valuable Triumph Herald Handicap, despite conceding up to 32lb to his 21 rivals. His last-to-first victory earned Farney Fox an invitation to represent Ireland in the Washington D.C. International.

also saw the Patrol camera Film of the race. Mr R. Kelly and Mr P. Dunne Cullinan (Stewards of Baldoyle) were also present.

"The Stewards of the Irish National Hunt Steeplechase Committee and the Stewards of the Turf Club are of the opinion that the inquiry by the Baldoyle Stewards was fully justified.

"They are not satisfied that the horse was deliberately stopped and consequently take no further action save to warn Mr Burns and J. Devine that they should be particularly careful in the running and riding of the horse in future."

Lucky on that occasion to escape with his licence, Jimmy Devine had come to Lumville as an apprentice on the recommendation of Mona O'Connor, Mrs Stella Burns' sister. Long accustomed to keeping one under wraps in public, Jimmy was also entrusted with 'bringing home the bacon' when required. Jimmy's biggest win was gained in the inaugural Martin Mahony Champion Novice Hurdle at Punchestown in 1961, on Danny St John Gough's rank outsider Glenity. Having spent his riding career in Lumville, Jimmy became a valet's assistant on hanging up his boots. He had only just retired to his native county, to mind an ailing brother, when he died.

TP's 31 Irish winners in 1960 included Tula Ban for Colonel Blake and Gloir Anna for John Oxx in his role as presidential jockey. However, John Oxx had been quick to recognise the expertise of Bill Williamson, putting him up on Lynchris to win the Irish Oaks and St Leger. Indeed, had Liam Ward not managed to get Anne Biddle's Zenobia home by a short head in the Irish 1000 Guineas, the three resident Aussies would have completed a clean sweep of the Irish classics.

Happily for TP, Charlie Weld was prepared to look further afield for decent prizes. They combined to land the Triumph Herald Handicap with Mrs M. E. Donnelly's Farney Fox at Birmingham at the end of September. Handicap or not, it was worth more than any race run in Ireland in 1960, other than the Irish Derby. Thus did Farney Fox progress from the Grattan Cup at Navan in March 1959 to become Ireland's representative in the Washington D. C. International at Laurel Park, Maryland eighteen months later. In going over to ride Farney Fox in the Washington International, TP emulated his father, who had made the same journey to ride Chamier, unplaced in the race for Vincent O'Brien back in 1953. He carried TP into sixth place behind Bald Eagle, winner for the second time. "Farney was a real good stayer and they were always going too fast for him at a mile and a half round Laurel. No disgrace."

Farney Fox was by Archive, a beautifully bred but undistinguished racehorse. His stock had begun to demonstrate that Archive was successfully transmitting more of his genes than his own racecourse ability. Moreover, his stock had begun to attract good prices in the sale ring. That was one aspect of lot 148 in the catalogue for Goffs Horse Show Week sale in Ballsbridge on August 4th 1960 that appealed to the 'Scotchman' and his family. Far closer to their hearts was the fact that the three-year-old gelding by Archive was out of Bright Cherry. Moreover, Bright Cherry's association had been exclusively with TP, who had won on her over hurdles and fences. The deeper attraction in Lumville lay in the fact that Bright Cherry was a half-sister to their great favourite and Punchestown hero, Lucca Prince.

The association impelled the 'Scotchman' and TP to make the journey to Malahow to inspect the three-year-old, with a view to buying him on the spot, should the Baker family be disposed to sell before auction. Their mission proved fruitless. The Bakers were determined that their horse should go through the ring. Mr Burns would have

Trainer Charlie Weld (left), 'Staff' Ingham and a thoughtful TP (right) at the post-race reception

LAUREL PARK, MARYLAND, November 11, 1960 – jockeys for the Washington D.C. International: TP (top right), Scobie Breasley (bottom left) and Manuel Ycaza (bottom right).

every opportunity to bid for him in Ballsbridge, should he wish. The Bakers did not see the need to reveal that the gelding would be put on the market at just 500 guineas, for they had already decided that he was going to Ballsbridge to be sold. They had no intention of taking him home to feed over another winter.

The Bakers' decision proved correct, for the three-year-old realised 1,150 guineas, the highest bid so far that day. Alison Baker was ecstatic. They had never obtained such a price for any horse they had put on the market. When the identity of the successful bidder became known the press photographers swarmed round to the gelding's stable. Any purchase by the Duchess of Westminster was newsworthy. This one she called Arkle.

The *Directory of the Turf* listed TP's retainers for 1961: H.E The President of Ireland, K. Bell, T. Burns, D. Rogers, C. Weld and R. McCormick. Unless something very special swam to the surface, it was a case of little fish tasting sweetest. One of the least fashionable of TP's workhorses of that era was Fawcett's Bridge. Foaled in 1950, 'Ted' Browne's old stager won his first flat race in 1957, and then got better with age. He proved the point by winning handicaps at Ballinrobe and Mullingar with TP aboard, now aged eleven. Moreover, his advanced years invariably ensured that 'Ted' Browne got a decent price about his old warrior. TP's ability to empathise with old warhorses seemed to coax the best out of not just Fawcett's Bridge, but a whole succession of evergreens throughout his lengthy career.

However about provincial success, which included the sponsored Carroll Hurdle at Dundalk on Coniston for Charlie Weld, TP had yet to visit the winner's enclosure on the Curragh that season when lining up for the Irish St Leger on Vimadee, trained in Lumville for Tommy McCairns. Out of that great servant Upadee, Vimadee was by the Irish National Stud horse, Vimy, French-trained winner of the 1955 King George VI & Queen Elizabeth Stakes. "The Old Man went for those Vimys. Not just Vimys either, he always liked to patronise the National Stud stallions. Those Vimys were all hot, sweaty bastards. If you tried to rush them, you'd lose them completely."

CURRAGH, September 13, 1961 – Vimadee (TP) winning the Irish St Leger from Irish Derby winner Your Highness (Paddy Powell) and Silver Moon (Garnie Bougoure), Mister Moss (Bill Williamson), Erskine (Willie Robinson) and Baynard (Ron Hutchinson).

Owner 'Gertie' McCairns leading in Vimadee, flanked by Lumville jump jockey Jimmy Devine and assistant trainer John Burns. Winning trainer 'Scotchman' Burns had ridden the first of his record 6 Irish St Leger winners as long ago as 1916.

While he could be peremptory in his manner with people, the 'Scotchman' would exercise endless patience with the horses in his care. Ridden by Jimmy Devine, Vimadee had a quiet introduction at the Curragh in October 1960. A promising fourth at Leopardstown in November completed Vimadee's juvenile programme. On his reappearance Vimadee was noted running on steadily under Lumville apprentice Vivian Kennedy to finish third at the Curragh in April.

It was a dramatically different Vimadee that opened his autumn campaign, dividing Baynard and Royal Avenue in the Desmond Stakes. Two weeks later, again on his local course, Vimadee ran Silver Moon to less than a length in the Blandford Stakes. Now regarded as the best three-year-old maiden in Ireland, Vimadee faced formidable opposition in the Irish St Leger, notably Your Highness, winner of the Irish Derby, Silver Moon and Baynard.

Vimadee's starting price would have been considerably shorter than the 100/9 available, but for two factors. He was rumoured to have coughed on the morning of the race. Those closest to Vimadee knew that the colt coughed a couple of times every day or so, for no apparent reason. That was no cause for concern. More pressing was the matter of what to tell Tommy McCairns' wife Gertie, officially Vimadee's owner. The 'Scotchman' knew from experience that to alert Gertie to a horse's chances was tantamount to broadcasting the same information on Radio Eireann. Tommy persuaded himself that the excitement of leading in a classic winner would outweigh any suspicions Gertie might harbour that she had been 'put away' on this occasion.

Despite what an Irish St Leger would mean to the 'Scotchman' and all his family – had his sister Stella not been the making of Upadee? – TP refused to enthuse. "Yes, he was a good horse that day. But a cowardly bastard. It wasn't till we were coming off the hill into the straight that I began to believe he'd go through with it. He did. Thanks be to God!"

Whatever TP's private views, he shared his family's jubilation. The 'Scotchman' had ridden no fewer than six winners of the Irish St Leger between 1916 and 1948. Now, from a small family-run stable in which all three of his children played an important role, he had put his name on the final classic as a trainer.

Tony Sweeney, editor of *Irish Racingform*, was in no doubt as to Vimadee's place in the classic order of merit. "The Irish National Stud stallion Vimy, who was bought as a replacement for Tulyar, has been slow to make his mark. . . However, his fortunes appear to be on the rise and last month saw him achieve his first Classic success in the Irish St Leger through the medium of Vimadee. . . clearly the best of his age trained in Ireland this season."

At the end of 1961 Liam Ward had regained his riders' crown from Garnie Bougoure with 44 winners. TP's 37 left him in fifth place. That Irish St Leger constituted another tick in the box *vis-à-vis* his father's achievements: Irish champion jockey, Irish Derby, Irish St Leger, Galway Hurdle, Gloucestershire Hurdle. And there was that St Leger on Ballymoss, exactly forty years after his father had finished second in a wartime St Leger on Kingston Black. One up for TP.

Chapter Twenty Seven

The Irish racing world was consumed with the prospect of the inaugural Irish Sweeps Derby, the richest race in Europe. It promised to lift Irish racing from its provincial, backwoods level to a wider, more significant international status. This sense of anticipation was reflected in riding arrangements for the 1962 flat season. Ron Hutchinson and Bill Williamson moved over to ride for major English stables. There they faced an established coterie of fellow countrymen headed by the ageless Scobie Breasley, along with Eddie Cracknell, Val Faggoter and Russ Maddock. Garnie Bougoure moved from Ballydoyle to Paddy Prendergast at Rossmore Lodge, replaced by another Aussie in Pat Glennon. Stuart Murless trumped his rivals when signing Indian champion Pandu Khade. Herbie Holmes, longtime stable jockey to 'Brud' Fetherstonhaugh, had retired after winning the last 'old-style' Irish Derby, succeeded by former English champion apprentice Peter Boothman. Of the Irish flat jockeys, only Liam Ward could look forward to any regular supply of winners, retained as he was by glamorous Anne Biddle, for whom Tommy Shaw was private trainer.

Paddy Sleator's threat to campaign his horses in England, in protest at bumper winners no longer being eligible for handicapping on the flat on their bumper form, was another blow to TP's prospects of regaining his championship crown. Paddy had been a steady source of winners for TP since Domaghmore had done the business at Leopardstown back in 1951. Although generally regarded as a jumping trainer, Paddy had not turned out more winners than any of his rivals between 1955 and 1961 without collecting more than his share on the flat.

Getting on with it in his usual unflappable fashion, TP opened his annual account on Farney Fox over hurdles at Leopardstown. Good old Fawcett's Bridge, officially twelve years of age, then turned back the clock with a repeat success in the Cong Handicap at Ballinrobe. Paddy Norris, who provided the first leg of TP's double that day, was to prove a staunch ally. TP and Paddy went back a long way, to the early days in Ballydoyle, when Paddy was travelling head lad. Having ridden with fair success over jumps, Paddy began training in the Phoenix Park before moving to the Curragh. For three consecutive seasons Paddy would saddle more winners than any of his rivals. Despite Paddy's proven versatility, TP esteemed him for his ability with sprinters. "Paddy learned his trade in the Phoenix Park, where they specialised in sprinters. If you had ever ridden work in the 'fifteen acres' you'd understand what I'm telling you."

While the Aussies seemed to have gained a stranglehold on Ireland's feature races, Irish jockeys were well fit to ride classic winners, only given the chance. TP's chances of winning an Irish Guineas in 1962 looked slim indeed. Le Pirate might have run into fifth in the colts' classic behind Arctic Storm and Bill Williamson, but Shandon Belle would not get the stiff Curragh mile in a horsebox. By the sprinting sire, Hook Money, Brud Fetherstonhaugh's second string had run over five furlongs, which seemed to be her *métier*, only four days previously. Unsurprisingly, she was friendless in the market at 20/1, whereas Abermaid, winner of the One Thousand Guineas at Newmarket, was hot favourite to make it an Irish Guineas double for Bill Williamson. Twilight Time, the young Aga Khan's French raider, was next in demand.

After True Course had made it for five furlongs, Pat Glennon hit the front on Lovely Gale, stalked by Bill Williamson on Abermaid. The Aussies had it between them, until TP pounced close home to win by a length from Lovely Gale, with the favourite a neck adrift in third. Criticised for being caught close home by the 'Scotchman' in this event almost a decade previously, TP had just executed a waiting ride that his father could scarcely have bettered. "We knew she didn't get a mile, so I just waited and waited. And then waited some more. She had a terrific turn of foot. It was up to me to use that speed effectively."

Lucky owner S. B. Abbott, who had given just 1,800 guineas for Shandon Belle as a yearling at Ballsbridge, was now £3,360 richer, having taken the most valuable running of the Irish 1000 Guineas since its inception in 1922. Although she failed to win subsequently, Shandon

CURRAGH, May 16, 1962 – Shandon Belle (TP) swooping late to take the Irish 1000 Guineas from Lovely Gale (Pat Glennon) and Abermaid (Bill Williamson). Winning trainer 'Brud' Fetherstonhaugh and TP, lifelong friends, had been classmates at Newbridge College.

Belle further enriched Mr Abbott when purchased privately for the paddocks by whisky heir Johnny Macdonald-Buchanan.

By contrast, trainer and jockey went back a lot further, to their school days in Newbridge College and even prior to that, for their families had been friends and neighbours ever since Brud's late father, Bob Fetherstonhaugh, had moved from Westmeath to the Curragh in 1924. Earlier still, in 1920, the 'Scotchman' had ridden Irish Present a winner for Bob at the Phoenix Park. James, TP's brother, had been apprenticed to old Bob prior to enlisting at the outbreak of World War II. As Shandon Belle was to prove Brud's solitary classic winner, it was appropriate that TP should have been the winning jockey. Peter Hughes, who looked after the filly, would never forget his present from the winning jockey. Instead of the expected cash Peter was proffered a parcel of clothing, worn but still serviceable.

Back in the limelight, TP picked up a somewhat unlikely retainer, for wealthy American E. E. Dale Schaffer, a newcomer to racing on either side of the Atlantic. During a brief vacation in Ireland, Dale Schaffer had commissioned journalist Sean Murphy to find him some readymade winners, a trainer and a 'contract rider'. Despite declining the invitation to locate those readymade winners, TP agreed to accept £500 a year to ride the Schaffer horses that were sent to Michael Dawson in Rathbride Manor, where Michael had assumed control following the sudden death of his brother Joe, shortly after TP had won the 1941 Irish Cambridgeshire for him on Mill Boy. "That five hundred might sound like good money for the time, but I did have to ride work whenever required. It wasn't just a matter of turning up to ride them in their races. And time is money!"

Never one to wear his heart on his sleeve, TP did have one lifelong friend and confidante always happy to lend an ear to his grumbles. John O'Neill and TP had grown up together, reared on the intrigue between their respective fathers. Bill O'Neill had combined his official duties as stationmaster in Newbridge with a less public role as commission agent for the 'Scotchman'. Just as their seniors had shared confidences, so did John and TP down the years. So much so that in time John appeared the more accurate judge of TP's winning chances as each Saturday's racing approached. No man is an island.

That season continued well for TP, his total of 39 winners placing him third in the table to Pat Glennon and Liam Ward. One of TP's more unusual winners was Ben Stack, successful on the flat at Baldoyle for Tom Dreaper and Anne, Duchess of Westminster. Infinitely better known for his exploits over fences, Ben Stack would later fulfil his 'John the Evangelist' role to perfection when humbling Fulke Walwyn's much-vaunted and odds-on Irish Imp in the 1964 Two-Mile Champion Chase, just forty-eight hours before Arkle clashed with Walwyn's other invincible champion, Mill House, in that unforgettable Cheltenham Gold Cup.

Mickey Rogers weighed in with some decent winners in Sir Victor Sassoon's colours, while Stuart Murless filled one of the few remaining blanks in TP's Curragh dossier when Sicilian Prince won the Desmond Stakes. Vimadee got his head in front in the Leinster Handicap, his first success since taking the final Irish classic twelve months previously.

TP signed off over hurdles on a winning note when riding Hopeful Hero to victory at Limerick's old Greenpark course in March 1963 for trainer Larry Keating. Jimmy Devine took over on the Lumville hurdlers, as did Tony Redmond on Paddy Norris's timber-toppers.

Vimadee won his annual race, this time at the Irish Sweeps Derby meeting. He was subsequently sent over to Manton trainer George Todd, a master at rejuvenating aged flat horses, notably Trelawny. Vimadee eventually added to his Irish laurels when winning at Newbury as a seven-year-old.

By far and away TP's most publicised riding engagement in 1963 was Arkle, in a fourteen-furlong flat race at Navan. Tom Dreaper often brought his good chasers back in a flat race after their summer break and Arkle was no exception. Well, that was not quite true. Arkle was already an Irish icon. "I had to go to Dreapers' to sit on him, beforehand, just because he was so special. Why did they choose me for the job? Well, I ridden the dam a few winners. Maybe more to the point, the Duchess always had a soft spot for me. Once Tom told her I was riding Arkle, that was fine by her."

It's all safely enshrined in the Arkle legend that he started odds-on for the Donoughmore Maiden Plate at Navan, on October 9th, 1963 and duly obliged by five lengths. While it may have looked all plain sailing from the grandstand, it was far from so for the man in the hot seat. "Going down the back towards the final turn we weren't travelling at all. He wasn't on the bridle and I could see the leaders beginning to get away from me. I kept telling myself not to panic. Even across the top we were still going nowhere. As we turned for home I had to get after him. Nothing happened for a few strides. Then Arkle clicked into gear. He had the lot of them beat in the next hundred yards. Thinking back on it, I believe the horse missed seeing a fence in front of him, something to get him fired up. If you remember, he always took a hold with Pat and I think it was the fences and the exhilaration of jumping at speed that turned Arkle on.

"The Duchess was delighted with Arkle's performance that day. She asked me what I thought of her horse. I told her he was a lovely horse. And every time we'd meet after that she would always remind me of how right I was in my opinion. Ah, well.

NAVAN, October 9, 1963 – Arkle (TP) winning the Donoughmore Maiden Plate as an odds-on favourite should, five lengths clear of Descador (Johnnie Roe) and Pearl Lady (Tommy Kinane).

"Actually, Arkle was supposed to go on for the Irish Cesarewitch, which would have been very interesting. But something happened and he didn't make it to the Curragh. For me he was a super staying horse, but Knock Hard would always have done him for sheer speed."

Dermot O'Brien agreed with TP's assessment of the two horses. As Vincent's trusted aide told 'Buster' Harty, "Over the Gold Cup distance we could never have beaten Arkle. But if they'd met over two and a half miles, my money would have been on Knock Hard."

Perhaps it was his lengthy association with Ballydoyle that made TP selective with his information, in this instance on the reason for Arkle's non-participation in the Irish Cesarewitch. Nevertheless, when confronted, TP came clean. "Well, yes, now that you remind me. It was Pat Taaffe who rang me to say that Arkle wouldn't be going to the Curragh. He'd told Tom Dreaper that if Arkle got another run on the flat he'd become so fired up that he wouldn't be able to hold him in his chases. A pity, really. Because now we'll never know."

Yet another previously untold Arkle anecdote was accompanied by a shy smile, a little shrug and an involuntary wrist motion, indicative of rather different memories of the greatest chaser of all time. Far from struggling to restrain Arkle at Navan, TP had sat and suffered, wondering would his famous steed ever pick up the bit and do what all Ireland expected him to do – win. "All the other horses I rode for Tom took a tug, ran nearly too free. But they stayed on like buggery. Big and fresh they'd always be. He was an amazing trainer. Don't try to follow Tom. What worked for him doesn't work for other men."

To those who lived through the Arkle era, TP's pride in having ridden him a winner is all too easy to respect, understand, even envy. To younger generations that achievement is perhaps more difficult to comprehend. After all, was Arkle much more than a steering job that day, as it turned out? Well, in truth, he was just that. But this is to miss the point. Arkle was much more than the best steeplechaser of his time. He was even more than the greatest steeplechaser of all time. Arkle transcended any standards by which horses had ever been appraised. Universally admired and adored, Arkle acknowledged that adulation, playing to the gallery with his unique blend of hauteur and *joie de vivre* that moved many to wonder whether he was somehow more than flesh and blood. Arkle knew he was a star. His sense of theatre was manifest on entering a parade ring, halting until all heads should turn to hail his appearance. Hero-worshipped in his lifetime, Arkle had long become an icon when his career was halted by injury in December 1966. From all over the world 'Get Well' cards poured in, many addressed simply 'Arkle, Ireland'.

Perhaps TP's pride of association with this wonder horse is best illustrated by counterpoint. Mark Hely Hutchinson rode Arkle in his two bumpers, without winning. Mark has often been quoted on what he fears may be his epitaph: Here lies the only man to have ridden Arkle; and not won on him.

Chapter Twenty Eight

The vogue for Australian stable jockeys had become so widespread as to make them seem like fashion accessories. Pat Glennon had departed from Ballydoyle to ride for Etienne Pollet in France. While he had become Irish champion in the first of his only two seasons here, Pat Glennon had his critics, among them one TP. "Of all of those Australians that came here, he was the worst. Couldn't even keep hold of the reins."

Pat Glennon was succeeded in Ballydoyle by Jack Purtell, who earned TP's respect. "You couldn't meet a nicer or more modest man. Of course his best years were well behind him when he came to ride for Vincent, but he made up for any lack of strength with a great racing brain. He wasn't as wily as old Bill Williamson, who must have been some operator in his prime. Bill was well past his best when he came here, but he could still make fools of the rest of us!"

Kevin Bell, Michael Dawson and Paddy Norris provided TP with the majority of his thirty winners in 1964, though there were two notable exceptions. In June Vincent O'Brien put TP

PHOENIX PARK, April 17, 1965 – Prominer (TP) coming in after a scrambling victory in the Player's Navy Cut Trial Stakes. Prominer did not run again that season.

up on Bally Joy in the Powhatan Stakes at Limerick Junction, with Jack Purtell on the shorter-priced stable mate, Ballymartin. TP's booking was only appropriate, for John McShain had bred Bally Joy by mating Ballymoss with Gladness. To complete this happy tale, Bally Joy ran out a comfortable winner on his seasonal debut.

Bally Joy had gone off second favourite, quite unlike Prominer, a rare P. J. Prendergast booking for TP in the National Stakes at the Curragh in September. "You'll find Darkie ran three or four in the race. If they didn't win the

National Stakes, that was hardly a disgrace. But if they got turned over in an ordinary maiden. . . That was the way Darkie looked at things like that. Anyway, Prominer skated in. Won like a good horse."

Garnie Bougoure was in the saddle when Prominer kept his unbeaten record in the Royal Lodge Stakes at Ascot. However, TP regained the mount the following season when Prominer won the 1965 Players Navy Cut Trial Stakes at Leopardstown. Otherwise it was as before, with Kevin Bell, Michael Dawson and Paddy Norris providing the bulk of TP's twenty-nine winners, which included a treble at Laytown in August.

Was there perhaps one exceptional animal, trained just down the road in Stepaside, that TP might have expected to ride, the first dual Derby winner since Orby? After all, the Burns and Rogers families went back a long way. . . TP's mood turns sombre at the recollection. He had ridden a lot of work alongside Santa Claus. But that was as close as he had got to the

BLESSINGTON, February 10, 1966 – TP and Chris cut their wedding cake

tall, leggy, angular brown bombshell that obliged Ladbrokes to pay out a world record on a single bet when landing the 1964 Derby - £69,375 to Bernard Sunley. It seems like an old sore reopened, a bugbear disturbed. It wasn't so much a matter of who didn't ride Santa Claus, as who did. Professional pride was affronted. Diffident suggestion that Mickey Rogers wanted to keep all his options open concerning Epsom only deepens the gloom. Santa Claus remains a taboo topic in Landfall.

A discreet little notice in the Social & Personal column of *The Irish Times* in January 1966 startled not a few who read it. "A quiet wedding will take place on 10 February 1966 between T. P. Burns and Christine, eldest daughter of Mr and Mrs T. Phelan, Kiltegan." Thus did TP, with masterful understatement, inform the world at large that he was forsaking his 42-year-old bachelor status, to marry the nurse that he had met while visiting patients in the nearby Drogheda Memorial Hospital. As his brother John wryly observed, the 'Jockey Hospital' had long proved a source of wives for Curragh bachelor boys.

'Chris', together with sisters May, Anne, Kathleen and brother Tommy had enjoyed an idyllic upbringing in the fairytale surroundings of Humewood Castle, Kiltegan, where their father, Tommy Phelan, was estate steward. Built in 1867 by English architect William White for William Wentworth Fitzwilliam Hume Dick, Humewood was originally conceived as a comparatively modest hunting lodge, set in 450 acres with the Wicklow Mountains as its backdrop. The original budget of £15,000 overran to a total of £25,000, as the 'modest hunting lodge' grew into one of the last great houses to be built in Ireland, a Victorian gothic fantasia. White's unsuccessful lawsuit against the builder ruined the plaintiff, who spent his latter years trying to prove that Shakespeare was in fact Francis Bacon. During Tommy Phelan's tenure as estate steward Humewood belonged to Madame 'Mimi' Hume-Weygand, French-based daughter-in-law of controversial General Maxime Weygand.

TP and Chris were married in Baltinglass, John Burns acting as best man. Kathleen Phelan and Stella Burns were bridesmaids. Following a reception in Downshire House, Blessington, the newlyweds departed on honeymoon to Scotland – "the land of my forefathers". TP's uncles John and Billy extended traditional Scots hospitality, doubtless adamant that alcohol flowed in Ayr only to welcome visitors.

Charlie Weld joined the Aussie jock league in 1966 when importing Lawrie Johnston, to which Paddy Prendergast responded by bringing over dynamic Des Lake. Vincent O'Brien had made other plans, whereby Liam Ward became his first jockey in Ireland, with Lester Piggott riding the Ballydoyle runners overseas. As TP tells it, the situation had become comical, were it not for the loss of earnings for those trying to compete without the mandatory Aussie twang. "It got so that if a trainer rang an owner to say his horse was going to run on the flat, the first question would be, 'Which Australian have you booked?' And if no Australian could be got, they'd nearly say 'Don't run him so'."

In a career, which had come increasingly to mirror his father's, TP had ridden just one winner in 1966 when injury to Paddy Powell led trainer David Ainsworth to book him for Paveh in

CURRAGH, May 14, 1966 – Paveh (TP) holding Ultimate II (Paddy Sullivan) at bay to win the Irish 2000 Guineas, with Not So Cold (Joe Mercer) eight lengths back in third.

the Irish 2000 Guineas. If the market was any guide, that classic was a formality for Mickey Rogers' Democrat. Third in the National Stakes on his only racecourse appearance eight months previously, Democrat was already acclaimed the successor to Santa Claus, Rogers' champion of 1964. Ridden by Willie Burke, Democrat started odds-on, with Paveh, already a three-time winner, available at 9/1.

When Time Gail charged the tapes and broke them, the Irish 2000 Guineas was started by flag. Well away, TP kept Paveh in the forefront,

Crotanstown trainer David Ainsworth greets Paveh and TP, echoing earlier classic-winning associations between the Burns of Lumville and the Rogers of Crotanstown.

taking it up fully three furlongs out. Headed by Joe Mercer on Not So Cold, but only on sufferance, TP sent Paveh into the lead again two furlongs from home. It proved a winning ploy, for hard as Paddy Sullivan drove Ultimate II in pursuit, Paveh passed the judge three-quarters to the good. Democrat finished a remote fourth. Frigid Aire, the best horse to carry Dale Schaffer's colours, made it a day to remember for TP when winning the concluding May Scurry Handicap.

Other red letter days in 1966 included an Ulster Harp Derby on My Kuda, trained in Rangers Lodge by Aubrey Brabazon and a Beresford Stakes on Sovereign Slipper for Sunnyhill trainer Paddy Murphy, better known for his front-running jumpers, notably Fredith's Son. "Paddy Murphy was some character. Liable to say anything. A very good trainer for all that." A total of 39 winners saw TP share third place in the jockeys' table with Tommy Carberry, bettered only by Johnnie Roe and George McGrath. TP signed off on a winner, Sagaris in the Final Handicap at Thurles on November 10th. Eight days later Chris made TP a father for the first time when James Gerard entered the world.

An impressive string of retainers in 1967 – Michael Dawson, Dale Schaffer, T. Burns, A. Brabazon, P. Murphy and G. Wells virtually guaranteed TP a respectable season, albeit devoid of any headline

Trainer's wife Sarah Ainsworth adding a touch of elegance to a memorable moment.

KILLARNEY, May 25, 1966 – Stella poses with Lully Boy, successful in the feature race of the day under Lumville apprentice Vivian Kennedy, the first leg of a hat trick for this dependable son of Beau Sabreur.

winners. One that TP could be proud of came through Tu Va at the Phoenix Park. Although 'Buster' Harty's charge was only three, he had already shown definite signs of duplicity. Riding him like a non-trier, TP codded the grey into doing more than usual before whooshing him to the front in the only place that matters. It was a masterpiece of crafty jockeyship. Twenty-eight winners placed TP sixth in the combined Irish jockeys' championship, which lightweight Johnnie Roe had made his own by mid-season.

Continuing his love affair with Vimy's stock, the 'Scotchman' came up with another good one in Normandy, three times successful at Leopardstown in 1968. In carrying the colours of one W. Burns, Normandy revived a long-dormant family connection with Ayr. Uncle Billy, as he was to TP, had ridden a little as an amateur almost forty years earlier. Indeed, he had ridden Lt-Commander Leake's Mardin II to win chases at Bogside and Catterick in 1931, his first two rides over fences. Unfortunately, Uncle Billy didn't always ride to win, which led to his being banished from Applehirst in disgrace. An opportune marriage to Jessie Duncan, heiress to the Dalblair Hotel in Ayr, saw Uncle Billy driving a Rolls Royce and living in splendid style. The marriage was childless, so, when Jessie died, Uncle Billy promptly sold the hotel. Determined to obtain some of his brother's affluence, the 'Scotchman' had got him into a horse. With Uncle Billy's luck, it turned out to be a very good horse, which he happily sold on to Fred Rimell at a handsome profit. When Fred brought Normandy back to the land of his birth to win the 1969 Sweeps Hurdle at Fairyhouse it represented one of those rare horse deals in which all parties could take pleasure.

Chapter Twenty Nine

Now the senior member of the jockeys' brigade, TP could reflect that he had taken more mounts in 1968 than all but two of his rivals, while his 33 winners placed him fifth in the overall table behind Johnnie Roe. Much of the credit for TP's prolonged appeal to trainers belonged to Chris. While she did not actually book her husband's rides, Chris was scrupulous in recording telephone calls to Landfall and equally insistent that TP return them as soon as he came home. Long before the days of jockeys' agents and mobile telephones, but also in that era when telegrams had entered terminal decline, the landline telephone was the only means of rapid communication. By the same token, confidentiality was important. Had those calls been fielded elsewhere, "well, too many would have known my business. And you wouldn't want that."

It helped, too, that the Curragh telephone exchange had become automated by the early 1960s. Curiously, one who might not have agreed that automation constituted an improvement was Cecil Brabazon, the Burns' neighbour in Rangers Lodge, who had done so much to get TP going again in those post-war years. Earlier still Cecil had trained for 'Boss' Croker's son and namesake, Richard Croker. The younger Croker's horses all had 'C' as their initial – Carey Dennis, Celebrator, Chelsea, Chieftain, Claremorris, Clendennen, Clonford, Cloverdale, Corcy, Countess Royal and Custodian. And they were just one year's occupants of Rangers Lodge. Croker's nocturnal telephone conferences invariably got Cecil into a hopeless muddle, all those names becoming rapidly indistinguishable. Happily, the night operator in the Curragh Camp telephone exchange happened to be an avid racing fan. His timely interjections soon proved indispensable in maintaining a smooth owner-trainer relationship.

LANDFALL, 1971 – Three generations – L to R: Chris, Stella, TP, Tom, 'Scotchman' and James.

*LEOPARDSTOWN, 1969 – Chris and Stella following
TP's fortunes keenly as ever.*

Fit and healthy as ever and also finding it easier to keep his weight in check, TP got 1969 off to a flying start with a treble at Baldoyle on the opening day of the new season. Thereafter his best winners were supplied by his near neighbour Mickey Rogers. Candy Cane obliged in the Royal Whip and Barrons Court did likewise in the Blandford Stakes. TP's seasonal total of 22 winners saw him down the rankings behind 'Buster' Parnell and Johnnie Roe, whose struggle went to the wire, with 'Buster' coming out one ahead on the final day. Reindeer got TP back into the Irish Derby frame for the first time in many years when finishing third to Prince Regent and Ribofilio. To do so he had to repel Blakeney, the Epsom Derby winner, by a short head to claim the £7,048 prize money for third place.

In 1970 TP had a very distant view of Liam Ward winning the Irish Sweeps Derby on Vincent O'Brien's outstanding Nijinsky, as Honest Crook reflected his 300/1 SP when beating just three home. From being the new kid on the block some thirty years before, TP was now riding winners for trainers like Paul Doyle and Andy Geraghty, who had not even been born when TP began his riding career. For all of that, TP still had mounts in four of the five Irish classics, proof that his skill in the saddle continued to be in strong demand on the days that mattered. In common with all his flat racing brethren, TP silently applauded the abandonment of flat racing in Kilbeggan. He had been one of the luckier ones in that melee that had claimed 'Mut' Conlon's life – May 12th, 1952. Besides, TP now had two sons to rear, as James had been joined in Landfall by young Thomas Joseph, born April 6th, 1970.

The vogue for Australian stable jockeys sprang to life again in 1971. Kevin Prendergast retained Lawrie Johnson. Gordon Spinks replaced Lawrie in Charlie Weld's Rosewell stable. Lance Harvey and then Hilton Cope teamed up with John Oxx in Creeve. Alan Simpson joined Stephen Quirke in Mountjoy Lodge. The Aussies were similarly in demand in France, where Bill Williamson, Bill Pyers and Gary Moore rode for some of the most powerful stables. Liam Ward's retirement saw Johnnie Roe become Vincent O'Brien's contract rider in Ireland.

TP's career got another extension with Michael Fogarty's return to the Irish racing scene after a lengthy sojourn in America. Leasing TP's yard in Landfall, 'Fogo' soon began to turn out winners, some of them ridden by his evergreen landlord, notably that speedy filly Fiery

Diplomat, successful in the featured Park Stakes. Mrs Redmond Gallagher's Fiery Diplomat advertised both her trainer and Landfall Stables when going on to become only the second Irish-trained juvenile to score in England, Ireland and France. 'Fogo' employed American training methods, one of which, as young James Burns observed, fascinated, involved walking horses round the yard, hour after hour until both horses and handlers appeared on the point of collapse. Another rising trainer happy to entrust his blue-blooded Nelson Bunker Hunt runners to TP was Ted Curtin. They combined to win the Ulster Harp Derby with Falaise and the Phoenix 'Fifteen Hundred' with Marble Arch.

PHOENIX PARK, August 12, 1972 – TP winning his second Phoenix '1500', now Group 2, on Nelson Bunker Hunt's Marble Arch (USA) for trainer Ted Curtin.

Baldoyle staged racing for the final time in August 1972, with TP unplaced on his only mount. Despite his good record on the seaside course, TP refused to mourn its passing. "Baldoyle was a very sharp, tight track, always on the turn. A lot of good horses failed to act there. Could make you look foolish, or worse."

Around the same time Kevin Prendergast was also starting to feel foolish. He had won the Irish 1000 Guineas with Norman Butler's smart grey filly, Pidget. But Pidget had since decided that she had seen quite enough of the Curragh, resolutely refusing to go on the gallops. When all others had failed, Kevin resorted to TP. The ploy proved successful, as Pidget went through her paces unruffled on the only occasion that TP rode her a piece of work.

Lest familiarity induce contempt, TP only sat on the quirky grey to finish second in the Desmond Stakes until she appeared to contest the 1972 Irish St Leger. F. E. Fetherstonhaugh's account in the *Bloodstock Breeders' Review* warrants repetition in full.

"Had the Irish St Leger on September 23 been run in France there would have been rather more than considerable doubt that Pidget would have retained her verdict. Indeed, there were many doubting Thomases present that day following her in-and-out progression in the straight.

"This controversial blemish in no way detracts from the gallantry and season-long enthusiasm of the filly which kept the rich prize at home in a race otherwise dominated by the two English-trained colts, Our Mirage and Fire Red. Manitoulin, best of the other four home-trained runners, was beaten a dozen lengths in a processional finish.

CURRAGH, September 23, 1972 – Pidget (TP) turning the Irish St Leger into a procession, chased home by Our Mirage (Bill Williamson) and Fire Red (Brian Taylor).

"The colour patrol film viewed from head-on at the end of the day showed clearly that Pidget deviated from a straight path, not once but twice. First she cut across Our Mirage, whom Williamson had to switch to the outer; then, in the closing stages she reversed the procedure, seeming again to baulk the colt. At those points Our Mirage – an even money favourite following his close second to Boucher in the Doncaster St Leger – was the only serious challenger. Naturally, a lengthy inquiry ensued but the Stewards decided to make no change in the placings.

"Apparently the Stewards use discretion over this breach if they are satisfied that the crossing did not lessen the loser's chance of winning, but that is an enigma I do not propose to try and unravel."

"Lady Exbury set off in front, her nearest attendant being Pardner, with the others many lengths behind. The filly retained her lead at half-way but the wide gaps were closing with Pardner still second, followed by Our Mirage, Pidget and Manitoulin. Lady Exbury lost her place coming down to the turn, where Pardner was still holding on, but was joined by Our Mirage and Pidget into the straight.

"Pardner folded up, leaving Pidget and Our Mirage to fight it out, and it was the filly who took the initiative. She established a two lengths' advantage before the controversial incidents occurred and with veteran Tommy Burns keeping her up to her task, her unbounded courage and tenacity were rewarded."

When TP's licence for the 1973 flat season appeared in the *Irish Racing Calendar* many assumed that he aimed to exceed his father's forty-one-year riding career. Indeed, if one took into account all the breaks the 'Scotchman' had taken, voluntary or involuntary, TP had already matched his father. The 'Scotchman' had ridden his first winner in 1913, been suspended for most of 1918 and retired for the first time in 1927. He had come out of retirement very briefly in 1928, only to become a trainer the following year. In 1930 he had returned to ride a classic winner, only to lose his licence in September. Reinstated in 1931, he became Irish champion jockey the next season. The Raeburn episode at Royal Ascot had seen him retire again in 1937, only to resume in 1939. Thereafter he had ridden continuously until finally hanging up his boots in 1954, having landed that Royal Ascot gamble on Upadee.

Embarking on his 36th season in the saddle, TP had long since ceased to be 'fashionable'. Not that he had ever made much concession to fashion. His carefully preserved tweeds and cavalry twills had seen so much service that he was dubbed "Patches" by the irreverent. Nevertheless, as with his father, Canty and Wing in their time, TP had achieved well-nigh iconic status with trainers who needed to know the time of day. He was a simply outstanding judge of a horse's prospects. John Murphy has fond memories of Curragh gallop post-mortems.

"Well, TP, what do you think? Can we back this lad?"

"I think you could have a little on him."

"When you heard him say that, you could head for the bank, get all they'd let you have, and back it down to your last fiver. It wouldn't get beaten." Habitess and Fiona's Slipper proved that point in fine style. Sue Doyle has similar memories, citing Patent Slipper, Border Hero and Bluehel as examples of gambles landed with the ageless TP on board. Ted Curtin and Willie Robinson, then TP's neighbour in Stepaside, were two more to rely on his enormous reserves of experience. Willie made sure of TP's availability by inducing Bert Firestone, his principal patron, to retain TP. The Tormey brothers wanted no one else on Grand Visier when their money was down. Richard Annesley never missed the opportunity to pick the veteran's brains about Curragh gallops and how to use them to greatest advantage. Michael Fogarty, TP's tenant in Landfall, got some very rewarding turns through such as Raptor and Royal Racquet with his landlord in the saddle.

Younger generations of jockeys who thought TP an oddity in the weighing room quickly learned the perils of underestimating the old-timer, with his tiny flask of coffee and carefully rationed quota of Fox's Glacier Mints. Still fitter and considerably stronger than many half his age, TP rarely sought or gave any quarter from start to finish. And if he did proffer a quiet word of advice or reproach to a junior, the latter ignored it at his peril. TP had learned his trade in a harsher world, holding his own in the cut and thrust that was race riding before the advent of camera patrols. Pat Eddery was renowned for his will to win, but even he had to accept a code of discipline to which his father could never have begun to conform. TP spanned both eras, bringing to the 'seventies a repertoire of tricks from an earlier age of which younger men had no experience and thus no defence. While it was said that TP had no peers in riding Leopardstown, to many trainers it was TP's encyclopaedic knowledge of country tracks in all types of underfoot conditions that made him an invaluable ally.

Uncharacteristically coy on the merits of those he rode against latterly, TP resorts to anodyne categorisation. Liam Ward was "very stylish, perhaps not the strongest". Johnnie Roe had that indefinable gift – "horses ran for him. Bit like Frankie Dettori." 'Buster' Parnell – "Well, you just never knew with Buster. Brilliant, sometimes". Lester Piggott was "a fantastic judge". Paddy Powell was "very good over hurdles", Nicky Brennan "an excellent lightweight", Jackie

Power "the ideal stable jockey" and Peadar Matthews a "far better jockey than he was ever got the chance to show". Christy Roche – "a clever rider". As for those invasive Australians – "Bill Williamson could cod you every time, even though well past his best. Must have been some jockey in his prime. Jack Purtell could ride too. Hilton Cope was very strong but got it hard to do the weights." Right. So who did TP least like to do battle with? George McGrath. "George was incredibly strong in the saddle. He would never get tired before his horse did. The last hundred yards against George was always a battle."

Going back in time TP is more forthcoming. Joe Canty had "no style, but had everyone eating out of the palm of his hand." Jack Moylan was "very, very good, remarkable really, considering he was elderly when I started riding." Morose Morny Wing was "a good enough jockey, but not as cunning as the Old Man, in my book anyway." Dan Moore was "an excellent horseman. Couldn't ride a finish if his life depended on it." The 'Brab' was "very, very good on a horse that would carry him through a race. Not great on a lazy bugger that needed driving." Martin Molony was "the exact opposite. Martin would kick and drive for four miles if need be. Never gave up. Won races no one else would have."

CURRAGH, October 20, 1973 – Sir Penfro, a reformed character in TP's hands, cruising home in the Stayers' Stakes. Vincent O'Brien's 'funny' charge was to give TP his final Group success in the 1974 Desmond Stakes.

The Aussie vogue continued in 1974, with Keith Watson riding for 'Long Paddy' Prendergast, Paul Jarman for Kevin Prendergast, John Murray for Willie Robinson and Alan Simpson for John Oxx. Nonetheless, TP's solid support base enabled him to ride a very respectable 26 winners that season, of which Vincent O'Brien supplied five, notably Sir Penfro in the Desmond Stakes. Sir Penfro marked a turning back of the clock, as TP had not ridden a winner for Vincent for quite some time. It transpired that Vincent had previously brought Sir Penfro up to the Curragh in a draft of post-racing gallopers. When the colt refused to go backwards or forwards, the trainer merely directed the staff to box him up and take him back to Ballydoyle.

Sir Penfro was brought up again for a subsequent race meeting, with similar post-racing exercise in prospect. However, on this occasion Vincent sent for TP from the jockeys' room. "Ah, Tommy. Perhaps you would be good enough to sit up on Sir Penfro after racing. A funny horse. Giving me a lot of trouble." Just as the old magic had worked on Pidget, so it did on Sir Penfro, with gratifying results for all concerned.

It really did seem that TP had discovered the secret of eternal youth, in his case attributable to a sober, careful life style on a strict and unvarying diet that virtually excluded alcohol. "Oh, I'd take a glass of sherry if I was at a party. But I never cared for the taste of alcohol and any more than one glass would have me off colour for three days and sometimes more."

That regime saw TP in the saddle once more in 1975, but by now the winners had begun to dry up to a trickle. Irrespective of trainers' views, owners demanded younger, more fashionable jockeys. While it may not occur so much in flat racing, it is certainly true on the jumping front that trainers begin to fight shy of using senior jockeys, no one wishing to have it on his or her conscience that it was a fall from one of their charges that caused permanent incapacitation, or worse. Festive Diplomat for Willie Robinson at Bellewstown in August proved to be the last of TP's 1,000-plus winners. There were even those with the temerity to suggest that Lester Piggott give up the game. And he had ridden his first winner in 1948, a decade after TP had first heard "Winner all right" applied to him.

November 1975 – Chris and TP admire the silver salver presented to him by his fellow jockeys at the dinner to mark his retirement

Chapter Thirty

So many jockeys traditionally turned their hand to training when they retired from the saddle, considering that the logical, perhaps the only, progression. TP had seen far too many instances of former jockeys dissipating their hard-earned savings in that endeavour to have contemplated it seriously. Moreover, the most successful trainers employing his services down the decades had not been notable jockeys in their earlier days. Cecil Brabazon, Charlie Rogers, Tom Dreaper, Joe Osborne, Vincent O'Brien, Mickey Rogers, Michael Fogarty, Paddy Mullins and Brud Fetherstonhaugh had ridden with varying success as amateurs. Paddy Prendergast, Kevin Bell, Michael Dawson, Charlie Weld and Paddy Norris were infinitely more successful as trainers than they had been as professional jockeys. Colonel Blake, John Oxx and Ted Curtin had never donned colours. True, there were exceptions – Dan Moore, Danny Morgan, Aubrey Brabazon, Georgie Wells and Willie Robinson. Besides, the 'Scotchman' was still active on that front in Lumville, assisted by John and his sister Stella. John had ridden his last winner back in 1966 on Black Justice, having ridden out his claim seven years previously. Successful in his first two bumper starts, Black Justice had routed strong opposition, winning by eight lengths each time.

"The best horse I ever rode in public. Won his two bumpers at Leopardstown. I couldn't do the weight the first time, so Tommy Finn got the ride. There was a queue of customers for him. But he failed the veterinary examination five times, each time for a different reason. In the end a fellow fresh out of veterinary college gave him a sound certificate. He won his first three hurdle races in England, but never reached the heights we felt he should have."

Vivian Kennedy had also become an integral part of the closely-knit Lumville team, maturing from raw apprentice to seasoned 'job' jockey. "Twenty-one years I was there. Pure hardship, and never any money, but a great grounding. It stood to me. The old Scotchman would think nothing of hanging on to a horse for a year or more. 'No, not today,' he'd say to me. When one was to his liking, word would go to his brother John in Ayr. John would arrive on the Friday, due to return on the Saturday evening after racing. But if the horse did the business...

Well, it could be the following Saturday before John would leave. The Scotchman would see first or second lot. Then it was off to the Grand Hotel in Newbridge with the pair of them. They'd come back for evening stables in a right old state."

John Burns rarely made the journey from Ayr unless accompanied by bibulous fellow dealer Sandy Davison. Stella Burns came to dread the effect of their visits on her husband's liver, from which the entire household would subsequently suffer. Happily, domestic relations in Lumville improved when Johnny Duffy succeeded Sandy as John's travelling companion.

Apart from riding work for the 'Scotchman', TP had moved on from the Lumville scene a long time ago. In any case, the fact that he no longer held a jockey's licence was no barrier to his riding work for Vincent O'Brien as he had always done. "Vincent liked to get value for his money. Besides, he trusted me, one of the very few he did trust."

TP had expressed those sentiments in other words to Raymond Smith when interviewed for Raymond's best-selling *Vincent O'Brien – the Master of Ballydoyle*. "As Assistant Trainer I found

CURRAGH, 1970s – two heads being (sometimes) better than one, Vincent O'Brien concentrating on his assistant's opinion, momentarily oblivious to Robert Sangster's proximity.

that if he trusted you, he left things up to you. He expected you to know your business and that there would be no slip-ups. You were on your honour and there could be no messing. His demands were pretty high. He expected you to keep up with them, for the standards he set for others he maintained himself. There was no place in his set-up if you could not meet those standards."

Elizabeth Bowen might have had Vincent O'Brien in mind when penning this character sketch in *A World of Love*. "As master he had the name of being a terror, throwing out what he detected to be a slack man as soon as look at him; but as against that he had been bred here and knew fundamentally what he was working with: men he chose to keep chose to stay – it was recognized that himself was the one he drove hardest of all."

However, that lay in the future. John Gosden was then Vincent's assistant, in the heady days of The Minstrel. Purchased for $200,000 as a yearling the gritty little chestnut was sold back to America two years later for $9,000,000, The Minstrel laid the foundation for the new Ballydoyle-Coolmore axis that set out to buy potential stallions as yearlings. That transformation depended upon the genius of Vincent O'Brien and Vincent depended in turn on the skill and judgement of his key lieutenants and work riders, notably TP, Johnny Brabston and Vincent 'Benjy' Rossiter.

Despite his crucial role in those glittering Ballydoyle successes, TP made a bid for freedom. He took out a trainer's licence, specifically to train Snowy Creek for John and Mary Murphy from Rathangan. "But Vincent never left me alone, ringing up about the going on the Curragh and any other thing that was on his mind. He got Tim Rogers to talk me into going back to him, as his assistant."

EPSOM, June 1980 – TP exercising Derby hopeful Monteverdi, The colt's Derby flop caused a lengthy rift between Vincent O'Brien and Lester Piggott.

Snowy Creek accordingly moved from Landfall to Lumville. He duly paid the Christmas expenses and more besides when winning a maiden hurdle at Limerick in December 1978. Four years later the Murphys and the Burns were to experience the darker side of racing when Barton, nursed back to his best in Lumville, incurred fatal injuries at the second last fence in the Irish Grand National when travelling like a winner. Barton's tragic end and the swarm of ghoulish onlookers that it attracted was to become an abiding memory for young James Burns – TP's elder son.

TP's return to the Ballydoyle fold coincided with Alleged's consecutive Prix de l'Arc de Triomphe victories and Golden Fleece's smashing Derby success. Alleged had been greeted in Ballydoyle without any great enthusiasm, for Robert Sangster had bought him in California at Billy McDonald's urging when the colt was already in the breeze-up phase of his career. "Johnny Brabston rode him out the first couple of days. I rode him the next two days. When Vincent asked me my opinion, I recommended he keep him."

From his winning debut at the Curragh in November until he won his second Arc two years later Alleged was only ever beaten once in ten races, when second in the St Leger. TP retains a very high opinion of Alleged. "He was possibly the best horse Vincent ever had." And TP had seen them all.

The association between Vincent O'Brien and Lester Piggott, stretching back to the days of Gladness, came to a temporary end during TP's term as assistant. "Lester was a dangerous man to let in around the place in those days. He and Vincent were forever trying to out-smart each other. You knew it was going on, even if you never quite got the whole picture. The only place you wanted Lester on your side was on the racecourse. He didn't ride much work in Ballydoyle, but any he did he'd make a mess of it. Work in Ballydoyle was the most precise I've ever experienced. It had to go exactly according to plan. That didn't suit Lester, who simply wanted to get on the best horse in every big race. He had an extraordinary intelligence network. Lester knew the whereabouts of every good horse in England, Ireland and France and the form they were in."

Tom Gallagher, whose father Gerry travelled so many of those Ballydoyle champions since joining the team in 1953, recalled TP's pivotal role in Ballydoyle, where woe betide messengers bearing bad tidings. "If anything had gone wrong we'd always get TP to go into the office and break it. TP was the only man who could put it across in language the Boss could understand. They went back a long time, so they did."

EPSOM, June 2, 1982 – Danny Schwartz, Vincent O'Brien, Jean Pierre Binet and Robert Sangster savour Golden Fleece's majestic Derby triumph, while TP nurses a broken foot, incurred in a fall from Golden Fleece just days earlier.

But not even TP's diplomacy could disguise the ongoing problems with Golden Fleece, a truculent, temperamental son of the

EVRY, July 2, 1983 – deputy Burns shares Yves Saint-Martin's delight following Glenstal's 'short neck' success on his racecourse swansong in the G3 Prix Daphnis. Vincent was doing likewise at Sandown, where Solford won the Eclipse Stakes, by a head.

magnificent Nijinsky. Pat Eddery, already the first Irishman ever to become champion flat jockey in Britain, had succeeded Lester as Ballydoyle contract rider. Contrasting in character to his predecessor, Pat Eddery represented that continuity so valued by Vincent O'Brien. He just happened to be a grandson of Jack Moylan, the veteran jockey who had set up those crucial gambles in Vincent's early days. Pat rode the colt in his four lifetime starts and occasionally in his work. The rest of the time Golden Fleece was entrusted to TP, then in his fifty-eighth year. "He was a bad-tempered bastard and you couldn't have a row with him. He'd go down the all-weather once and canter up. But no way would he go down to do a second canter. He planted one day shortly before the Derby and Johnny Brabston hit him. He whipped round and dumped me, broke my instep."

While he won the 1982 Derby in spectacular style, Golden Fleece returned to Ballydoyle a very sick horse. He had coughed on the morning of the race and only took part after a tense telephone conference between his fraught trainer and Bob Griffin, Vincent's trusted veterinary surgeon back on the Curragh. Bob had advised that if the colt had only just begun to cough, he should still be healthy enough to run to his best. That advice had proved sound. However, when Vincent consulted Bob subsequently about Golden Fleece's future prospects, the advice was very different, as TP could recall. "Bob Griffin put it to Vincent that he'd got his Derby, which had always been the object. However, Bob did not believe that Golden Fleece's fragile temperament would stand further training demands. He should be retired to stud. And so he was."

By 1983 TP had grown tired of travelling between his home on the Curragh and Ballydoyle. Apart from the prolonged absences from Chris and their sons, TP had fallen foul of the traffic police, to general hilarity in Ballydoyle. Tom Gallagher recalled the incident. "None of us could believe that TP had been done for speeding, even if it was in Cullahill, which is notorious for speed traps. TP explained at length the importance of his mission, hinting strongly to the prosecuting garda that he knew a stone-cold certainty for one of the races that day. One that should not be allowed to run unsupported. The garda was wise to him. 'Mr

Burns, if I were you, I'd be having enough on yourself to pay this speeding fine I'm about to give you!'"

Much of the amusement derived from the fact that TP, motorist, has always been the antithesis of the daredevil jockey profile that has seen his profession classified as 'highest risk' by motor insurers ever since cars became commonplace. His penchant for Austins, Hillmans, Datsuns and Volkswagens – all driven with care and economy – effectively ensured that the only conceivable place TP could ever be convicted for speeding was in Cullahill's 30mph zone, a partly hidden hiccup on the main Dublin-Cork road.

LUMVILLE, Summer 1976 – Germanicus (Vivian Kennedy), 3-y-o son of Barrons Court – Agrippina, recent Curragh winner for owner-breeder Rosaleen Tonson-Rye. TP had won the Blandford Stakes on Barrons Court, besides winning on Agrippina, trained by John Tonson-Rye for Rosaleen. Agrippina subsequently won the 1965 Irish Cesarewitch.

Chapter Thirty One

When TP wished Vincent O'Brien, Jacqueline, their family and the staff in Ballydoyle 'Happy Christmas' in December 1983 his departure brought one of racing's longest and most successful associations to a close. Forty-two years had elapsed since a youthful TP had made that wearisome wartime train journey to Churchtown to ride work on Astrometer, his prospective mount in the Irish Cesarewitch. While that plan had not materialised – for TP anyway – he had ridden Astronomic to victory at Limerick Junction the following year.

Change had taken place on the home front, too. Stella, TP's mother, died on November 24th 1980, leaving the 'Scotchman' lonesome after nearly sixty years of happy marriage. True, daughter Stella and son John were on hand for company, but life in Lumville could never be the same.

His desire to spend more time at home also meant that TP turned his back on what was already acclaimed as the very best of all Vincent's numerous champions – El Gran Senor. Named in honour of legendary trainer Horatio Luro, who had trained his sire Northern Dancer, El Gran Senor had gone through his juvenile season unbeaten. His character and sunny temperament had endeared him to the Ballydoyle team. After their trials and tribulations with Golden Fleece they found this short-priced Guineas and Derby favourite a joy to have in the stable. Equally smitten, Vincent and Jacqueline featured the charming colt on their 1983 Christmas card. Actually, TP had a softer spot for Caerleon, recently retired to stand at Coolmore. "Caerleon was a gent. He won the French Derby in spite of Pat Eddery. He would have gone to the very top as a four-year-old."

By the time TP left Ballydoyle at Christmas 1983, the gallops that he had seen created from an old-fashioned farm that Vincent had purchased from two elderly sisters who continued to reside in Ballydoyle during its painstaking remodelling, now accommodated another string. High on a hill and away from his childhood home, young David O'Brien had created his own stable and had already carved out a name for himself at the highest level. He had won both the French Derby and the Irish Derby with Assert in 1982, the year in which his father had won

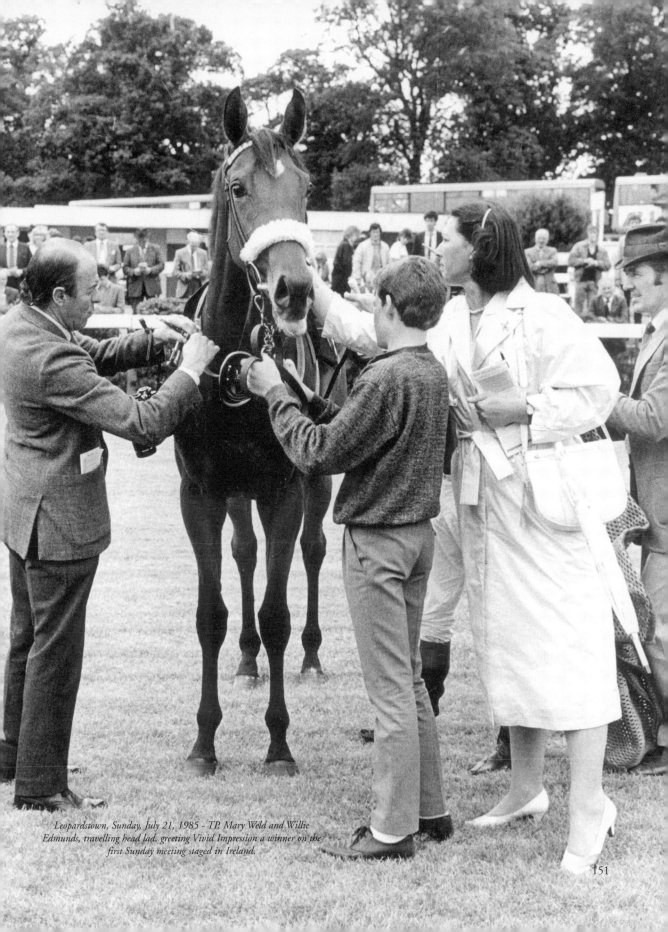

*Leopardstown, Sunday, July 21, 1985 - TP, Mary Weld and Willie
Edmunds, travelling head lad, greeting Vivid Impression a winner on the
first Sunday meeting staged in Ireland.*

151

TIPPERARY, July 21, 1988 – Tipperary Veteran's Race
left to right standing: TP, John Harty, Ron Barry, Dessie Hughes, John Francome, D. O'Connell, Tommy Carberry.
Kneeling: J.J. Kinane, Tom Enright, Tommy Murphy, Paddy Sullivan, Pat Hanly, Jonjo O'Neill.

his sixth Epsom Derby with Golden Fleece. David had not yet been born when Vincent and TP had gone so close in the 1957 Derby with Ballymoss. TP had watched the boy grow into his own man. "I wouldn't be up in David's yard that often, but I got the impression that he was a young man destined for success. No 'back of the clock' was David."

Far from retiring to look after his farm near Clonbullogue, twenty miles north-west of the Curragh, TP soon joined Dermot Weld as his assistant trainer in Rosewell, hard by the Curragh grandstands. TP could clearly remember Morny Wing building his house and stables, named after what Morny considered the best of his six Irish Derby winners. Furthermore, TP could recall Rosewell's appearance prior to that 1938 Irish Derby, for which his preparation had been confined to precisely one gallop. "Rosewell was as big as a whale. It was all they could do to get girths to go round him."

TP had been a spectator that day, when his brother Jimmy had ridden Gay Cottage for their father, then training in the run-up to the Raeburn case. It was the following day that TP had ridden Prudent Rose to win the opener, while Jimmy had taken the final race on Kilglass, his solitary winner.

In going to work for Dermot Kenneth Charles Weld, TP turned back another clock. He had ridden Listen In to win a Curragh handicap for Charlie Weld in 1952, when Dermot, Charlie and Gita Welds' only child, was all of four years old. Thereafter TP had ridden numerous winners for Charlie, notably Farney Fox and Coniston, actually giving Charlie fifth claim on his services in 1961. Then came that craze for Australian stable jockeys.

Charlie had retired to his Piper's Hill Stud in 1971, handing the Rosewell stable over to Dermot, then champion amateur in Ireland for the third time, having ridden his first winner aged fifteen. From the start Dermot had sent

48 years after winning here on Slightly Slow, TP reliving the moment with owner/trainer Dermot Weld, son Mark and Willie Edmunds

out a stream of winners, heading the table for races won in Ireland eight times, saddling over one hundred winners in 1974 and 1977. In 1983 he had claimed his first overall championship, thereby bringing Vincent O'Brien's six-year reign to a temporary halt. For all of that, life in Rosewell could never compare to Ballydoyle, not least because Vincent O'Brien was seven years TP's senior, whereas Dermot was twenty-four years his junior.

It was not by chance that TP found employment in Rosewell. Ever in search of competitive advantage, as he had already demonstrated to dramatic effect, Dermot Weld had been making overtures to TP for some time. Dermot's campaign to recruit TP to his Rosewell banner found a willing accomplice in Chris Burns, who was increasingly anxious to have her husband return home and play his part as paterfamilias. James, their elder son, might be boarding in Newbridge College and thus out of mischief, but young Tom was not subject to similar strictures. While TP might have withstood pressure from either party, he had no chance against both.

TP was back in action on those Curragh gallops that he knew from childhood when that extraordinary Greek tragedy was played out on Epsom Downs. El Gran Senor, unbeaten winner of the Two Thousand Guineas appeared to have Vincent's seventh Derby in the bag, only to be worried out of it by a tigerish Christy Roche and Secreto. Also a son of Northern Dancer, Secreto was trained in Ballydoyle, but by David O'Brien. TP could only marvel from afar, fretful that this upset might bring out a darker side of his old ally's character.

Meanwhile, TP adjusted to his new employer's policy of winning as many races as possible.

PUNCHESTOWN, July 7, 1989 – Old Man River, Old Man River, just keep rolling along.

However, it had its compensations too. On July 21st 1988, TP donned colours for the first time in thirteen years, to ride Dermot's Midsummer Gamble in the Tipperary Veterans' Race over 1m 6f in Limerick Junction. Well, it had been called Limerick Junction since its inception. Now it was known as Tipperary. Apart from its title, not a lot had changed since TP had ridden Slightly Slow to belie his name in the Croker Cup all of forty-eight years previously.

Midsummer Gamble opened odds-on to justify his name, easing marginally to 5/4. Perhaps punters were reluctant to put their faith and their cash on a 64-year-old jockey, pitted against such doughty younger rivals as Ron Barry, Tommy Carberry, John Francome, John Harty, Dessie Hughes, Tommy Murphy, Jonjo O'Neill and Paddy Sullivan. They need not have worried. The formbook recorded: "waited with; head-way to 3rd over 5f out; led 3f out; clear last furlong." The judge gave it to Midsummer Gamble by five lengths. He went on to win in Galway and completed his hat trick in the Irish Cesarewitch, ridden each time by stable jockey Michael Kinane.

Michael – his preferred mode of address – remembers TP's role in Rosewell with gratitude and affection. Reflecting on his comparative youth and inexperience when appointed stable jockey to an ambitious and exacting taskmaster, Michael Kinane readily gives credit to TP for the unstinting benefit of his advice and assistance. "I never met anyone as good at finding the key to any horse, the best way to ride him. Being that bit heavier than the rest of us, TP would generally ride the lead horse in a gallop. He wasn't easy to pass!"

To Michael Kinane TP even more crucially proved a steadfast ally in smoothing over any tension between trainer and stable jockey. "Dermot wasn't easy to ride for. Grand when things were going well, but of course that can't always be the case. . ." Michael Clower made that abundantly clear in his authorised biography: *Michael Kinane – Big Race King.*

While not given to talking for talk's sake, Michael Kinane offers two anecdotes of his old friend that bear repetition. TP was still in action when Michael Kinane was a rising apprentice. "I was coming down the hill in Clonmel one day when TP came by – and turned my horse sideways!" And the flip side? "I got a bad fall in Gowran Park. Serious facial injuries. Brought to St James's Hospital to be operated on. When I came round after surgery, the first person I saw was TP, sitting beside the bed with a bottle of something or other and a bag of sweets."

Midsummer Gamble was surely TP's swansong in colours? Wrong again. "I won on Old Man

River – chestnut with a parrot mouth – at Punchestown the following summer. Look it up."
Sure enough, Punchestown, July 7th, 1989, the Milka Lilapause Trainers Race, worth £1,382
to the winner, as were all but two of the races on that card. Even money favourite Old Man
River (T.P.Burns) "Led early; 2nd till led again under 4f out; not extended." Owned by
Bertram R. Firestone and trained by D. K. Weld, Old Man River won by eight lengths. TP
was followed home on this occasion by Mr P.J.Finn, T. Carberry, Capt. D.G.Swan and Mr
S.Shanahan.

Thus did TP ring down the curtain on a race-winning career that had begun at the Curragh
in June 1938, fifteen months before Britain declared war on Nazi Germany. In the intervening
fifty-one years racing in Ireland had ceased at Baldoyle, Claremorris, Longford, Mullacurry,
Mullingar, Rathkeale and Tuam. On the credit side: Sligo had closed in Hazelwood, but
reopened in Cleveragh, while Wexford had also come into being, marked by an opening day
riding double for TP and his brother John. Others may have ridden in colours for a greater
span than TP's fifty-one years. 'Old' Harry Beasley in Ireland and Bobby Renton in England
certainly did, but neither rode winners over a comparable span.

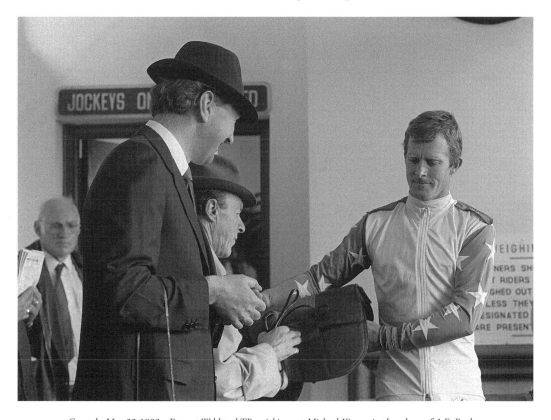

Curragh, May 22 1993 - Dermot Weld and TP weighing out Michael Kinane in the colours of A.E. Paulson,
subsequently carried by Zagreb

Chapter Thirty Two

Having ridden a winner in the same year in which he qualified for free travel on public transport, TP saw no reason to put his feet up. In any case, inactivity was anathema to the man's nature. Moreover, Chris had no particular desire to have her restless husband under her feet all day, every day. She had taken full advantage of TP's absences to landscape Landfall. The vast majority of men consider their duty done when providing comfortable accommodation for their spouses and offspring. TP was no exception, oblivious to the lunar waste surrounding his hearth and home.

After all, had he not created expanses of lawn, which it was his delight to mow at every opportunity? Lawn mowing, with an old-fashioned push mower, had long been TP's way of shedding any unwanted ounces that might have crept on to his spare frame through age rather than over-indulgence. Indeed, he had reduced John Oxx's team to helpless laughter on that very subject. The late Paddy Sullivan, a lynchpin of the Oxx stable for years, recounted the scene on the Flat Rath as the string circled at the end of a gallop. Low-key as ever, John Oxx murmured to TP that his particular mount was due to run the following day. TP could have the ride. Taken completely by surprise at this unexpected development, TP spluttered in amazement. "Ah, John. Now I'll have to go and mow the lawn!"

When the coast was clear Chris seized every opportunity to transform TP's bleak sauna substitute into the friendly, secluding gardens that surround Landfall today. Unlike so many Kildare gardens that invariably peak in riotous colour round Irish Derby time, Landfall provides a pleasing array of colour throughout the growing seasons. At other times the mature trees and shrubs combine with the flanking rear wall of one stable block to provide a welcome buffer against those whispering breezes, forever part of that unique micro-climate caressing the Curragh of Kildare.

Those whispering breezes, in which he had lived the greater part of his 92 years, bore Tommy 'Scotchman' Burns to his eternal reward in February 1991. The master of the waiting game had long since outlasted all his former rivals in the saddle. His passing prompted widespread appreciation of the feats and foibles that had made the 'Scotchman' a legend in his time. All too few of his obituaries were penned by those who could personally recall the glory days when Irish racing thrilled to the artistry of 'Canty, Burns and Wing'. By then the Lumville yard accommodated others, as John had taken over the training mantle for only a brief period in 1985 before moving to live permanently in west Cork. Sister Stella became the sole custodian of Lumville, with all its memories. Philip McCartan, Nick Bell and Frank Lacy rented the stables in their turn.

TP soldiered on as the only non-family assistant Dermot Weld ever employed until reaching another milestone, his 'threescore years and ten,' in 1994. Had he perhaps outstayed his welcome, surpassed his usefulness? Chris had always insisted that her husband's invaluable skill was his ability to assess a horse's potential from the saddle – "looking through a horse's ears. That's his great contribution."

Michael Kinane echoed Chris's assessment. "TP was really only happy on horseback, riding work. He didn't like being on the ground, not comfortable in that role. Yes, he did stay on too long."

Could that have coloured octogenarian memories? So it seemed.

What were the memorable horses from his decade in Rosewell? A quizzical glance intimated a mixture of incredulity and amnesia. "Well, Committed was a very good sprinter. I could take some of the credit for that. You see, she was to be taken out of training at the end of her three-year-old season. I told Dermot he was daft. We hadn't seen the best of her at all yet. And the rest you know. Wasn't she European champion?"

Theatrical and the Moyglare Stud homebreds Brief Truce and Big Shuffle surely warranted a mention? Happily, Big Shuffle, crack sprinter and later successful sire, had endeared himself to TP.

Diffident mention of Vintage Crop induced a visible frown of recollection and a weighing of words. In TP's estimation Vintage Crop warrants respect primarily for his courage and toughness in overcoming more physical disabilities than any other ten horses might experience. Two Irish St Legers, leading up to TP's retirement, surely made Vintage Crop a bit special, one should have thought. Clearly one would have thought wrongly. Classic races were instituted for three-year-old colts and fillies, a formula that had surely stood the test of time. As for the Melbourne Cup, discretion overcame valour. No medals for becoming the bravest corpse in the cemetery. Michael Kinane would not be drawn.

Zagreb seemed safe to mention, since TP's allegiance had shifted by then from Rosewell to Landfall, where son James had begun training in 1992, after six years understudying John Dunlop in Arundel, plus a stint in Australia with Bart Cummings and Colin Hayes. Bull's-eye. "Zagreb? Irish Derby. Those things happen once in every fifty years!"

LEOPARDSTOWN, May 11, 1996 – TOSSUP (Pat Shanahan), being led in victorious by Maria Wilmot accompanied by James and TP.

The bull's-eye later became a left-and-right when put to Michael Kinane. He vividly recalled Zagreb's final gallop as so dismal that he immediately asked to be released in order to accept the proffered mount on Dr Massini. While Michael has since won that coveted Irish Derby not once but twice, on Galileo and High Chaparral, those hallmark sandy eyebrows still elevate, incredulous in recollection of Zagreb's transformation on the day that counted.

By the time Zagreb caused mass incredulity at the Curragh, young Tom Burns had followed his father and brother into the bloodstock business, though not before learning about life in foreign lands at first hand. In his case Tom opted for regular employment, spending the greater part of his career to date under the Darley banner. Tom is presently assistant manager in Blackhall Stud, where yearlings complete their transition from frolicsome weanlings to fledgling racehorses. He shed his bachelor status when marrying Helen Nunan in December 2002.

Modest to the point of evasion on his training achievements – "this is Dad's book" – James mentioned just once that he fancied one of his to win. Duly it did. His father would have been disconcerted. Interviewed twelve months earlier for *The Irish Field*, TP summarised his lifetime on the Turf. "I have had a great innings. I never had a bet even though my father would plan a coup a year in advance. He did give me one valuable piece of advice: 'Never give tips, because you can't win'."

When James was setting out to learn the trainer's art in Arundel, the 'Scotchman' had amplified that advice, reflecting that a lifetime's punting had left him no richer, and wiser only at eighty-six.

In the light of his grandfather's belated renunciation of gambling, his father's lifelong refusal to bet and John Dunlop's philosophy of training as a business, it was almost inevitable that James would adopt an equally commercial approach to the management of Landfall Paddocks. Meanwhile, Landfall has experienced *Months of Misery, Moments of Bliss*, as former trainer Bill Wightman so aptly entitled his memoirs. Such as Laurentia, Memories, Romanylei, Sagar Pride, Tossup and Vinthea have flown the flag for the fourth generation of the Burns family to train on the Curragh of Kildare. Curiously, those called James have made their reputation as trainers, whereas the intervening Thomases achieved their renown in the saddle. To heighten the distinction still further – TP never trained a winner, and James never rode one. It makes for an equitable working relationship.

Indeed, TP's continued involvement in the stable's activities provides a therapeutic distraction following Chris's life-threatening stroke, which rendered her seriously incapacitated and in need of constant nursing care. Her family's reaction to Chris's predicament says more about their upbringing than words could convey.

Biographers of living subjects inevitably feel intrusive, even subversive, in their search for the 'real story', whatever that might be. Seldom can the word 'voyeur' seem more appropriate. This sense of intrusion is even more marked in the ephemeral world of horseracing, where virtually every topic and every issue is essentially subjective. More often than not carefully prepared agendas are thrown into disarray by unexpected, disarming disclosures. All too frequently the Red Herring mesmerises, swimming across the angler's chosen stretch of water, dorsal fin clearly visible. Unable to resist, the angler casts, and so becomes caught, as his real quarry swims smirking out of sight.

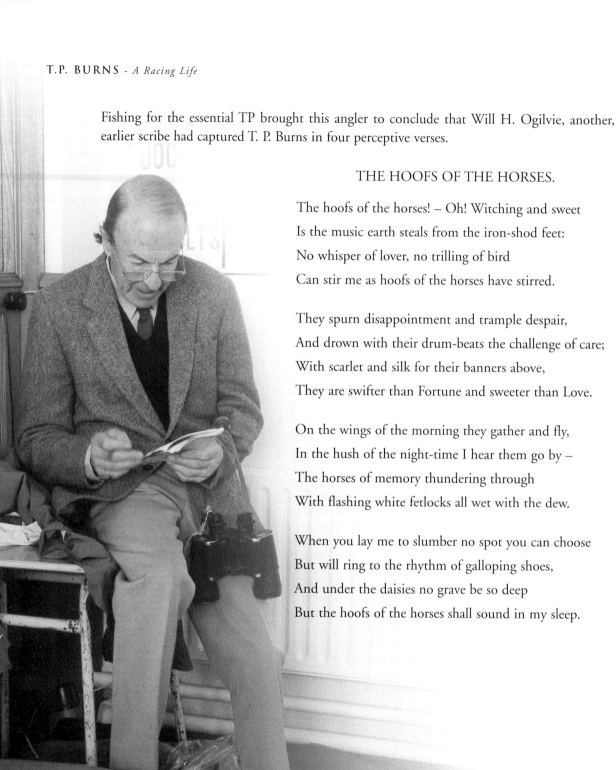

Fishing for the essential TP brought this angler to conclude that Will H. Ogilvie, another, earlier scribe had captured T. P. Burns in four perceptive verses.

THE HOOFS OF THE HORSES.

The hoofs of the horses! – Oh! Witching and sweet
Is the music earth steals from the iron-shod feet:
No whisper of lover, no trilling of bird
Can stir me as hoofs of the horses have stirred.

They spurn disappointment and trample despair,
And drown with their drum-beats the challenge of care;
With scarlet and silk for their banners above,
They are swifter than Fortune and sweeter than Love.

On the wings of the morning they gather and fly,
In the hush of the night-time I hear them go by –
The horses of memory thundering through
With flashing white fetlocks all wet with the dew.

When you lay me to slumber no spot you can choose
But will ring to the rhythm of galloping shoes,
And under the daisies no grave be so deep
But the hoofs of the horses shall sound in my sleep.

T. P. BURNS
& Tommy BURNS
Feature Race Successes

IRISH CLASSICS

IRISH 2000 GUINEAS
1921 . . . . Soldennis (T)
1923 . . . . Soldumeno (T)
1939 . . . Cornfield (T)
1947 . . . . Grand Weather (T)
1948 . . . . Beau Sabreur (T)
1959 . . . . El Toro (TP)
1966 . . . . Paveh (TP)

IRISH 1000 GUINEAS
1927 . . . . West Indies (T)
1933 . . . . Spy-Ann (T)
1934 . . . . Kyloe (T)
1953 . . . . Northern Gleam (T)
1962 . . . . Shandon Belle (TP)

IRISH DERBY
1936 . . . . Raeburn (T)
1957 . . . . Ballymoss (TP)

IRISH OAKS
1916 . . . . Captive Princess (T)
1917 . . . . Golden Maid (T)
1926 . . . . Resplendent (T)
1941 . . . . Uvira (T)

IRISH St LEGER
1916 . . . . Captive Princess (T)
1917 . . . . Double Scotch (T)
1919 . . . . Cheap Popularity (T)
1931 . . . . Beaudelaire (T)
1940 . . . . Harvest Feast (T)
1948 . . . . Beau Sabreur (T)
1961 . . . . Vimadee (TP)
1972 . . . . Pidget (TP)

ENGLISH CLASSICS

St LEGER
1957 . . . . Ballymoss (TP)

IRISH SEMI-CLASSICS &c

TETRARCH STAKES
1948 . . . . Beau Sabreur (TP)
1951 . . . . Signal Box (T)
1953 . . . . Treetops Hotel (T)
1955 . . . . Bright Night (TP)

ATHASI STAKES
1958 . . . . Minou (TP)

GALLINULE STAKES
1949 . . . . Bird Watcher (T)

PRETTY POLLY STAKES
1953 . . . . Northern Gleam (T)
1955 . . . . Free Model (TP)

INTERNATIONAL STAKES
1956 . . . . Beau Chevalet (TP)

ROYAL WHIP
1931 . . . . Sahabelle (T)
1932 . . . . Cloverdale (T)
1952 . . . . Beau Sire (TP)
1969 . . . . Candy Cane (TP)

DESMOND STAKES
1947 . . . . Spring Offensive (T)
1950 . . . . Galatian (T)
1962 . . . . Sicilian Prince (TP)
1974 . . . . Sir Penfro (TP)

IRISH CHAMPION STAKES
1947 . . . . Turkish Tune (T)
1948 . . . . Heron Bridge (T)
1950 . . . . Heron Bridge (T)
1952 . . . . The Dane (T)
1953 . . . . Northern Gleam (T)
1957 . . . . Gladness (TP)

BLANDFORD STAKES
1955 . . . . Nile Bird (TP)
1969 . . . . Barrons Court (TP)

IRISH JUVENILE GROUP RACES

RAILWAY STAKES
1933 . . . . Kyloe (T)

ANGLESEY STAKES
1932 . . . . Black Wings (T)

1939 .... Eyrefield (T)

1946 .... Grand Weather (T)

PHOENIX STAKES

1925 .... Allets (T)

1926 .... Archway (T)

1939 .... Eyrefield (T)

1941 .... Fair Crystal (T)

1959 .... Gigi (TP)

1972 .... Marble Arch (USA) (TP)

NATIONAL STAKES

1921 .... Soliman's Orb (T)

1944 .... Solid Pact (T)

1956 .... El Minzah (TP)

1964 .... Prominer (TP)

BERESFORD STAKES

1920 .... Ballyheron (T)

1924 .... Capture Him (T)

1927 .... Wavetop (T)

1946 .... Grand Weather (T)

1949 .... Dark Warrior (T)

1952 .... Northern Gleam (TP)

1966 .... Sovereign Slipper (TP)

MAJOR IRISH HANDICAPS

MADRID

1917 .... Double Scotch (T)

1922 .... Barrackton Lad (T)

1923 .... Soldumeno (T)

1927 .... Caustic (T)

1943 .... Wykehamist (T)

1948 .... Grey Abbey (T)

1968 .... French Serenade (TP)

LINCOLNSHIRE

1943 .... Foam Crest (T)

1950 ... Knock Hard (TP)

McDONOGH, Galway

1971 .... Greek Waters (TP)

CAMBRIDGESHIRE

1941 .... Mill Boy (TP)

CESAREWITCH

1927 .... Old Orkney (T)

1955 .... Reinstated (TP)

NAAS NOVEMBER

1952 .... Sontogo (TP)

NATIONAL HUNT - IRELAND

KERRY NATIONAL

1949 .... Sadler's Wells (TP)

MUNSTER NATIONAL

1949 .... Confucius (TP)

ULSTER NATIONAL

1951 .... Miss Steel (TP)

GALWAY HURDLE

1920 .... King Eber (T)

1923 .... Smoke Cloud (T)

1952 .... Warrenscourt Lad (TP)

NATIONAL HUNT – ENGLAND

CHELTENHAM

1933 .... Gloucestershire Hurdle – Cobequid (T)

1954 .... Spa Hurdle – Lucky Dome (TP)

1955 .... Birdlip Hurdle – Ahaburn (TP)

.... Gloucestershire Hurdle (II) – Ilyric (TP)

1956 .... Gloucestershire Hurdle (I) – Boys Hurrah (TP)

.... Gloucestershire Hurdle (II) – Pelargos (TP)

1957 .... Gloucestershire Hurdle (II) – Saffron Tartan (TP)

1958 .... Gloucestershire Hurdle (I) – Admiral Stuart (TP)

.... Gloucestershire Hurdle (II) – Prudent King (TP)

1959 .... Gloucestershire Hurdle (I) – York Fair (TP)

T. P. BURNS' CHAMPIONSHIPS

~ 1954 ~

21/1. . . Gowran, Sgt Murphy M Hdle – Bon Secour (W. T. O'Grady) T. E. Hallinan 5/1

18/2. . . NEWBURY, Compton Nov Hdle – Knockabout (M.V.O'B) H. M. Stanley 4/6F

18/3. . . Gowran, Lower Grange M Hdle – Flowery Path (R. Shanahan) L. O'Byrne 9/4

20/3. . . Leopardstown, Killiney H – Spring Beauty (C. L. Weld) E. C. Grey 5/2F
     Bray H Hdle – Ahaburn (M.V.O'B) J. A. Wood 13/8F

25/3. . . Clonmel, Clonmel H – Flowery Path (R. Shanahan) L. O'Byrne 4/1

31/3. . . Mullingar, Rathconnell M Pl – Cranacrower (Lt-Col P. J. Hilliard [P]) 100/8

6/4. . . . Ballinrobe, Rathcarron M Hdle – Waving Comet (W. T. O'Grady) P. Stokes 6/4F

17/4. . . Phoenix Park, Athboy H – Garryvoe (K. Bell) W. J. Kelly 8/1

5/5. . . . Phoenix Park, Finglas Pl – Beau Sejour (J. Oxx) N. S. Macnaughton 4/6F

8/5. . . . Mullingar, Westmeath M Hdle – Irish Mist (K. Bell) Mrs C. A. Ryan 4/1JF

20/5. . . Lmk Jct. Queen's Pl – Beau Sire (J. Oxx) N. S. Macnaughton 4/6F D/H

22/5. . . Naas, Carlow H Hdle – Rose Ward (Capt D. A. R. Baggallay) E. Malone 10/1

2/6. . . . Navan, Simonstown 2-y-o Mdn Pl – Nanga Parvat (K. Bell O/T) 5/1

3/6. . . . Gowran, Goresbridge H Hdle – Lady Walk (D. Kirwan) F. Deegan 10/1
     Ballyragget M Hdle – Cliffordene (W. T. O'Grady) P. Bell 4/6F

8/7. . . . Bellewstown, Shallon H – Reinstated (G. Robinson) Mrs J. Bourke 7/2

14/7. . . Phoenix Park, Currage Cup – King's Melody (C. A. Rogers) John Dunlop 2/1F

15/7. . . Clonmel, Slievenamon H Hdle – Alltheway Inn (W. T. O'Grady) P. G. Grey 7/1

17/7. . . Leopardstown, Leopardstown H Hdle – Ballinlee (C. Brabazon) H. Wilton 10/1

20/7. . . Killarney, Lake H Hdle – Cliffordene (W. T. O'Grady) Mrs N. Dunne 7/4F
     Kenmare H – Jenny Pearl (J. C. Tonson-Rye) Miss R. Tonson-Rye 5/2JF

24/7. . . Down Royal, Sir Thos Dixon Cup – Evening Belle (J. Oxx) Sam Fawcett 11/4

2/8. . . . Mallow, Banteer H Hdle – Alltheway Inn (W. T. O'Grady) P. G. Grey 3/1

11/8. . . Tramore, Dungarvan H – Miss Mustang (K. Bell) R. B. Beaumont 4/1

13/8. . . Tramore, Southern H – Jingo (D. Kirwan) Mrs P. J. Loughlin 7/2

14/8. . . Leopardstown, Dundrum H Hdle – Red Column (Capt D. A. R. Baggallay) 7/1

17/8. . . Gowran, Blanchville H – Help Yourself (P. Sleator) Col J. McLaughlin 7/4F
          Lower Grange H – Cranacrower (M. Connolly) Lt-Col P. J. Hilliard 6/4F

19/8. . . Lmk Jct. Parkinson Cup H Hdle – Cliffordene (W. T.O'Grady) Mrs N. Dunne 6/4F

21/8. . . Curragh, Tyros 2-y-o Pl – Bright Night (K. Bell) M. A. Wing 3/1JF

26/8. . . Clonmel, Blackwater H – Alltheway Inn (W. T. O'Grady) P. G. Grey 1/1F

8/9. . . . Tralee, Corkaguiney H Hdle – Jenny Pearl (J.C.Tonson-Rye) Miss R.T-Rye 5/2JF

9/9. . . . Tralee, Iveragh Mdn Pl – Orage (M.V.O'B) Mrs M. V. O'Brien 4/5F

15/9. . . Curragh, Moy 2-y-o Mdn Pl – Bohermeen (J. Oxx) N. S. Macnaughton 5/2F

25/9. . . Baldoyle, Stewards' Nursery – Guess Who (K. Bell) J. J. Thompson 10/1

28/9. . . Listowel, Dingle Mdn Pl – Limereagh (K. Bell O/T) 10/1

29/9. . . Listowel, Castleisland H Hdle – Jenny Pearl (J.C.Tonson-Rye) Miss R.T-Rye 4/1

30/9. . . Listowel, Shannon Pl – Brisk (P.J.Hartigan) S.Coughlan 3/1JF

2/10. . . Curragh, Autumn Nursery – Bright Night (K. Bell) M. A. Wing 7/2

7/10. . . Limerick, Delmege Mdn Pl – Coventry Girl (M.V.O'B) Mrs M. V. O'Brien 5/1

9/10. . . Leopardstown, Annamoe H – Limereagh (K. Bell O/T) 5/2

16/10. . Curragh, Moorefield Nursery – Bright Night (K. Bell) M. A. Wing 6/1

21/10. . Lmk Jct. Knocklong H – Coventry Girl (M.V.O'B) Mrs M. V. O'Brien 3/1

28/10. . Gowran, Tullaroan 2-y-o Mdn Pl – Lisnaskea (K. Bell) J. J. Thompson 5/4F
          Eire Og Mdn Hdle – Good Berth (Capt D. A. R. Baggallay) P. McCann 4/1

30/10. . Naas, Newbridge Mdn – Clive-Sullish (M.V.O'B) Mrs A. P. Reynolds 4/5F

3/11. . . Mullingar Streamstown Hdle – Good Berth (Capt D.A.R.Baggallay) P. McCann 3/1JF

4/12. . . Navan, Brownstown Hdle – Roddy Owen (D. J. Morgan) Lord Fingall 1/1F

18/12. . Naas, Oughterard Hdle – Ron's Lace (J. C. Tonson-Rye) Mrs M. Fitzgerald 8/1

27/12. . Limerick, St Stephen's Day Hdle – Eleanor M (D. Kirwan) Mrs D. Kirwan 5/2

50 + 1 winners (total career wins to date – 370)

~ 1955 ~

15/1. . . Leopardstown, Delgany Hdle – Illyric (M.V.O'B) R. Mulrooney 10/1

9/3. . . . CHELT. Birdlip (S) Hdle – Ahaburn (M.V.O'B) J. A. Wood 2/1

10/3. . . CHELT. Gloucester Hdle II – Ilyric (M.V.O'B) R. Mulrooney 3/1F

17/3. . . Limerick, Munster H – Irene Dale (J. C. Tonson-Rye) Miss R. Tonson-Rye 7/1

19/3. . . Naas, Fishery 3-y-o Mdn – Star One (C. Brabazon) A. W. S. Adams 7/1

20/4. . . Curragh, Tetrarch Plate – Bright Night (K. Bell) M. A. Wing 8/1

21/4... Lmk Jct.Tipperary M Hdle – Ruby Brick (W. T. O'Grady) Mrs P. G. Grey 1/1F

5/5.... Limerick, Ballincurra H – Canterbury Flower (T. Donnelly O/T) 2/1F

11/5... Leopardstown, Milltown 2-y-o Pl – Otterburn (C. L. Weld) W. I. Billig 4/1

26/5... Gowran, Thomastown Mdn Pl – Rembrandt (E. M. Quirke) N. Halley 1/1F
        Ballyhale H – What-Ho (K. Bell) Brig C. M. Stewart 2/1F

28/5... Ph. Park, Glengarriff Pl – Clive-Sullish (D. J. Morgan) Mrs M. Erlanger 15/2
        Glendalough H – Manaos (J. A. Mangan O/T) 7/1

31/5... Tramore, Whit H – Kansas City (K. Bell) C. Scott 4/5F
        Holiday H – Alltheway Inn (W. T. O'Grady) Mrs P. G. Grey 4/5F

9/6.... Naas, Athy H – Galatian (M.V.O'B O/T) 7/1

16/6... Thurles, Tipperary Hdle – Ruby Brick (W. T. O'Grady) Mrs P. G. Grey 5/4JF

23/6... Wexford, Carne & Kilmore Hdle – Rocint (C. L. Weld) Capt W. Townsend 6/4F

25/6... Phoenix Park, Laidlaw H – Ivy Green (J. W. Osborne) J. G. Duggan 4/1JF

29/6... Lmk Jct. Cashel H Hdle – Alltheway Inn (W. T. O'Grady) Mrs P. G. Grey 3/1F

5/7.... Phoenix Park, Rathgar H – Flashaway (W. Ronaldson) A. Duncan 5/4F

6/7.... Bellewstown, Hilltown H – Rocint (C. L. Weld) Capt W. Townsend 4/1JF

9/7.... Curragh, Erne 2-y-o Mdn Pl – Barlass (C. L. Weld) E. P. Douglas 10/1
        Pretty Polly Pl – Free Model (J. M. Rogers) Sir V. Sassoon 9/2

16/7... Leopardstown, Leopardstown H Hdle – Camo Fly (G. A. Barry) P. Purfield 7/1
        Lambay H – Tullamore (C. L. Weld) M. J. O'Neill 5/1

21/7... Killarney, Dunloe H Hdle – Ruby Brick (W. T. O'Grady) Mrs P. G. Grey 1/1F

23/7... Curragh, Maddenstown H – Belle de ma Coeur (J. Oxx) N. S. Macnaughton 2/1F

27/7... Galway, Salthill H Hdle – Rocint (C. L. Weld) Capt W. Townsend 1/1F

1/8.... Leopardstown, Three Rock H – Rasper (J. M. Rogers) Sir V. Sassoon 5/4F

6/8.... Phoenix Park, Naul Mdn Pl – Ballybrittas (M.V.O'B) Lord Dunraven 1/2F

9/8.... Gowran, Lower Grange H – Rocint (C. L. Weld) Capt W. Townsend 5/4F

13/8... Baldoyle, Balbriggan H – Help Yourself (P. Sleator) Col J. McLaughlin 3/1JF

25/8... Clonmel, Corrib Mdn Hdle – Mary Chess (C. L. Weld) P. J. Clarke 1/2F

31/8... Mallow, Ballymagooly Hdle – Fair Faction (J.C.Tonson-Rye) Mrs M. Egan 7/4F

3/9.... Curragh, Blandford Pl – Nile Bird (J. M. Rogers) H. H. Maharani of Baroda 1/2F

7/9.... Tralee, Corkaguiney H Hdle – Jenny Pearl (J. C. Tonson-Rye) Miss R.T-Rye 5/4F
        Clanmaurice H – Mary Chess (C. L. Weld) P. J. Clarke 4/1

14/9... Curragh, Turf Club H – Iberia (M.V.O'B) W. J. McEnery 4/1

15/9... Curragh, Shannon 2-y-o Pl High Heels (K. Bell) Mrs C. M. Stewart 2/1

26/9... Mullingar, Rathganny Mdn Pl – Fairfield Lad (K. Bell) D. P. Tyndall 5/2F

27/9... Listowel, Abbeyfeale Mdn Hdle – Kansas City (K. Bell) C. Scott 1/1F

6/10... Limerick, Adare H Hdle – Cliffordene (W. T. O'Grady) W. D. Darrer 4/7F

Garryowen H – Constant Pearl (G. V. Wellesley) Mrs A. H. Watt 8/1

Delmege Mdn Pl – Rose Profit (J. C. Tonson-Rye) John O'Mahony 7/1

8/10... Leopardstown, Johnstown H Hdle – Athenian (D. Kirwan) W. J. Hutchinson 6/1

Annamoe H – Kingfisher Bridge (C. L. Weld) Mrs G. Gilroy 100/8

13/10.. Clonmel, Nore M Hdle – Irene Dale (J.C.Tonson-Rye) Miss R. T-Rye 6/4F

22/10.. Phoenix Park, Yew Tree H – Reinstated (G. Robinson) Mrs J. Bourke 8/1

27/10.. Gowran, HE President's H Hdle – Gallerio (C.L.Weld) Mrs M. E. Donnelly 6/1

29/10.. Naas, Monasterevan H – Garryvoe (K. Bell) W. J. Kelly 7/1

5/11.... Curragh, Swilly 2-y-o Mdn – Belle Sabot (J. Oxx) Mrs I. M. Macnaughton 100/8

Irish Cesarewitch – Reinstated (Geo Robinson) Mrs J. Bourke 100/9

23/11.. Mallow, Mallow November H – Cockatoo (M. V. O'B O/T) 4/1

26/12.. Limerick, Holiday H Hdle – Mel's Flame (L. J. Mahon O/T) 1/1F

27/12.. Leopardstown, Stand M Hdle – Colorado Prince (M.V.O'B O/T) 1/1F

54 + 2 winners (total career wins to date – 426)

~ 1957 ~

1/1.... Baldoyle, Sutton M Hdle – Maranboy (P. J. Prendergast) John Huston 7/4F

16/2... Baldoyle. Killester Hdle – Saffron Tartan (M.V.O'B) Lady Cottenham 10/11F

28/2... Thurles, Fethard H Hdle – Ballyknock (W.T.O'Grady) Duchess of Westminster 3/1JF

2/3.... Naas, Kilcullen H Hdle – Valley Spring (M.V.O'B) Harry Lane 6/4F

13/3... CHELT, Gloucestershire Hdle (II) Saffron Tartan (M.V.O'B) Lady Cottenham 10/11F

14/3... Wexford, Gay Count (M. Connolly) G. J. Byrne 4/5F

18/3... Limerick, Ardnacrusha H Hdle – Easter Glory (T. Burns) T. McCairns 6/4F

9/4.... Ballinrobe, Cong H – Come Again (P. Norris) W. Leddin 9/4F

22/4... Mallow, City Pl – Courts Appeal (M.V.O'B) J. McShain 1/1F

9/5.... Limerick, Ardnacrusha M Hdle – Norwood (W. T. O'Grady) W. D. Darrer 5/4

16/5... Clonmel, Tipperary Cup H – Owen's Image (W.T.O'Grady) B. Naughton 5/2

18/5... Dundalk, Clermont M Hdle – Domont (P. Norris) T. A. Ronan 5/4F

30/5... Curragh, May Sprint H – Gorm Abu (J. Oxx) H. E. The President 4/6F

Mountjoy H – York Fair (M.V.O'B) J. McShain 2/1

10/6... Baldoyle, Collinstown H – Beggar Princess (T. Burns) T. McCairns 3/1

11/6. . . Tramore, Castletown M Hdle – Ballybrittas (M.V.O'B) Col G.R.Westmacott 8/15F
    Holiday H – Anothergram (P. Sleator) Clifford Nicholson 2/1F

13/6. . . Thurles, Southern H – Brimstone (T. W. Dreaper) Mrs John Thursby 4/1

19/6. . . Mallow, Mitchelstown 2-y-o Mdn – Strong Rage (M.V.O'B) J. McShain 3/1

26/6. . . Curragh, IRISH DERBY – Ballymoss (M.V.O'B) J. McShain 4/9F

29/6. . . Lmk Jct. Cashel H Hdle – Ballybrittas (M.V.O'B) Col G. R. Westmacott 5/2F
    Juvenile Pl – Panabelle (M.V.O'B) Mrs M. V. O'Brien 2/5F
    Holiday Mdn Pl – Honey Butterwick (M.V.O'B) Mrs M. V. O'Brien 11/4

11/7. . . Clonmel, Galtee M Hdle – Bruff Bridge (M.V.O'B) Mrs J. A. Keith 4/6F

18/7. . . Killarney, Dunloe H Hdle – Blue Gum (W. T. O'Grady) A. Kennedy 6/1
    Kerry H – Anothergram (P. Sleator) Clifford Nicholson 11/10F

20/7. . . Phoenix Park, Rathgar H - Courts Appeal (M.V.O'B) J. McShain 4/1

24/7. . . Navan, Mellifont H Hdle – Key of the River (T. Burns) H. Roberts 9/4

1/8. . . . Galway, Renmore Mdn Pl – Trudeau (T. Burns) Mrs T. Burns 10/11F

2/8. . . . Tuam, Flying H – Kansas City (K. Bell) C. Scott 11/8F

5/8. . . . Mallow, Newmarket Mdn Pl – Merry Deb (M.V.O'B) J. McShain 1/2F

7/8. . . . Phoenix Park, Park Selling Pl – Toujours No 1 (K. Bell) P. J. Kilmartin 6/4F
    North Wall H – Stephanotis (J. M. Rogers) Arpad Plesch 4/5F

14/8. . . Tramore, Dungarvan H – Hurry Daisy (W.Roche) Mrs B.Harcourt Wood 8/1 DH

16/8. . . Tramore, Guillamene Mdn Pl – Knocknagole (M.V.O'B) S. T. Alexander 6/1

20/8. . . Gowran, Clashwilliam Mdn Pl (I) – Chance Tip (M.V.O'B) J. McShain 4/5F
    Clashwilliam Mdn Pl (II) – Meriel Jane (K. Bell) R. B. Beaumont 7/2

26/8. . . Kilbeggan, Clara H Hdle – Fortlass (P. Mullins O/T) 11/10F

28/8. . . Phoenix Park, Skerries 2-y-o Mdn Pl – Julie (K. Bell) C. A. Ryan 11/4

29/8. . . Clonmel, Blackwater H – Anothergram (P. Sleator) Clifford Nicholson 13/8F
    Shannon Mdn Pl – Bernice (W. J. Byrne) M. Macabe 4/1

31/8. . . Curragh, Rangers Pl – Ishbelle (M.V.O'B) N. Galway-Greer 4/6F

3/9. . . . Tralee, Oakpark Nursery – Strong Rage (M.V.O'B) J. McShain 3/1

5/9. . . . Tralee, Corkaguiney H Hdle – Everest Twenty-one (K.Bell) Col C.K H Bury 1/1F

11/9. . . DONCASTER, St LEGER – Ballymoss (M.V.O'B) J. McShain 8/1

19/9. . . Curragh, Leinster H – Gladness (M.V.O'B) J. McShain 4/5F

28/9. . . Leopards. Johnstown H Hdle – Roddy Owen (D. J. Morgan) Lord Fingall 13/2
    Laragh 2-y-o Mdn Pl – Even Money (M.V.O'B) C. H. Palmer 1/1F
    Arklow Mdn Pl – Anson (T. W. Dreaper) Lady Fingall 9/4JF

1/10. . . Listowel, Dingle Mdn Pl – Jacques Coeur (P. Sleator) Prince Aly Khan 2/5F

2/10. . . Listowel, Limerick Pl – Honey Butterwick (M.V.O'B) J. McShain 4/6F

10/10. . Limerick, Garryowen H – Quick Approach (M.V.O'B) J. A. Wood 5/1

19/10. . Curragh, Champion Stakes – Gladness (M.V.O'B) J. McShain 2/9F

October H – Floor Show (P. Sleator) Thos C. Coleman 1/1F
24/10. . Lmk Jct. Bansha M Hdle – Quick Approach (M.V.O'B) J. A. Wood 30/100F
30/10. . Downpatrick, Ardglass Pl – Solfanello (K. Bell) H. B. Farmer 5/1
23/11. . Leopardstown, Blackrock H – Can't Say (T. Burns) B. P. McCormack 5/1JF
27/12. . Limerick, County M Hdle – Ragd (M.V.O'B) Mrs J. Forrestal 4/6F

56 + 2 winners (total career winners to date – 541)

CURRAGH, September 6, 1975 – TP entrusted with the racecourse debut of Navarre by owner-trainer Anne Brewster in the National Stakes.
Unplaced on that occasion, Navarre went on to win five times for his glamorous owner-trainer.

INDEX
People

Abbott, S. B., 128

Ainsworth, David, 134, 135

Ainsworth, Sarah, 135

Allen, Geoffrey, 33, 34

Annesley, Richard, 141

Anthony, Algy, 13

Armstrong, Robert 'Bob', 47

Armstrong, 'Sam', 45, 60

Arnott, Maxwell, 16, 18, 65,

Aspell, Paddy, 30

Auld, D. A. C., 96, 112

Aylin, Clyde, 14

Baker, Alison and June, 82, 123, 124

Baker, Mrs Mary, 123, 124

Barnett, D. William, 21, 41, 43, 44, 52

Barry, Ron, 154

Barthropp, 'Max', 45

Beary, Michael, 18, 35, 40, 61, 64

Beary, P. J. 'Paddy', 66, 84

Beasley, Harry, 13, 155

Beasley, H. R. 'Bobby', 113

Beaumont, Mrs L. D., 63

Behan, Philip, 13, 25, 45

Bell, Kevin, 94, 96, 98, 124, 132, 133

Bell, Nick, 157

Biddle, Anne, 122, 127

Binet, Jean Pierre, 147

Birkett, Sir Norman KC, 52, 57

Blake, Col Arthur, 61, 65, 66, 67, 70, 71, 74, 100, 122

Boothman, Peter, 127

Bougoure, Garnie, 115, 116, 120, 126, 127, 133

Boussac, Marcel, 74

Boyd-Rochfort, Capt Cecil, 62

Brabazon, Aubrey, 71, 73, 79, 82, 84, 103, 111, 135, 142

Brabazon, Cecil, 39, 44, 46, 72, 77, 78, 79, 103, 137

Brabazon, Leslie, 20

Brabston, Johnny, 146, 147, 148

Braime, H., 10

Breasley, A. R. 'Scobie', 112, 113, 115, 123, 127

Brennan, Nicky, 141

Brewster, Anne Biddle, 169

Britt, Edgar, 107

Browne, E. F. 'Ted', 124

Browne, Dr Noel, 75

Bulger, D. D., 93, 95, 117, 121

Bullock, 'Bert', 75, 76

Bullock, William, 75, 76

Burke, Willie, 135

Burns, Chris (nee Phelan) 133, 134, 135, 137, 138, 143, 148, 153, 156, 157, 158

Burns, Helen (nee Nunan) 159

Burns, James I, 2, 3, 4, 5, 7, 8, 10, 11, 13, 14, 15, 16, 17, 18, 21, 22, 24, 25, 27, 33, 38, 40, 43, 60, 94

Burns, James II, 14, 15, 16, 18, 31, 40

Burns, James III, 1, 21, 33, 37, 41, 50, 54, 55, 57, 59, 63, 73, 74, 75, 128, 152

Burns, James Gerard, 135, 137, 139, 148, 153, 157, 158

Burns, Jane (nee Tait), 3, 38, 40

Burns, Jessie (nee Duncan) 40, 136
Burns, John I, 2, 5, 17
Burns, John II, 10, 40, 134, 144, 145
Burns, John III, 23, 36, 70, 78, 83, 86, 87, 91, 112, 117, 125, 133, 134, 144, 150, 155, 157
Burns, Stella (nee O'Connor) 18, 19, 20, 21, 22, 23, 29, 36, 50, 52, 57, 77, 83, 98, 122, 137, 150
Burns, Stella, 23, 36, 69, 70, 83, 94, 126, 134, 136, 138, 144, 150, 157
Burns, T. H. 24, 25
Burns, Thomas I, 2, 18
Burns, Thomas Joseph, 137, 138, 148, 153, 158
Burns, William (Billy), 3, 40, 134, 136
Bury, Lady Mairi, 91
Butchers, Don, 120
Butler, Norman, 139
Byrne, Larry, 82
Byrne, W. J. 'Rasher', 66
Cannon, Dominic, 75
Cannon, Noel, 46
Cannon, P. F., 71, 72
Canty, James, 55, 74
Canty, Joe, 16, 25, 27, 34, 40, 41, 43, 67, 69, 70, 72, 141, 142, 157
Canty, Lena (nee Dawson), 25
Carberry, Tommy, 135, 154, 155
Carslake, Bernard 'Brownie', 94
Chawke, Justice, 58
Chevalier, Mrs 'Chev' 30, 77
Childs, Joe, 24
Clark, Edward C., 3
Clarke, Fred, 44, 76
Clibborn, Captain C. J., 48
Clifton, Harry de Vere, 44
Clower, Michael, 154
Collins, Con, 50, 89,
Collins, Michael, 19
Collins, Michael C., 50, 70
Compton, Major P. H., 22, 23
Conlon, P. 'Mut', 138
Coonan, P. J., 86, 87

Cooper, Brian, 88
Cope, Hilton, 138, 142
Cosgrove, Joe, 35, 40
Cosgrove, Stan, 40
Cottrill, Harry, 45
Coulthwaite, Tom, 76
Cox, Paddy, 98
Cracknell, E. J. 'Ted', 127
Croker, Richard, 137
Crotty, Paddy, 100
Cullinan, Paddy, 27
Cummings, Bart, 157
Cundell, Leonard A., 10
Curran, Bernard, 32, 33, 34
Curtin, T. G. 'Ted', 139, 141
Daly, James, 6
Davison, Sandy, 145
Dawson, Joseph, 44, 65, 67, 129
Dawson, Michael Sr, 13, 21, 23, 25
Dawson, Michael Jun, 77, 129, 132, 133, 135
Dawson, R. C. 41
Dawson, S, C., 26, 41
Delany, Eamon, 86, 117
Derby, 17th Earl, 15, 42, 94
De Valera, Eamon, 41
Devine, Jimmy, 121, 122, 125, 129
Dewhurst, Capt R.H. 'Bob', 16
Dixon, Sir Thomas, 67
Dobell, R. B., 3, 4, 10
Donnelly, Mrs M. E., 122
Donoghue, Ethel, 74
Donoghue, Steve, 23, 29, 32, 42, 46, 47, 52, 59, 60, 61, 62, 63, 64, 66, 74, 94, 116
Donoghue, Stephen jun., 74
Doran, Jacqueline, 20
Doran, Johnny, 20
Douglas, Lady James, 24
Doyle, Jimmy, 32
Doyle, John Sr., 10, 13
Doyle, John 'Chalk', 32, 40
Doyle, Paul, 138
Doyle, Sue, 141
Drake, John, 38
Dreaper, T.W., 69, 83, 111, 129, 130, 131

Duffy, Johnny, 145
Duggan, D. J. 'Dinny', 88
Duggan, Mrs D. J., 89
Dundas, Lord George, 20
Dunlop, John, 157, 158
Dunne, James 'Fairy', 13, 14,
Dwyer, T. Ryle, 19
Earl, Walter, 32
Easterby, Walter, 53
Eddery, Jimmy, 73, 76, 77, 96, 98, 141
Eddery, Pat, 141, 148, 150
Edmunds, Willie, 151
Edward VII, 7,
Elliott, E. C. 'Charlie', 63
Elsey, Charles, 60, 76
Emery, Rene, 92
Faggoter, Val, 127
Fairfax-Blakeborough, Jack, 3, 76
Fallon, John 'Jack', 10, 13
Farquhar, Betty, 112
Farrissey, Mick, 88
Fetherstonhaugh, F. E., 139
Fetherstonhaugh, R. 'Bob' 39, 42, 44, 48, 50,
    55, 59, 128
Fetherstonhaugh, R. 'Brud', 50, 127, 128, 129
Fingall, Oliver, Lord, 96
Finn, P.J., 155
Finn, Tommy, 144
Firestone, Bertram, 141, 155
Fitzgerald, Peter, 28
Fleming, T. 'Baron', 18
Fogarty, Michael, 138, 139, 141
Fordyce, Ted, 79
Formby, George, 15, 94
Francome, John, 154
Freeman-Jackson, Dorothy, 82
Freeman-Jackson, Harry, 82, 83
Freeman-Jackson, Virginia, 83
Furness, Viscount, 41
Gallagher, Gerry, 147
Gallagher, Mrs Redmond, 139
Gallagher, Tom, 147, 148
Gallivan, Barney, 76, 88, 91, 94, 95, 96
Gardner, Major Laurie, 116, 118

Gardner, Ted, 49
Geraghty, Andy, 138
Gilpin, Geoffrey, 38, 39
Gleeson, Mickey, 86
Glennon, T. P. 'Pat', 127, 128, 129,
Gooch, Capt Dick, 29
Gorman, Jimmy, 38
Gosden, John, 146
Gough, Danny St John, 122
Grant, Howard, 113
Greenwood, Hamar, 19
Greer, Sir Henry, 12
Griffin, Joe, 111
Griffin, R. 'Bob', 148
Grundy, Fred, 16, 17, 18, 31, 50
Hallinan, T. E. 'Tim', 113
Hamilton, Blaney, 111
Hanley, M., 13
Hannon, George, 55
Hardwidge, Bobby, 67, 69
Hartigan, Frank, 45
Hartigan, Hubert M., 39, 41, 43, 66, 79
Harty, C. B. 'Buster', 131, 136
Harty, Henry, 82
Harty, John, 154
Harvey, Lance, 138
Hastings, Sir Patrick, KC, 52, 54,
Hawkins, Charles, 10
Hayden, Paddy, 60
Hayes, Colin, 157
Healy, T. E., 96
Hely Hutchinson, Mark, 131
Hill, William, 112
Hogan, P. P., 69, 70
Hollingsworth, Sydney D., 47, 58
Hollingsworth, Mrs Sydney, 48
Holmes, 'Herbie', 64, 127
Hope, R. E., 54
Hughes, Dessie, 154
Hughes, Peter, 112, 129
Hulme, George, 37
Hunt, Nelson Bunker, 139
Hunter, Joseph, 13
Hurley, T. J. 93, 121

Huston, John, 112

Hutchinson, Ron, 116, 121, 127

Ingham, 'Staff', 123

Jarman, Paul, 142

Jarvis, Jack, 1, 51, 52, 54, 56, 57, 91

Jeffery, S. C. 'Shem' 20, 25

Joel, 'Solly', 32

Johnston, Lawrie, 134, 138

Johnstone, Rae, 107

Keating, Larry, 129

Kelly, Andy, 91

Kelly, W. J., 55, 68

Kennedy, Vivian, 125, 136, 144, 149

Keogh, Harry, 84, 85, 93

Kerr, Bert, 61, 62, 66, 74, 79

Keswick, H. G., 15

Khade, Pandu, 127

Khan, Aga III, 55

Khan, Aga IV, 128

Khan, Aly, 84, 120

Kinane, Michael, 154, 155, 157, 158

Kline, C. Mahlon, 115

Lacy, Frank, 157

Lake, Des, 134

Lambton, Hon George, 15

Lane, Freddie, 29

Lane, Harry, 111

Lascelles, Lord, 18

Lawson, Joe, 47

Leach, Felix, 3,

Leake, Lieut-Commander, 136

Lombard, Jack, 88

Loraine, Sir Percy, 41, 44

Lowry, Albert, 16

Luro, Horatio, 150

MacCabe, F. F., 16

McCairns, Gertie, 124, 125

McCairns, Tommy, 91, 95, 124, 126

McCartan, Philip, 157

McCavana, P., 54

McCormack, Count John, 32, 33, 35, 37, 38, 39, 40, 42

McCormack, Gay, 20, 78

McCormack, Capt Paddy, 19, 20

McCormack, Mollie (nee O'Connor), 19, 78

McCormick, Dick, 60, 118, 124

McDonald, Billy, 147

McGovern, Hughie, 75

McGrath, George, 135, 142

McGrath, Joe, 69, 70, 76, 117, 119

McGrath, Seamus, 109, 116,

McGregor, Sidney, 101, 105

McGuigan, John, 3,

McKeever, Mr F. E., 43

McKie, W. A., 10

McShain, John, 100, 107, 108, 114, 132

McShain, Mary, 107, 108, 109

McVey, James, 72

Macauley, Arthur H., 26, 27, 28, 29, 57, 70

Macdonald-Buchanan, Johnny, 128

Macnaughton, Barney, 79, 88,

Macnaughton, Norman, 92, 96

Madden, Otto, 24

Maddock, Russ, 127

Magee, Capt Louis, 121

Magnier, Clem, 111, 114

Maher, Peter, 32, 40, 45, 50

Mahon, R. A., 13

Mahon, Sir Bryan, 31

Malone, Joe, 122

Mangan, J. A. 'Gus', 54

Markey, J. R., 14

Marsh, Jim, 115

Marshall, Bryan, 92, 93

Massard, Jean, 109

Matthews, Peadar, 142

Mercer, Joe, 135

Milbanke, Lady, 39

Miller, Mrs G. B., 47

Miller, Thomas, 13

Milton, Lord Peter, 53

Molony, Martin, 73, 77, 79, 82, 86, 87, 88, 142

Moore, D. L. 'Dan', 82, 87, 111, 142

Moore, Gary, 138

More O'Ferrall, Dominic, 37

More O'Ferrall, Frankie, 35, 38
More O'Ferrall, Nancy, 34, 37, 38
More O'Ferrall, Roderic, 32, 33, 34, 35, 38, 39, 40, 42, 43, 45, 46, 49, 72, 97
More O'Ferrall, Rory, 38
Morgan, D. J. 'Danny', 86, 96,
Moylan, Jack, 27, 28, 43, 55, 73, 142, 148
Mullane, Jimmy, 81, 88
Mulrooney, Bob, 97, 98
Mumford-Smith, H. F., 112
Murless, Noel, 64
Murless, Stuart, 127, 129
Murphy, Jack, 43, 44
Murphy, Jas J. 44
Murphy, John, 141
Murphy, John and Mary, 146
Murphy, J. J., 29
Murphy, Paddy, 135
Murphy, Sean, 129
Murphy, Tommy, 154
Murray, John, 142
Musker, John, 25
Myerscough, Fred, 18, 50, 55, 57, 72
Nagle, Florence, 47
Neil, Jane (nee Burns), 3,
Neil, Jean, 3,
Neil, William, 3
Norris, Paddy, 127, 128, 129, 132, 133
Nugent, Barney, 77
Nugent, Tommy, 69
O'Brien, A. S. 'Phonsie', 92, 93, 97, 104, 121
O'Brien, Dan, 28, 46, 67, 69
O'Brien, David, 150, 152, 153
O'Brien, Dermot, 92, 93, 102, 105, 131
O'Brien, Jacqueline, 150
O'Brien, M. Vincent, 67, 69, 74, 84, 85, 87, 92, 93, 94, 96, 97, 100, 103, 104, 105, 106, 107, 108, 109, 110, 111, 112, 113, 114, 115, 120, 121, 122, 132, 134, 138, 145, 146, 147, 148, 150, 152, 153
O'Connor, Gerald, 18, 19
O'Connor, James, 18, 21
O'Connor, Katherine, 18
O'Connor, Mona, (nee Fleming) 18, 19

O'Grady, W. T. 'Willie' 44, 46, 85, 94, 96, 113
O'Hehir, Michael, 106
O'Kelly, Sean T., 90, 100, 102, 124
O'Neill, Bill, 129
O'Neill, John, 129
O'Neill, Jonjo, 154
O'Sullevan, Peter, 106, 107, 109
Osborne, J. W. 'Joe', 87
Oxx, John, 72, 88, 92, 96, 100, 112, 122, 138, 142, 156
Paget, Hon Dorothy, 49, 65, 67, 69, 68, 71
Parkinson, Emmanuel, 54, 80, 81, 82
Parkinson, J. J. 'Jim' 10, 13, 16, 25, 61, 64, 66
Parkinson, Mrs Margaret, 79, 80
Parkinson, Joe, 59
Parkinson, W. J. 'Billy' 10, 20, 28, 43,
Parnell, R. F. 'Buster', 138, 141
Patton, R. G. 'Bobby', 100
Paulson, A. E., 155
Peacock, Dobson, 5, 18, 19
Perry, Tom, 86
Persse, H. S. 'Atty', 27
Phelan, Anne, Kathleen and Tommy, 133, 134
Phelan, Mr and Mrs Thomas, 133, 134
Pickering, Sam, 14
Piggott, Lester, 94, 95, 106, 112, 134, 141, 143, 147, 148
Plunket, Hon Mrs Brinsley, 38
Pollet, Etienne, 132
Powell, Paddy jun, 96, 134, 141
Power, John 'Jackie', 72, 90, 105, 117, 142
Power, Paddy, 80, 81, 82
Power, Patsy, 80
Powney, Hugh, 16
Prendergast, Kevin, 79, 138, 139, 142
Prendergast, Maurice G., 7
Prendergast, Paddy Junior, 142
Prendergast, P. J. 'Paddy', 64, 68, 72, 79, 86, 105, 115, 116, 121, 132, 133, 134
Price, T.W., 13
Pullin, George, 4
Purtell, Jack, 132, 142
Pyers, Bill, 138
Quinlan, R. 'Bobby', 117

Quirke, Denis, 'Dinny', 94

Quirke, E. M., 25, 28, 34, 43, 44, 45, 75, 76, 94

Quirke, Stephen, 138

Rank, James V., 45, 46

Reavey, Eddie, 64

Redmond, Tim, 55

Redmond, Tony, 129

Reidy, Maurice, 13

Renton, Bobby, 155

Renwick, John, 18

Richards, Gordon, 25, 40, 47, 50

Rickaby, Bill, 51

Rimell, Fred, 136

Roantree, Dr Joe, 75

Roberts, John, 64

Robinson, George, 98

Robinson, G. W., 113, 141, 142, 143

Robinson, W. T. 'Jack', 7, 10

Roche, Christy, 142, 153

Roe, Johnnie, 135, 136, 137, 138, 141

Rogers, Bryan, 32, 62, 63

Rogers, C. A. 'Charlie' 39, 48, 65, 66, 67, 68, 69,

Rogers, 'Darby', 57, 63, 64, 65, 76, 79, 84, 89, 111, 124

Rogers, J. M. 'Mickey', 84, 98, 129, 133, 134, 138

Rogers, J. T. 'Jack' 10, 13, 27, 32, 36, 49, 52, 62, 63, 65, 84

Roll, Gordon W., 61

Rosebery, 6th Earl, 52, 57, 91

Rossiter, V. 'Benjy', 146

Ruttle, Jack, 60

Ruttledge, D. 27

Ryan, J. R., 10

Ryan, Mrs T. V., 111

Saint-Martin, Yves, 148

Sangster, Robert, 145, 147

Sassoon, Sir Victor, 52, 62, 129

Schaffer, E. E. Dale, 129, 135

Schofield, Thomas, 10

Schwartz, Danny, 147

Shanahan, S., 155

Shand, Mrs J., 47

Shaw, Tommy, 127

Sheehan, Michael, 100, 106, 112

Simpson, Alan, 138, 142

Sleator, Paddy, 101, 116, 127

Slocock, Oliver, 50

Smirke, Charlie, 47, 64, 66

Smith, Eph, 51, 57

Smith, John, 6, 7,

Smith, Raymond, 92, 102, 145

Smyth, Victor, 94

Snow, Donald, 49

Snow, May (nee Paget), 49

Spinks, Gordon, 138

Sprague, Harry, 100

Springfield, Maurice, 104

Stanley, Hugh, 92

Steele, Gilbert, 3

Sullivan, Paddy, 135, 154, 156

Sunley, Bernard, 133

Svedjar, Frankie, 87

Swan, Capt D. G., 155

Sweeney, Tony, 80, 126

Swinburn, Wally, 115, 116

Taaffe, Pat, 91, 92, 93, 98, 121, 130, 131

Taaffe, Tom, 44, 56

Taaffe, 'Toss', 100, 101, 103, 109, 111, 115

Thackeray, Major, 8, 22

Thomas, Patsy, 60

Thomas, 'Tommy' 61, 64

Thomson, Robert, 3

Thompson, J. W. 'Jackie', 86, 116

Tierney, Peter, 25, 26, 27

Tindall, Bill, 51

Todd, George, 130

Tonson-Rye, John, 91, 112, 149

Tonson-Rye, Rosaleen, 149

Tormey, Jimmy and Tom, 141

Torrington, Eleanor, Lady, 47

Traill, W., 4

Turner, Major R., 95

Turtle, W. 'Billy', 79

Tuthill, Captain, 14

Tuthill, F. F., 117

Turnbull, W., 4

Ussher, Harry, 16, 65

Volterra, Leon, 47

Wadia, C., 27

Walker, Sir Andrew Barclay, 6

Walker, John Reid, 24

Walker, William Hall (Lord Wavertree), 5, 6, 7, 11, 12, 14, 24, 30, 44

Wallace, Edgar, 35, 36

Walwyn, Fulke, 129

Ward, Liam, 91, 100, 101, 103, 109, 113, 116, 122, 126, 127, 129, 134, 138, 141

Watson, Keith, 142

Weld, Charlie, 115, 122, 123, 124, 134, 138, 152

Weld, Dermot, 152, 153, 154, 155, 157

Weld, Gita, 152

Weld, Mark, 153

Weld, Mary, 151

Wellesley, Hon H. G. 32, 39, 40, 44, 45, 46, 47, 64, 66, 67, 76

Wellesley, 'Toby', 72, 76, 77

Wells, G. H. 'Georgie', 64, 66, 71, 135

Westlake, Joseph, 13

Westmacott, Colonel G. R., 104, 107

Westminster, Anne, Duchess, 124, 129, 130

Weston, Tommy, 42, 94

Wightman, Bill, 159

Williamson, Bill, 116, 117, 122, 127, 128, 132, 138, 140, 142

Willoughby de Broke, Lord, 97

Wilmot, Maria, 158

Wing, M. A. 'Morny' 37, 44, 67, 70, 82, 91, 98, 141, 142, 152, 157

Wing, Wally, 50

Winter, Fred, 97, 99

Wood, John A., 87, 92, 93, 97, 102

Woods, A., 96

Wragg, Harry, 40

Wyllie, William, 2, 15

Ycaza, Manuel, 123

INDEX
Horses

Abermaid, 128
Abbot of Hainault, 67, 69, 74
Abrupt, 62
Admiral Stuart, 110, 111
Agrippina, 149
Ahaburn, 87, 97
Albergo, 114, 120
Alberoni, 103
Alleged, 147
Allets, 26, 27, 45
Alletsoi, 45, 48
Another Flash, 120
Archway, 27
Arctic Prince, 119
Arden Link, 81
Arkle, 69, 86, 123, 124, 129, 130, 131
Assert, 150
Astrologer, 69
Astrometer, 67, 69, 150
Astronomic, 69, 150
Athasi, 21, 43, 60
Athlone, 26, 27
Balladier, 79, 80, 81, 82
Ballybrittas, 107
Bally Joy, 132
Ballymoss, 101, 103, 105, 106, 107, 108,
109, 110, 112, 113, 126, 132
Barfelt, 103
Barney VI, 84
Barrons Court, 138
Barton, 146
Beau Co Co, 90, 91

Beaudelaire, 38
Beauford, 79
Beau Sabreur, 78, 79, 82
Beech Hill, 94
Ben Stack, 129
Big Berry, 94, 95
Big Shuffle, 157
Black Cherry, 7
Black Eagle, 117
Black Justice, 144
Black Speck, 45
Bluehel, 141
Bold Maid, 63, 65
Bonanza, 32
Border Hero, 141
Boys Hurrah, 100, 112
Braydore, 61
Brief Truce, 157
Bright Cherry, 81, 83, 86, 123
Bright Night, 98
Brioche, 107
Brown Jack, 29
Brush, 55, 56
Bursary, 87
Caeleon, 150
Candy Cane, 138
Captain Cuttle, 23, 24, 42
Captain Hardy, 32
Captive Princess, 14, 48, 77, 91
Cataract, 4
Chamier, 103, 122
Chamour, 120, 121

Cheap Popularity, 16
Cherry Lass, 7
Clair Soleil, 97
Coastward, 88
Cobequid, 42, 97
Cockatoo, 92
Colombella, 64
Columbia, 65
Colonia, 7
Committed, 157
Confucius, 82
Coniston, 152
Cornfield, 60
Coronach, 20
Cottage Rake, 84, 86, 103
Courier Belle, 14
Courts Appeal, 114
Crepello, 106, 107
Democrat, 135
Denizulu, 4, 8
Dimorphodon, 4
Dolabella, 12
Domaghmore, 127
Double Bell, 39
Double Scotch, 14
Dr Strabismus, 39
Dunnock, 110
Early Mist, 93, 103
East Galway, 16
El Gran Senor, 150, 153
El Toro, 113, 115, 116
Ethland, 49
Eyrefield, 62, 63
Fanai Tire, 100
Fair Crystal, 66
Fairlight, 5
Fair Time, 114
Fairy Lantern, 18
Falaise, 139
Fanny's Way, 79
Farney Fox, 115, 121, 122, 123, 152
Farranjordan, 47
Fawcett's Bridge, 124, 127
Fearless Fox, 1, 51, 57

Festive Diplomat, 143
Fiery Diplomat, 138, 139
Fiona's Slipper, 141
Fireside, 48
First House, 66
First League, 3, 4
Flash of Steel, 12
Floor Show, 101
Flower Song, 31
Flying Aero, 8
Flying Top, 32
Foam Crest, 72
Fooled Again, 60
Forest Guard, 18, 94
Four Ten, 64
Franz Hals, 42
Frigid Aire, 135
Fuel, 103
Gainsborough, 24
Gardenia, 60, 61
Gay Cottage, 152
Gay Crusader, 24
Genevieve, 14
Germanicus, 149
Gigi, 116, 118
Gladness, 101, 102, 103, 105, 109, 110, 111, 112, 132
Gleniry, 122
Glennameade, 83
Glenstal, 148
Gloir Anna, 122
Golden Fleece, 147, 148, 150, 152
Golden Lancer, 50
Golden Maid, 14, 15
Good Morning, 73
Gorm Abu, 100, 101
Grand Vizier, 141
Grand Weather, 76, 77
Great Sport, 12
Greek Pie, 43
Greek Star, 76
Greenogue Princess, 69, 83
Habitess, 141
Half Caste, 4, 8

Harar, 63
Harina, 21
Harinero, 21, 43
Harmachis, 76
Hatton's Grace, 84, 86, 103
High Grass, 77
Hindu Festival, 106, 107
His Reverence, 44, 46, 47
Honest Crook, 138
Hopeful Hero, 129
Hyperion, 42
Ilyric, 97, 98
Jackaleen, 38
Jack Mytton, 32
Jack o' Down, 82
Jean's Folly, 7
Jolly, 63
Kellsboro' Witch, 104
Kilbelin Gap, 87
Kilglass, 1, 55, 152
King Eber, 18
Kingston Black, 24, 126
Kitty, 36, 37
Knight of Tully, 7
Knockabout, 92
Knock Hard, 84, 85, 86, 93, 103, 131
Kopi, 32
Kyloe, 44
L'Aine, 25
Laurel Hill, 86
Laurentia, 159
Lily Rose, 7
Lindley, 48
Listen In, 152
Lotus Lass, 31
Lovely Gale, 128
Lucca Prince, 69, 83, 123
Lucky Dome, 92, 93, 100
Lucky Range, 55
Macross, 56
Mahmoud, 47
Manhattan, 41
Maranboy, 112
Marble Arch, 139

Mardin II, 40, 136
Martin Griffin, 67
Memories, 159
Merry Moment, 7
Midsummer Gamble, 152, 154
Mignonne, 35
Mikado, 66, 68
Mill Boy, 67, 69, 129
Mill House, 129
Millennium, 38, 39
Minoru, 7
Minou, 111
Miss Marlhill, 32
Miss Steel, 86, 87
Modest Sunny, 54
Monteverdi, 146
Morning Wings, 77
Motliba, 55
Mum, 45
Museum, 45
My Kuda, 135
My Land, 15
Navarre, 169
Nellie Mac, 20
Night Hawk, 7, 12
Nijinsky, 138, 148
Nile Bird, 98
Noreast, 89, 90
Normandy, 136
Northern Gleam, 89, 90, 91
Not So Cold, 135
No Wonder, 64
Nuxford, 32
Old Man River, 154, 155
Old Orkney, 28, 29, 30
Oola, 73
Our Mirage, 139, 140
Over Yonder, 61
Pacifier, 73
Passage, 48
Paveh, 134, 135
Pelargos, 100, 110
Pericardium, 5
Phantom Bold, 20

Philip's Fancy, 34, 35, 36
Pidget, 139, 140, 142
Pitched Battle, 34
Plutarch, 60
Polyfoto, 64
Predominate, 105
Pretty Polly, 30
Primero, 21, 44
Prince Boudoir, 86
Prince Lionel, 24
Prominer, 132, 133
Prudent King, 110, 114
Prudent Rose, 1, 55, 152
Quack, 4
Quare Times, 93, 103
Queen's Park, 32
Raeburn, 47, 48, 49, 50, 51, 58
Raptor, 141
Rathcoffey Pride, 86
Reindeer, 138
Reinstated, 98
Resplendent, 27
Result, 82, 83
Rising Spring, 121
Roddy Owen, 96
Roisterer II, 62
Roman General, 32
Romanylei, 159
Rose Royale, 109
Rosewell, 152
Ross Sea, 115, 116
Royal Racquet, 141
Royal Realm, 12
Royal Tan, 93, 103
Sadler's Wells, 81, 82
Saffron Tartan, 104, 105, 111, 114, 120
Sagaris, 135
Sagar Pride, 159
Sail Anair, 100
Sandy Grey, 47
Sangre Grande, 116
Santa Claus, 133, 135
Sarragossa, 45
Sea Count, 78

Secreto, 153
Senor, 52
Shady Girl, 16
Shandon Belle, 128, 129
Sicilian Prince, 129
Signal Service, 85
Simon Ashton, 14
Sir Crispen, 32
Sir Penfro, 142
Slide On, 73
Slightly Slow, 65, 154
Smart Aleck, 39
Smoke Cloud, 25
Smokeless, 45
Snowy Creek, 146
Solar, 84
Soldennis, 20, 21, 25, 41
Soldumeno, 25
Solferino, 72
Solford, 46
Song o' My Heart, 38
Sovereign Slipper, 135
Spion Hill, 50
Spy-Ann, 42, 43
Star of Egypt, 33, 34
Stella Aurata, 117
Stratford, 41
Stroller, 92, 97, 100, 111
Strong Rage, 107
Take Time, 59
Tansy, 113
Tetra Nell, 55
Thankerton, 47
Theatrical, 157
The Minstrel, 146
The Phoenix, 72
The Soarer, 6
The Squire, 15
Tillywhim, 12
Timobriol, 120, 121
Tossup, 158, 159
Towanda, 20
Trigo, 21, 41, 43, 60
Triguero, 62

Tula Ban, 122
Tula Riona, 112
Tu Va, 136
Ultimate II, 135
Upadee, 91, 94, 95, 140
Uvira, 66, 67
Vatellor, 47
Vimadee, 124, 125, 126, 130
Vindore, 97
Vintage Crop, 157
Vinthea, 159
Vivid Impression, 151
Warrenscourt Lad, 88, 89
Watch Tower, 3
Wavy Stripe, 17
Wet Kiss, 20
White Eagle, 12
White Hawk, 7
White Lie, 12
White Mixture, 32
Wildwood, 14, 15, 94
Windsor Slipper, 70, 72
Witch Elm, 7
Woology, 44
Wykehamist, 72
York Fair, 114
Zagreb, 157, 158